"I have dedicated my life to [ ]
Christ while simultaneousl[y]
It's because I am a follower of Jesus that I'm compelled to be involved in the work of justice. In *Redeeming Justice*, Christina has masterfully unpacked the importance of a biblically based approach to social justice. This book is engaging, thought-provoking, and transparent, and it reflects the heart of God for a lost and broken world. As she poignantly writes, 'Biblical justice work is redemptive work.'"

—**Christine Caine**, founder of A21 and Propel Women

"The concept of justice is contentious in our deeply polarized society. This is especially true of social justice, which is a volatile flashpoint in our increasingly rancorous political debates. In *Redeeming Justice*, Christina Crenshaw offers a vision of justice—including social justice—that is rooted in a biblical worldview rather than postmodern academic theories or progressive identity politics. *Redeeming Justice* offers the perfect balance of Christina's personal story, engagement with Scripture, examples from Christian history, reflections on current events, and practical application. The result is an accessible book that will help many believers to think Christianly about justice and to engage in the hard but necessary work of pursuing justice for the glory of God and the sake of authentic human flourishing."

—**Nathan A. Finn, PhD**, professor of faith and culture and executive director of the Institute for Faith and Culture, North Greenville University

"The biblical word *justice* has often been hijacked by unbiblical movements. As a result, many Christians shy away from the topic. Christina Crenshaw's work helps us lean into genuine, biblical, godly justice. Not only does she refute bad arguments, but she also helps Christians live out a life of justice where they have influence. If you care about truth, if you care about the vulnerable, and if you care about following Jesus, you'll want to read this book."

—**Daniel Darling**, director of the Land Center for Cultural Engagement and author of several books, including *The Dignity Revolution, Agents of Grace*, and *In Defense of Christian Patriotism*

"In *Redeeming Justice*, Dr. Crenshaw does what few writers can—she raises the biblical call to social justice while holding accountable the ways Western culture has attempted a counterfeit of God's heart. This book is timely, revealing Dr. Crenshaw's deep personal awareness of the division in church and culture on social issues and calling the reader to take action—not performatively but scripturally. I will return to its wisdom often and recommend this book to those who feel caught in the tension of desiring justice and activism while remaining dedicated to a truly biblical worldview."

—**Phylicia Masonheimer**, founder and
CEO of Every Woman a Theologian

"In *Redeeming Justice*, we get a much-needed return to Jesus, the gospel, the church, and the Bible as the solution for the transformation of hearts, families, poverty, and pain that we find throughout our world. I've had the privilege of walking side by side with Christina and her family in our local church as we have wrestled together with how to impact society holistically, with Jesus and the gospel at the center. This theological and practical book should be a mainstay for every believer, as we look to do good, seek justice, walk humbly with our God, and truly fulfill the ministry of Jesus to bind the brokenhearted, set the captives free, and preach the gospel to the poor."

—**Jimmy Seibert**, pastor of Antioch Church, Waco, TX

"The Psalmist tells us, 'Righteousness and justice are the foundation of your throne. Unfailing love and truth walk before you as attendants' (Psalm 89:14 ESV). As justice is the foundational twin for Heaven's authority, it should be reflected for His glory here on earth. I have watched Dr. Christina Crenshaw choose truth when it would have been easier for her to kowtow and side with lies. This choice was costly, one that resulted in felt betrayals by those she had worked with and walked alongside for years. *Redeeming Justice* is a book that was well lived before it was well written. On its pages, I believe you will find the courage to rise above signals and embrace the true virtue of justice."

—**Lisa Bevere**, New York Times bestselling author
and co-founder of Messenger International

REDEEMING JUSTICE

CHRISTINA CRENSHAW, PhD

HARVEST HOUSE PUBLISHERS

EUGENE, OREGON

Cover design by Faceout Studio

Cover images © oksanka007 / Shutterstock; Spencer Fuller / Faceout Studio

Interior design by KUHN Design Group

For bulk, special sales, or ministry purchases, please call 1-800-547-8979.
Email: CustomerService@hhpbooks.com

This logo is a federally registered trademark of the Hawkins Children's LLC. Harvest House Publishers, Inc., is the exclusive licensee of this trademark.

Redeeming Justice
Copyright © 2025 by Dr. Christina Crenshaw
Published by Harvest House Publishers
Eugene, Oregon 97408
www.harvesthousepublishers.com

ISBN 978-0-7369-8984-8 (pbk)
ISBN 978-0-7369-8985-5 (eBook)

Library of Congress Control Number: 2024935691

Printed in the United States of America

25 26 27 28 29 30 31 32 33 / VP / 10 9 8 7 6 5 4 3 2 1

To my boys: Craig, Christopher, and Corban

I pray our family continues to seek what the Lord deems good. May we do justice, love kindness, and walk humbly according to His holy and sanctifying standard, not the world's. Thank you for being my support and inspiration this side of eternity.

CONTENTS

PART 3: DOING GOOD FOR GOD'S GLORY

FOREWORD

Jonathan Pokluda

In times of crisis, the world watches to see how Christians will respond. In the early centuries of the church, plagues swept through the Roman Empire, bringing devastation. Some accounts speak to bodies being piled up by the thousands. In those days, when disease struck, people often fled—leaving the sick behind to die alone.[1] But the Christians? They stayed.

They cared for the suffering, risking their own lives to tend to strangers. They fed the weak, comforted the dying, and buried the dead. They shared the love of Christ, accompanied with the message of Christ. Many of them died alongside those they nursed, but they did so with peace and joy, believing they were following the example of Jesus. Their radical love was so countercultural that even their enemies took notice. While others abandoned the sick, Christians embodied sacrificial care. That's part of our history. That's part of our calling. You might think the faith would die out under this harsh reality, but on the contrary, it exploded.

Moments like that remind me why the church cannot afford to sit out on justice. There's a whole generation passionate about doing good, about defending the vulnerable, about making an impact in the world. And that is a good thing. But in many evangelical circles, *social justice* has become a loaded term. Some embrace it uncritically, absorbing secular ideologies without testing them against Scripture. Others reject it outright, wary of cultural distortions.

But here's the thing: Biblical justice isn't optional for the people of God. He calls each of us to global and local justice work for His glory.

Across the world and across the country, I've had the privilege of witnessing God move through His people in powerful ways. But there's something especially sweet about seeing that fruit in my own Waco community.

I think about those at Mission Waco and Compassion Waco stepping into the lives of those experiencing poverty and homelessness—not just handing out help, but restoring dignity. The Shepherd's Heart Food Pantry, faithfully partnering with churches to feed families who aren't sure where their next meal is coming from. Mentoring Alliance and STARS Book Clubs, making sure kids don't just learn to read, but know they're seen, valued, and loved. Isaiah 117 House and Together for Good, standing in the gap for vulnerable children and families, embodying the gospel in the messiness of foster care. Baylor Missions, organizing local and international service opportunities throughout the year. And Care Net Pregnancy Center, walking alongside women facing unplanned pregnancies with truth, love, and real support. All these works attach the good deeds of service to the eternity shifting message of the gospel.

That is what it looks like to be the hands and feet of Jesus. Biblical justice work is redemptive work. That's why *Redeeming Justice* is so important. Dr. Christina Crenshaw isn't just talking about justice—she's lived it. She's navigated these conversations in classrooms, churches, and cultural spaces where biblical conviction and cultural ideology often collide. And I've had the privilege of seeing her walk in that tension with both truth and grace.

Christina is a friend, but long before that, I was their family's "teacher" at summer camp, a small-world connection that still makes us laugh. I've watched her faith in action, from her work at Baylor to her engagement in the local church. And I've seen her stand for truth, even when it cost her.

This book is more than just a defense of justice; it's a roadmap. Christina lays out a clear, theologically rich framework for engaging justice in a way that aligns with Scripture, not shifting cultural trends. She doesn't demonize or romanticize justice work. Instead, she offers a balanced, compelling vision for how Christians can step into this space with wisdom and discernment.

In *Redeeming Justice*, you'll find a:

- Biblical framework for justice that is rooted in God's character, not culture's definitions

- Historical perspective on how the church has engaged justice—both faithfully and imperfectly

- Challenge to reclaim justice work instead of retreating from it out of fear or frustration

- Vision for gospel-centered cultural engagement that leads to transformation, not just activism

- Call to pursue justice in ways that honor God and draw others to Christ

This book will challenge you. It will push you to examine your own motives, to test cultural narratives against biblical truth, and to engage in justice work that is both wise and winsome.

My prayer is that as you read, you will be both encouraged and convicted. Encouraged, because you have been called into a story far bigger than yourself. Convicted, because faithfulness to Jesus demands more than passive belief—it requires active obedience.

Christina, thank you for writing this. Thank you for reminding us that justice belongs to God, that it's central to the gospel, and that we can't abandon it just because the world misrepresents it.

To the reader: Get ready. This book won't just change how you think about justice—it will change how you live.

Jonathan Pokluda
Harris Creek Baptist Church
Waco, Texas

PREFACE

Light in the Darkness

Not a month passes when my husband, Craig, and I don't recall the young girl we witnessed being trafficked from an airport in Thessaloniki. The memory still brings tears to our eyes. She couldn't have been older than 13 or 14. We were returning to America after a two-week service trip in the summer of 2016, having joined nearly 2,000 others from our church in Waco to assist Syrian refugees fleeing civil war.

The Syrian refugee crisis, which began in March 2011, had reached catastrophic proportions by 2016.[1] The United Nations reported 4.9 million Syrians displaced, with over a million seeking refuge by making the perilous journey across the Mediterranean to Greece. An estimated 27,000 Syrian men, women, and children drowned during these desperate attempts to escape their war-torn homeland.[2] War inevitably displaces people, rendering vulnerable groups even more susceptible to crimes against humanity.

When we learned about children and women falling prey to

human traffickers, we felt compelled to leave our comfortable American lives and serve. At that point in my academic career, I had dedicated years to combating human trafficking through established agencies like Christine Caine's A21 Campaign, Antioch Community Church's Unbound Now, and Operation Mission's Freedom Climb. I had served as chair of our Waco Human Trafficking Prevention Coalition and participated in roundtable meetings with Texas Governor Greg Abbott's statewide Human Trafficking Task Force. Human trafficking prevention education became my research focus while on faculty at Baylor University. We arranged childcare for our young sons and joined a team trained to travel across the world to raise awareness about human trafficking in Syrian refugee encampments in Thessaloniki. What we witnessed was heartbreaking, but no training could have prepared us for encountering a human trafficker in action or the terror of confronting him.

Greece has long been a hotbed for trafficking—one reason Christine Caine founded the A21 Campaign there. Our team was well versed in recognizing signs of trafficking, particularly sex trafficking. We walked tent to tent in Syrian camps distributing literature in Arabic warning of trafficking schemes and providing the national hotline number. Often, we were invited inside for tea and conversation, listening to stories of trauma that overwhelmed our comprehension. We couldn't fathom living through civil war, abandoning possessions, traveling for weeks with small children without necessities, only to be confined for months in encampments with insufficient electricity, water, food, or privacy. The conditions were impoverished, lice was rampant, tribal fighting unbridled. That any semblance of hospitality and hope existed in such dire circumstances was confounding.

When our trip ended, we departed from Thessaloniki by plane, connecting through Athens en route to Dallas. In the Thessaloniki airport, I noticed a billboard of missing children's photos. As I scanned the wall, I recognized Madeleine McCann, who had disappeared nearly a decade earlier during her family's vacation in Spain. I was struck by a grievous sense of global solidarity—no decent human wants to see children harmed. I turned to show my husband but found he had wandered into a nearby duty-free shop.

As I moved toward him, a young girl caught my eye. She reluctantly emerged from the women's bathroom, walking toward a scowling man easily in his forties. She wore short shorts and a crop top, her hair styled in an unkempt bob. When within reach, he grabbed her forcibly by the arm, shook her steadily, and berated her in a language unfamiliar to me. Given their olive complexion and accents, I guessed they had Eastern European origins.

I likely stared longer than socially acceptable—after 30 to 60 seconds of witnessing this outrageous behavior, the man made eye contact with me. I was struck by his brazenness, his lack of embarrassment at being caught manhandling a young girl in public. His audacious glare only compounded my sense of injustice. So, I glared back until he looked away, yanking the girl toward the airport gates.

I rejoined my husband, incredulous: "Can you believe that? Can you imagine borderline abusing your daughter in public and then glaring at someone who witnessed it?" I have what friends call a high justice meter. But I'm confident any person, regardless of personality type, would have struggled witnessing such behavior.

Making our way to our gate for Athens, I was astonished to see that the man and girl were in line for our flight! But what I saw next paralyzed me. He was not the girl's father. He was kissing her shoulders and neck, caressing her lower back, while passengers stole disgusted glances before looking away. His mistreatment was on full display—clearly physical and sexual harassment, if not assault. The girl stood frozen, passive, resigned to abuse. Her expression matched what I'd seen earlier. At that moment, I knew he wasn't her father.

Angry tears welled up then, as they do now as I recount this. I felt genuinely frozen with horror—one of the few times I've truly been stunned into inaction. How brazen, how disgusting, how evil. I frantically scanned other passengers' reactions. Was I overreacting? What was I missing? A woman near the front of the line caught my eye, shook her head in disapproval, then turned away. Others did the same—stealing glances at this 40-year-old man sexually fondling a 13-year-old girl, then sheepishly looking away as if to say, "This isn't right, but it's none of my business." I've considered their inaction a hundred times without finding justification. Perhaps they feared entanglement with law enforcement in a foreign country. Maybe the Greeks felt compassion fatigue from years of refugee crises and trafficking. Maybe I was an overly emboldened, naive American expecting the world to share my justice-oriented lens. I cannot say. But I couldn't stay silent.

I tugged my husband's arm, pulling him close: "Craig, look! That's the father I told you about! But that girl isn't his daughter. He's molesting her in front of everyone!" Craig followed my gaze and shared my revulsion. We were both momentarily frozen with indecision—there's no guidebook for such a social breach. Abuse is rarely discussed outside the context of private settings. Within minutes, we decided I would approach the female gate agent for intervention.

Whatever boldness I'd shown earlier was gone. I shuddered passing within feet of this man—what emanated from him felt nothing short of demonic. With a lump in my throat and tears in my eyes, I explained the situation to the gate agent. She admitted seeing it, too, and agreed it was likely trafficking. But her response unnerved me: "What do you want me to do about it?" I had no framework for such apathy. Everything in my Christian and Western worldview taught intervention when witnessing injustice.

"I don't know," I replied firmly. "Call police or security. But we have to do something. We can't do nothing!"

She called someone, speaking Greek. I returned to my place in line, aware others had noticed my actions—including the man with the girl. My heart raced with uncertainty.

Minutes later, uniformed officers pulled the man aside. After initial resistance, he stepped away from the line. At that moment, the young girl bolted through the airport at full speed, clutching her backpack straps. Even the police seemed astonished. They took the man out of sight, and within seconds, another older man between us and the abuser chased after her. My jaw dropped in disbelief. I understood exactly what was happening but couldn't process it—the second man was "the spotter," textbook trafficking methodology. When reality matches training materials so precisely, it creates a cognitive dissonance hard to reconcile.

I wish I could report the victim escaped. As Christians, we long for redemptive endings. But painfully, that's not what happened. The police returned the trafficker to the line, apparently accepting whatever story he told. I watched him make a phone call, and minutes later, the older trafficker returned with the girl. They boarded our plane with us. By what seemed beyond coincidence, my husband and I were seated in 17A and B, with the trafficker and victim in 16C and D—in my side view for the hour-long flight. The older trafficker sat rows behind. I prayed through tears the entire time.

I tried repeatedly to intervene. When the girl rose to use the restroom, I followed, but the trafficker cut me off, standing outside the bathroom door. I approached a flight attendant, explaining the situation. She asked how I could be certain about trafficking. I explained I couldn't claim absolute legal authority but noted all the red flags from my training. She relayed this to the pilot, then returned to inform me they couldn't act without concrete evidence.

Upon deplaning, I waited to follow them. The girl darted for the restroom, and I followed, but her trafficker stood in the doorway— alarming other women but impervious to their reactions. He wouldn't let her out of sight or allow me access. Inside, the girl and I exchanged a sympathetic glance in the mirror as we washed our hands; she knew I was trying. We both knew there was nothing more I could do—not in a foreign country, not against two traffickers. They disappeared into Athens that day. But my heart has not forgotten her.

We didn't get the intervention we wanted, but that certainly doesn't mean God hasn't redeemed the story. I maintain hope that somehow, by God's grace and sovereignty, she found rescue. What I know with certainty is the work God did in me that day, cementing my understanding of the biblical mandate for Christians to pursue redemptive justice for His glory—even when misunderstood, even when we have no control over the outcome. This encounter compelled me all the more to courageous engagement with the world's darkest injustices. When we witness evil firsthand, we cannot retreat in fear. Instead, we must embrace the gospel through tangible action. The body of Christ stands uniquely positioned to enter these dark and broken spaces to offer light and restoration. The question isn't whether we should engage social justice; the question is, how can we answer Christ's call to do so in a manner that honors Him? I pray the following words move us closer to that answer.

INTRODUCTION

Anchoring Our Justice to Jesus

If it seems to you that the world has gone mad, that what was once considered widely accepted truth is now up for debate, this book is for you. If your heart beats for justice, for binding up the brokenhearted, for setting the captives free, for rescuing the lost and redeeming the enslaved, this book is for you. If you desire to do what is right, to engage what is just, true, beautiful, and good, but you are no longer certain how to define those terms according to God's framework, this book is for you. If it's becoming harder to discern what is biblical justice and what is political activism, I wrote this book with you in mind. You are not alone as you navigate your way through the social justice chaos and confusion.

In a culture that conflates justice with the latest cultural trends or political movements, we must anchor ourselves in the timeless truths of Scripture. We must remember that true justice flows from the very character of God, who is just and righteous in all His ways. When we seek to understand and pursue justice apart from God's revelation, we risk being swept away by the ever-shifting tides of human opin-ion and the deceptive allure of worldly wisdom. The gospel of Jesus Christ is not a call to conform to the patterns of this world, but to be transformed by the renewing of our minds (Romans 12:2). It is a call to see the world through the lens of God's Word, to rightly align our hearts with His priorities, and to pursue justice and righteousness as defined by His unchanging standard. And as followers of Christ, we must remember that our ultimate allegiance is to Him, not to any earthly ideology or agenda. In the pages that follow, we explore what it means to pursue biblical justice in a postmodern world. We will seek to discern the difference between the wisdom of God and the wisdom of this age, between the righteousness that comes from faith and the self-righteousness that comes from human effort. And as we do, my prayer is that we will be equipped and empowered to live out our calling as ambassadors of Christ's kingdom, bearing wit-ness to His truth and His love in a world that desperately needs both.

THE SHIFTING LANDSCAPE: NAVIGATING FAITH AND JUSTICE IN A POST-TRUTH ERA

For three years, I had the honor of serving as a research associate at Dallas Theological Seminary's Hendricks Center. In that role, I con-tributed to several podcasts, webinars, conferences, and staff and faculty meetings, and assisted with selecting seminary-wide supple-mentary readings. The projects I contributed to were focused on the intersection of faith, culture, leadership, and vocation. One of my projects entailed working on a grant application for a study exam-ining the connection between nonsectarian universities and col-lege students' experiences with faith. By sheer observation, I already knew these students—digital natives—were the most socially and globally connected generation in human history. But as I dove into the research, I was surprised to learn just how much younger Mil-lennials and Gen Z value social justice work. In fact, from papers published in peer-reviewed academic journals to trade articles published in outlets like *Christianity Today,* all told the same story: Social justice work is not simply more highly valued among Gen Z (those born from 1995 to 2012) than in other generations; social justice has become their professed religion.

From birth, Gen Z has been inundated with messages about being more compassionate, empathetic, and good. Those qualities are rarely ever defined, but they're socially established by demanding adages such as "Do better, be better, and speak up." Gen Z has come of age at a time when Black Lives Matter signs are planted in their neighbors' yards, virtue signaling has ostensibly supplanted being virtuous, and there is no greater offense than to verbally offend someone. This is the generation that has demanded safe spaces when they feel emotionally confronted or even merely uncomfortable, and yet, they will demand accountability for authority in the form of threats and violence and then consider it justice. I sincerely admire Gen Z's fight. They fight for themselves, their friends, and their neighbors. They fight for equal pay, treatment, and rights. They fight to improve our carbon footprint; they fight to end wars they believe are unjust; they fight to be a voice for the voiceless. And these are wonderful attributes of their generations. But in an increasingly secular, postmodern culture, it's apparent they are fighting for social justice from an increasingly secular, postmodern worldview.

If we're honest with ourselves, Gen Z is not the only generation conflating social justice narratives and biblical justice mandates. We've all been influenced more by culture than by Christ, at least more than we care to admit. And even those of us who profess Christ frequently struggle to articulate how our social justice fights align with God's Word or accomplish His purposes. In his letter to the Ephesians, the apostle Paul encourages the church to equip the saints for ministry, for building up the body of Christ, until we all attain to the unity of the faith and of the knowledge of the Son of God (Ephesians 4:12-13).

This call to shepherd and disciple believers toward spiritual maturity is particularly relevant for the church today. Discerning the difference between culture's false narratives and God's enduring truths is more challenging than ever in an increasingly secular society. We need better, more robust apologetics for cultural engagement. We need to cultivate a theological hermeneutic that not only addresses societal concerns and crises, but explains how the Bible's ancient truths still speak to contemporary social issues.

CULTURE CLASH: WHEN BIBLICAL TRUTH IS CONFLATED WITH COUNTERFEIT NARRATIVES

In the last few years, I've been discouraged by the shifting landscape. In terms of faith and civic engagement, the ground beneath my feet has changed so vastly and so quickly, it's been challenging to maintain my footing. To explain what seems to be occurring at the macro level, I'll offer a micro-level example. I've witnessed rising tensions between the state and church within the context of anti-human-trafficking efforts. When I first began engaging anti-human-trafficking efforts, I partnered almost exclusively with faith-based organizations such as Christine Caine's A21 organization, Unbound Now ministries, and Baylor University. I wasn't strategically wedging out nonsectarian groups; rather, for decades, faith-based organizations, ministries, and universities were spearheading efforts to end human trafficking. Christians were some of the first to organize efforts aimed at educating minors and other vulnerable people groups about the dangers of online and in-person traffickers. Christians were some of the first to provide rehabilitation to victims. And eventually, Christians were some of the first advocates to ask for increased punishment for traffickers and the decriminalization of victims.[1] Because our work, research, and data were all done with excellence, we received numerous government grants, and were positioned in front of Congress and other political officials. We were invited to attend academic conferences and present our work and suggestions for how best to address a growing global crisis. Essentially, churches, parachurch ministries, and people of faith were welcomed into decidedly secular or political spaces because of the good fruit of our steadfast labor.

And then, almost overnight, the terms of engagement shifted. It would be easy, albeit dishonest, to place the blame exclusively on the change in presidential administrations from President Trump to President Biden. I cannot speak to the sincerity, or lack thereof, of Trump's Christian faith. What I can suggest with confidence is that his 2016 to 2020 presidency embraced the church's efforts to combat human trafficking and partnered with Christians—all without a hint of hostility. It wasn't until the Biden administration took office in 2021 that I had ever heard the slanderous accusation *Christian nationalism*, and it was certainly the first time I can recall it being lobbed at church leaders who—as best I could discern from afar—had little interest in gaining political power or establishing any semblance of an American theocracy. Evangelicals who had spent decades on the front lines of prison reform, abuse rehabilitation, foster care, and pro-life advocacy were instantaneously and unjustly deemed Christian nationalists. There was a complete disregard for the years of good, faithful, and beneficial work they'd given for our common good. In sharing this observation, I am not undermining the reality of Christian nationalism. But as a threat, it is measurably insignificant. I have read the books, listened to the podcasts, and even spoken with a few of the primary progressive-thought leaders who assert the terror is large and looming.[2] Even after listening and learning, I am simply not convinced the problem of Christian nationalism is any more a problem than White supremacy, which is to say both are real and both are wrong, but neither actually dominates public thought or undermines America's democracy. The ideological pendulum swung so wildly and widely left after President Biden took office in 2021 that many Christians, including myself, wanted to just throw in the towel and call it quits. What was the point of working toward human flourishing and American's common good if we were going to be deemed Christian nationalists the moment we attributed our efforts to God's plans and purposes? If America was now a country that embraced pluralism—but only if that form of plurality denounced evangelical efforts—then why even try at all? Politically and theologically, the shifting landscape was not only disorienting but also demoralizing.

THE TRUTH IS WRITTEN ON OUR HEARTS

For as long as I can remember, a flame for justice has flickered within my heart. I can still recall the first time I encountered and attempted to reconcile sin and injustice when I was only five years old. My father had multiple affairs with women in the decade he was married to my mother. When I was in kindergarten, at an age he assumed I would be too young to discern the gravity of his unfaithfulness, he brought me along to the home of one of these women. He asked me to quietly play with toys in the living room with the woman's daughter, who was approximately my age, while he and the woman snuck off to a back bedroom. He was right in assuming what they were doing would be lost on me. At that age, of course I was unaware of what it meant to make a marital covenant before the Lord and then to break it. Certainly, I had no concept of affairs or infidelity, nor did I understand the theological and legal consequences of those immoral choices. But when they came out of the bedroom holding hands on that particular day, I knew I was witnessing an act that would break my mother's heart.

The weight of marital infidelity was far beyond my full comprehension at that age, but even then, I knew there was an air of secrecy in my father's words and actions. I could also rightly discern that the secrets would break my mother's heart, which is likely why I kept them for several years. Surely by five, I would have understood it was wrong to ask a child to hide something from her mother, a mother who had proved to be good, kind, dependable, and trustworthy. Likely by this age, I would also have had a framework for a healthy family unit that consisted of one dad and one mom, not a third-party participant. My father's blatant display of physical affection was forever solidified in my memory because I knew it was wrong. I knew it was an injustice against my mother and our family. Age, wisdom, and healthy biblical counsel have helped me forgive my father for this and many other transgressions. Although I have never committed adultery or harmed my family with the same gravity, I have come to recognize I am also a sinful human with a heart prone to wander from the Lord. I have forgiven my father as best I know how, but that is a difficult memory to forget.

It would be disingenuous to claim I'm in anyway thankful for the incident or the memory of it, but I am grateful the Lord makes beauty from ashes. In hindsight, the Lord used the offense I witnessed to plant seeds for God's framework for righteousness, goodness, and justice. As I look back over the four decades of my life, I can see the ways I've stepped out of my comfort zone to stand up for someone or something greater than myself. I was the kid who invited the new girl to sit at the lunch table; I was the teen who gave time in the summer to local and global mission work. I was the college student who mentored high school students through Young Life ministries because I wanted to spare as many high school students as possible from a life or death without Christ. For the same reasons, shortly after I married in my early twenties, my husband and I committed to taking mission trips every few summers. We traveled to foreign countries such as Tunisia, Lebanon, Uganda, Greece, and Mexico. We worked with local churches to serve in shelters, refugee centers, orphanages, and the like. We taught refugees about the dangers of human traffickers. We played with and cared for orphans, even bringing our own young children alongside. We painted; we cleaned; we listened; we shared.

We donated generously, always giving 10 percent of our income to our church and another 10 percent to faith-based, justice-minded ministries. But mostly, as best we knew how—imperfectly and sometimes awkwardly—we gave Christ in word and action. We knew our financial means were limited. Even if we poured out our entire savings account to every homeless man, single mother, or orphaned child, it would never be enough to meet their needs. But if we tried to meet their momentary needs and gave them Christ, we knew their greatest need would be met. They would have the assurance of salvation and the transformative power of the Holy Spirit, which far surpassed anything temporal and finite we could provide.

As we mature, our understanding of the world expands, and our sense of injustice also expands and matures. We begin to see that true justice is not merely about ensuring equality in rewards and punishments, but about upholding what is right and good. We start to recognize that our actions have consequences that extend beyond ourselves, affecting the lives of those around us. This realization is a crucial step in our moral development, since it helps us to shift our focus from our own desires and perceived entitlements to the needs and wellbeing of others. For followers of Christ, this growth in our understanding of justice is also related to our spiritual growth. As we deepen our relationship with God and immerse ourselves in His Word, we come to see justice not as a human construct, but as a divine imperative. We discover that true justice is rooted in love. The biblically rooted love that compels us is not the distorted version the world offers, which is a shallow and ever-shifting version. The love we're called to has eternal value. It is a love for God, a love for our salvation in Christ, a love for the sanctifying power of the Holy Spirit, and a love for the souls of our neighbors and enemies.

As we mature in our faith, we begin to see injustice not merely as a violation of some abstract principle, but as an affront to the image of God in every human being. We recognize that when we fail to treat others with the dignity and respect they deserve as God's beloved creation, we are not only wronging them, but we are also sinning against God Himself. This understanding deepens our commitment to justice and compels us to act, not out of a sense of self-righteousness or moral superiority, but out of a humble desire to love and serve others as Christ has loved and served us. In this way, our growth in faith and our growth in our understanding of justice are inextricably linked. As we seek to follow Christ more closely and to conform our lives more fully to His will, we cannot help but be moved by the injustices we see around us—and we cannot help but be compelled to do something about them. For the flame of justice that flickers within my heart—in all our hearts— is not merely a human impulse, but a divine calling, a calling to be agents of God's love and righteousness in a broken and hurting world.

WHY THE WORK STILL MATTERS

This book was written in a humble earnest effort to remind myself and the bride of Christ that social justice work matters. It matters to the Lord, for our Christian witness, and to a world desperately in need of Jesus. It has mattered since God created humankind in the garden. It mattered at the inception of the church when Christ walked the earth. And it matters today too. Pursuing social justice isn't an optional extra for Christians; it's a natural outworking of the transformative power of the gospel in our lives. As we experience more of God's heart for the broken and oppressed, we can't help but be moved to action, knowing that we're joining in the very mission of Jesus to proclaim good news to the poor, liberty to the captives, and freedom for the oppressed (Luke 4:18-19).

I have no interest in engaging trivial, inconsequential debates about the semantics of "social justice" over "biblical justice." Several books by far smarter thinkers already exist, and they have debated the definitions and philosophies ad nauseum. I am of the belief that

God is far less interested in our terms than our hearts' posture and purpose. As followers of Jesus, the distinction between the two terms matters not for the sake of semantics but for the sake of our apologetics. The ideologies, aims, and outcomes between secular narratives and Christian doctrines on social justice are vastly different. While social justice movements often focus on the redistribution of power and resources or elevating the oppressed and punishing the oppressor, biblical justice is rooted in the character of God, His righteous standards, and His love for all He has created. God has commissioned His followers to co-labor with Him and steward our influence unto His glory. Doing good work is one of the primary ways we fulfill God's mandate to love both our neighbors and our enemies. One of the most quoted Bible verses by Christians and unbelievers alike comes from the prophet Micah when he declares, "He has told you, O man, what is good; and what does the LORD require of you but to do justice, and to love kindness, and to walk humbly with your God?" (Micah 6:8 ESV). Even a secular world wants to believe there is a God who cares about righteousness, compassion, and humility. Even those who deny Christ want to believe, as Martin Luther King Jr. famously stated during the height of America's civil rights movement, that the arc of the universe is indeed bent toward justice.

UNDERSTANDING OUR CULTURE, WORLDVIEW, AND IMPETUS FOR DOING GOOD

This book is divided into three sections, each aimed at evaluating how Christians should think about engaging in social justice work and why our engagement with the world is distinctly different from other worldviews and perspectives. In section one, we will consider the contemporary conflict. We will examine our current American culture and why it seems harder than ever to claim Christ openly and overtly. Living in a post-Christian Western society presents a unique challenge for those who believe Christ as our Savior, identity, touchstone, and worldview. In such a diverse country, there are palpable tensions between our culture, government, and faith. But there is also hope for a way forward; there is enough common ground, through common grace, to do common good work. There is enough shared ground and mutual interest to link arms with people of different faiths and worldviews. There is room for unity within the context of work done for the sake of human flourishing. Questions at the end of the section prompt us to reflect on and discuss difficulties prohibiting us from authentically integrating faith into the public square.

Section two emphasizes the importance of a biblical worldview in navigating contemporary social issues and engaging in social justice efforts. This portion underscores that a Christian perspective should be rooted in Scripture, which provides a framework for understanding the world and our purpose within it. Here, we juxtapose Christianity and other major worldviews. We discuss that a biblical worldview is not a product of Western White privilege, Christian nationalism, or culture wars, but rather a comprehensive understanding of reality grounded in the timeless truths of God's Word. This worldview is derived from Scripture and transcends cultural, ethnic, and socioeconomic boundaries. And most importantly, section two highlights the importance of loving God first and then loving others as an overflow of that primary love, which should shape the way Christians approach social justice work. Ultimately, this section illuminates a biblical worldview that is rooted in the narrative of creation, fall, redemption, and restoration, and how this worldview guides us in our engagement with the world and the pursuit of social justice. At the end of section two, questions prompt us to consider how other major worldviews differ from a Christian and biblical worldview. Additionally, in these reflection questions, we contemplate where there is some shared ground to partner with others for the sake of engaging in good work, even when our worldviews differ.

In section three, our final section, we underscore the good work the church has done and continues to do. Christianity has been a powerful force for good in the world, despite the failures and hypocrisy of some who claim to follow Christ. I have often encountered people who are disillusioned by the abuse and injustice perpetrated by those who profess to be Christians. It is crucial that we acknowledge these failings and condemn them unequivocally, as Jesus Himself did. Even as we lament over our human hypocrisy, we also recognize that the very ideals of justice, freedom, and compassion that inspire our righteous indignation are deeply rooted in the biblical worldview, not in humanity. The Christian conviction that every human being is created in the image of God has been the foundation for the concept of universal human rights and the only long withstanding bulwark against the totalitarian claims of secularist, humanist ideologies. Throughout history, Christians have been at the forefront of the fight against slavery and oppression, driven by the belief that all people have inherent dignity and worth. From the early church fathers, to the abolitionists of the 19th century, to the modern-day anti-trafficking advocates, followers of Christ have challenged the prevailing cultural norms and worked tirelessly to defend the freedom of their fellow human beings. Today, this legacy of compassion and justice continues through the work of countless Christian ministries and organizations. Christians continue to lead the way in opposing oppression, redeeming the lost, and providing care to the marginalized and victimized.

Section three highlights research indicating that societies most influenced by Christian ethics are more likely to respect human rights, create and uphold just laws, resist mistreatment, and extend compassion. Christianity has also been a remarkable force for human flourishing in areas such as philanthropy, healthcare, and education. During times of plagues, poverty, and persecution, Christians have often been the ones to stay behind and care for the sick and dying, motivated by the love and compassion of Christ. Throughout church history and across the globe, Christians have been and continue to be known for their generosity; Christians are far more likely to give of their time, talents, and financial treasures.[3]

ENGAGING CULTURE WITHOUT LOSING OUR SOUL

As we reflect on this rich history of Christian service, we are reminded of why it matters for us to engage in social justice causes from a distinctly Christian worldview. When we work for justice, we do so not merely to alleviate suffering or to achieve certain social outcomes, but to bear witness to the redemptive power of the gospel and to point others to the hope that we have in Christ. In our pursuit of justice, we will often find ourselves working alongside those who do not share our faith or our biblical convictions. In such contexts, we must seek to find common ground, recognizing that God's common grace allows us to work together for the common good, even when our ultimate motivations may differ. As Jesus reminded us, we are called to be salt and light in a world that desperately needs both (Matthew 5:13-16).

Ultimately, our pursuit of justice as followers of Christ must be anchored in the gospel and in the hope of God's eternal kingdom. We recognize that true and lasting justice will only be achieved when Christ returns to make all things new. Until that day, we are called to live as citizens of that kingdom, bearing witness to God's righteousness and mercy in a world that is broken by sin and injustice. May we, as the body of Christ, be found faithful in this calling, always seeking to follow and apply God's teaching over the world's shifting narratives. May our lives reflect biblical orthodoxy (right thinking, according to Scripture and doctrine) and orthopraxy (right doing, according to Scripture and doctrine). May we be marked by a deep commitment to a biblical framework for justice that is rooted in God's Word. May our good works, done in the name of Christ, point others to the hope and healing that can be found in Him alone. I pray this book reminds all those who love the Lord that He has given us a sufficient framework and reason to do justice for His glory.

THIS CULTURAL MOMENT

1

FAITH UNDER FIRE

Christ and Culture

I cannot recall a time in my life when I didn't want to be an educator. I've always loved learning and then sharing what I had learned with others. My mother was a teacher throughout my childhood, and some of my fondest preschool memories include lining up my dolls and playing school. As I grew older and went to grade school, my love for education flourished, which eventually led me to pursue an English major with the hopes of teaching high school students.

That I could influence the trajectory of others' lives by empowering students to become agents of change within their spheres of influence was catalytic in my decision to become an educator. Early in my teaching career, I came to realize education is less about transferring knowledge and more about helping students steward their vocation, education, and opportunities for the sake of the common good and unto eternal purposes. A continued desire for learning and encouraging students led to further studies in education and English, and I eventually completed my PhD in these fields.

Perhaps the most fundamental and insightful lessons I have learned in 20 years of teaching and studying is how my personal development influences my students' growth. In short, I cannot offer my students what I do not possess. To cultivate the best in my students, as their professor, I had to first cultivate the best in myself. Parker Palmer's *The Courage to Teach* is one of the simplest and yet most profound books I have read on this topic. In it he states, "Good teaching comes from the identity and integrity of the teacher. As I teach, I project the condition of my soul onto my students, my subject, and our way of being together."[1]

My love for learning and teaching led me to a career in education, but my love for the Lord and my students' spiritual flourishing motivated me to teach at Christian universities. During my first teaching position at California Baptist University, the Lord led me to work on anti-human-trafficking curriculum and this opened the door to other justice efforts. Eventually the Lord moved my family to Waco, Texas, and He provided an opportunity to mentor students through my position at Baylor University, contribute to meaningful research, and continue my involvement in justice work. This was all I needed to feel fulfilled in my vocation.

In the last decade, I've worked with several faith-based ministries and non-faith-based organizations whose efforts were aimed at elevating women and children. And with each activist step, I invited my students into the journey. If my work entailed anti-trafficking efforts, I included students and anti-trafficking stakeholders in the research, the classes, and the meetings with activist leaders. In my work with Propel Women, a global ministry dedicated to equipping women to lead well in their vocational spheres of influence, I invited female students to conferences where I was speaking and shared articles I wrote for Propel's publications. Because Baylor is a Christian university, I intentionally selected faith-based articles for my students that highlighted how the church can better support women. Little did I know that the Lord was using my time in higher education and the justice arena to prepare me for a national platform.

STANDING ON TRUTH, WALKING IN LOVE, AND FORGIVING THROUGH GRACE

My former students would probably attest to my unwavering commitment to faith-driven justice work, particularly regarding protecting women and children. So, it was likely just as shocking for them as it was for me to witness my public assertion—that females need protected spaces that are separate from males—go viral on social media in January of 2021. At the time, I was serving as a university lecturer at Baylor University when my friend, Dan Darling, posted what I considered to be a sensible tweet on Twitter. He expressed his unease with the newly implemented Title IX executive order, stating it was unfair and unsafe for females and that we (the church) should all be concerned. I wholeheartedly agreed! The exchange went as followed.

Dan's Tweet:

The executive order on transgender issues and the expected overturning of the Mexico City policy on abortion are both anti-science and bad for human flourishing. And it will take some courage to say this publicly.

My response:

What if I don't want biological boys in the bathroom with my biological daughter? Do the 99% of us who do not struggle with gender dysphoria have a voice? No? Cool.

Then I retweeted the exchange. And that was it…for about a week. I don't recall an immediate response or outrage. There were a few civil and supportive comments and likes, mostly from like-minded

Christian colleagues and acquaintances. There were also the usual trolls and bots, which were especially prevalent on Twitter before Elon Musk bought and rebranded the platform the next year. I mostly muted or blocked those accounts. It was difficult to discern which accounts belonged to real people and which were spam, and I didn't have a reason or the energy to try and decipher. But unbeknownst to me at the time, a handful of students decided this exchange was precisely the fodder they needed for their fight to have the university sanction an LGTBQ+ student group on campus. For years, and mostly behind the scenes, a group of students advocated for one of the nation's largest Christian universities to affirm and sanction an LGTBQ+ student organization.

Just over a week after making the statement on Twitter, I awoke to nearly a hundred emails, social media messages, and texts from concerned former students and colleagues. I learned that morning from their outreach that the Baylor student paper, *The Lariat*, ran an article originally titled something along the lines of "Dr. Crenshaw is transphobic and needs to be fired." (The title was later updated to state *controversial* rather than transphobic.) The article claimed, that in spite of making the LGBTQ+ faculty safe list for years, I was no longer considered a safe person because I would not accept the transgender narrative wholesale. Concerned friends and stakeholders asked if I was doing okay, and they expressed their condolences for the student newspaper's dishonorable characterization of me. By the end of that spring semester, I received 788 forms of written communication, the majority of which were encouraging. I know the precise number of messages I received because the inpouring was so overwhelming, I hired a former student to triage the communication. It was too engulfing for me to tackle alone. And perhaps it's not too surprising, but the worst of the slander was committed under dark anonymous accounts.

There were dozens of hurtful messages, both public and private. I received messages accusing me of being transphobic, unsafe, privileged, evil—if you can imagine a slanderous comment along these lines, then I've probably heard it. The cruel commentary was hurtful, but the words that were hardest to shrug off were the ones directed toward my children. Some went as far as threatening to find them at their school and "hurt them like you've hurt us." Those are fighting words for any mama. There was also a university alum who worked for a leading Big Tech company who publicly bullied that she wanted me fired, that she would ensure I never stepped foot on her campus again. If you've followed J.K. Rowling's similar controversy and the world's response to her assertions that biological realities like male and female are fixed and not fluid, then you have some context for the messages I received as well. It was all quite painful. What I endured was much less viral or persistent, and the ramifications were less dire. An important distinction, though, is that Rowling's backlash wasn't crucifying her in the name of Christianity. Mine was. The support I received was comforting, but the outrage was cutting. And that's what I found most difficult to reconcile, if I'm being honest.

My husband and I amusingly refer to the *Lariat* article as, "the slander heard 'round the Christian world." Because the very day it went to press, a flood of supportive exchanges and media inquiries poured in too. For every threat or mischaracterization, I must have received ten times the number of supportive communications. I received welfare checkups from several colleagues who vowed to write character letters on my behalf. There were thoughtful undergraduate students who rallied to my support with a counter petition, publicly requesting I remain on campus and in my position. I am forever touched by their spiritual maturity—that these students, most of whom I had never met, would choose to comfort and pray for me; it was balm to my broken heart. In their grace, I saw Christ's love manifested. There were also a handful of presidents and senior administrators from other colleges and seminaries who called or emailed to express their sympathies. They shared in my reasonable concern that if this could happen at a Christian university like Baylor University, what could that mean for other colleges? These campus stakeholders wanted my advice for getting ahead of any potential theology breach or a media scandal.

To be charitable, I think these aggressive students believed they were "doing justice." Some even outright told me so. They believed canceling me was a form of advocating for anyone on campus who might identify as transgender. Their heart to care for marginalized students was admirable, but their methods were misplaced. Biblical justice seeks to do good work based on God's moral standard, holy Word, and plan for eternity. Its methods and outcomes evidence the fruit of the Spirit (Galatians 5:22-23). And to be fair to the student article, I should note about two weeks after it went to press and went viral, the Baylor provost released a faculty free speech statement. The statement was released not just on my behalf but for the sake of all faculty's right to their voice. For that, I was deeply appreciative. That there was no mention of faith informing the free speech statement was a bit disappointing. It was the sort of press release statement that could have come from any nonsectarian public university. I cannot imagine how difficult it was for the administration to navigate student outrage. In the last five to ten years, the news has highlighted the increase of campus protests. So, I sympathize with those at the helm of schools navigating choppy waters. Some factions of college students have become increasingly vocal and vindictive. But perhaps I naively thought Christian college students and stakeholders would respond differently. As journalist Brian Kilmeade noted during my *Fox and Friends* interview, we've seen this sort of cancel-culture behavior at Berkley and Baylor. His implication was that even Christian colleges are resorting to non-Christlike reactions in the public square, sometimes over issues of church orthodoxy.

I'm often asked if I chose to leave Baylor or if I was asked to leave. For the record, I left on my own accord. I finished teaching that spring's

Honors College course on human trafficking, but I declined an offer to teach a summer course or sign a 2021-2022 contract. My departure wasn't made in anger, but in recognition that healing required distance. My soul genuinely needed respite after the ordeal. *The Lariat* later issued a retraction for the article's title, which was responsible of them. I imagine that journalistic decision to change the title from "Dr. Crenshaw is transphobic" to "Dr. Crenshaw is controversial" was not one made easily. I applaud the student newspaper's efforts to be more honest in their reporting.

I wouldn't wish the experience on anyone. The old cliché "there is no such thing as bad press" is not true. I really could have done without that attention. Even still, through this experience, I'm thankful to have learned firsthand the power of Christ's example of forgiveness. I had to learn how to forgive professed fellow brothers and sisters in Christ who were being cruel and using His name to do so. But I recognize I am not alone in this, that most of us have felt this feeling of betrayal before. While at times I was tempted to harbor resentment, the Lord and my church family continually reminded me that I, too, have been forgiven much. And even when my flesh didn't want to, the Holy Spirit indwelling in me prompted me to pray for those who, in that moment of time, felt more like enemies than neighbors or brothers and sisters. My heart sincerely desired unity within the body of Christ. For the sake of the gospel and common good work, we have some reconciliation to do in the church body. I've also come to learn that the contemporary Western church needs a better apologetic to discern how to engage in social justice from a biblical worldview.

FORGIVING OTHERS

I have never experienced church hurt, at least not to the extent that it was deep enough to rock my faith in the Lord or question the love I've received from the body of Christ. But if Baylor is an extension of the church, as she professes to be, I have learned in a very painful and public way how to forgive those who intentionally malign your character, threaten your career and kids, and never come to you and ask your forgiveness. At some level, I imagine the experience was akin to what some have experienced by way of church hurt. After we came out of the fog of that semester, and the press storm subsided, and the job offers began to trickle in, I could feel the tangible presence and comfort of the Lord in a way I had not for months. As my husband and I sat on our back patio one evening in early May, the warmth of the setting sun on my face, I was enveloped in the Lord's peace. My husband and I decided that night we were going to be intentional and charitable with our forgiveness—even when someone hasn't asked or repented. Because how much more have we been forgiven by the blood of the Lamb? And how much less did we deserve it?

That isn't to say we don't establish boundaries. Healthy, biblically based boundaries protect us so we can engage in good work. One of the family boundaries we established after that season was reevaluating where we choose to give our time and money. Specifically, we still donate to and partner with various parts of Baylor's campus. Through the business school, my husband continues to guest speak, mentor students through a Christian leadership program, and judges an ethics competition each semester. I, too, guest speak and mentor students through the same Christian leadership program. We want to model how to bless someone who hurt you, even if that hurt is a whole university. And for this reason, we continue to frequent Baylor football and basketball games. As donors, we've taken our boys to the President's Suite for donor events. And when we hosted an event on behalf of the Museum of the Bible, we could have chosen several Waco venues, but we selected Baylor. Bringing even more of the Bible to campus was quite healing for my heart. But what was perhaps the most redemptive for me was coleading a Baylor Business School Chapel with my husband for the fall 2024 semester. Teaching

God's Word alongside my husband, who is my best friend and greatest cheerleader this side of eternity, was restorative to my soul. That redemption and restoration healed me so I can further partner with those desiring the same redemption and restoration through Jesus.

Forgive, Set Healthy Boundaries, and Be Fruitful

I've learned the hard way not to let the actions of a few dictate my feelings or distort the truth about the health of the whole. Judge a tree by the whole of its fruit, not by a few that have become infected, spoiled, or rotted. Those need attention, certainly, or they could infest the rest. But a few are not indicative of the whole. Hurt happens; it's inevitable. Hurt people will hurt you. And sometimes, however unintentional, you will hurt others as well. Either way, I can say now with more authority than I could have before the trial, we cannot stay hurt; by the blood of Jesus, we do not have the luxury or the right. No matter how the pain was inflicted, the only way to get from hurt to healed is by way of forgiveness. It doesn't matter if the offender apologized or not. It doesn't matter if the wrong was made right or not. It doesn't matter if the whole system is unjust or not. Forgiveness is less about them and more about you. It's about the condition of your heart. You can forgive with boundaries. You can forgive with accountability. You can forgive and still feel an ache in your heart. That's reasonable and biblical. But you have to forgive. Because how much more have you been forgiven? There is so much beauty and health to be found on the other side of bitterness and hurt. At the core of biblical justice is redemptive grace. As Christians, we extend grace to others because we know we have been given grace in the form of Christ's death and atonement for our sin, a gift we could never repay.

BUT CHURCH, HOW DID WE GET HERE?

Like our country, colleges have also undergone profound cultural shifts over the last few years. Namely, there have been changes in how students and administrators approach free speech, emotional and mental health, safe spaces, and power dynamics between authority and compliance. Particularly since 2020, we've witnessed a rise in accusations of microaggressions, or that a failure to agree with someone's perspective is hate speech. As a result, students have become conditioned to interpret any ideas they deem remotely controversial a form of violence against marginalized groups. Across the country, college campuses have scrambled to acquiesce to outraged students by way of trigger warnings, bans on microaggressions, a strict regulation of speech, and the crippling illusion of college campuses as a haven or "safe space." Social justice ideologies on campus have reinterpreted words, ideas, and behaviors as forms of violence. This frames subtle—or even perceived—insensitivities as dire threats to vulnerable students. In this kind of climate, emotional comfort takes priority over everything.

I'm not a particularly political person, at least not in the sense that I closely follow politics. Quite honestly, it was a bit of a political refresher when my fifth grader first began learning what the three branches of American government do. I may or may not have rewatched a few *Schoolhouse Rock!* videos on YouTube to sort out what branches and bills do. But in 2021, I was paying attention to the shifts in political policies as they pertained to Title IX. President Biden's executive order directed schools receiving federal funds include gender identity in Title IX protections.[2] Under those new guidelines, biological males who identify as transgender girls must be allowed to compete on girls' sports teams. With one executive order, the "expansion of protection" utterly undermined fair competition as well as Title IX's established purpose.

I maintained then and now that erasing historically protected sex-based spaces for females—restrooms, locker rooms, camps, prisons, and safe houses—leaves women and girls even more vulnerable to sexual assault. And efforts to allow biological males into female-only spaces threaten to undermine critical protections and privacy for women and girls. Research validates these concerns. In my anti-trafficking work, I learned the vast majority of sexual assaults are committed by males and against females. For example, 82 percent of juvenile sexual assault victims are female, with 90 percent of perpetrators male.[3] Opening restrooms and changing facilities based on gender identity rather than biological sex enables predatory males access to vulnerable females. The progressive retort I sometimes hear back to this argument is typically along the lines of, "Well, that's transphobic to assume trans-identifying females (biological males) would ever sexually assault biological females." Foremost, I disagree with how culture now defines "transphobic" as anyone who refuses to accept the narrative wholesale.

That rhetorical misappropriation aside, even if we were to suspend our disbelief that all trans females are safe, we are still at a loss for how to gatekeep predators who have evil intentions. Comprehensive research is lacking in this area, but estimates converge around 10-15 percent on the percentage of sexual assaults against young females occur specifically in bathrooms or locker rooms. And unsurprising, 96 percent of those assaults were committed by men.[4] The risk of assault is amplified for incarcerated women primarily because prison staff consists of males.[5] But there is also reason to consider how housing transgender prisoners according to gender identity rather than sex could further expose female inmates to assault. In her *Wall Street Journal* article, "Male Inmates in Female Prisons," journalist Abigail Shrier notes the spike of reported sexual assaults in California prisons correlated with the same year biological males were allowed to transfer to biological female prisons.[6] Housing transgender prisoners according to gender identity rather than sex could expose female inmates to assault. Likewise, up to 63 percent of homeless women have experienced violence or trauma from men.[7] Removing female-only shelters leaves abused women without refuge. Given this data, it's no small wonder 56 percent of women surveyed expressed concern about their safety, privacy, or comfort if required to share spaces like bathrooms or locker rooms with men.[8]

To be clear, I am not opposed to transgender identifying people, and my heart aches listening to stories of their distress and trauma. I believe every human being deserves dignity, compassion, respect, safety, and protected rights no matter how one identifies. Gender dysphoria is real, it causes severe emotional distress, and it is an increasingly diagnosed disorder in counseling. When studying gender identities for a biblical counseling certificate at Southwestern Seminary, I read several respected Christian counselors' thoughts and approaches to this growing ailment. If you're interested in further reading, I recommend the works of Drs. Mark Yarhouse, Preston Sprinkle, and Andrew Walker. For a less academic but theologically trustworthy source, Jackie Hill Perry provides a biblical perspective on finding identity in the Lord rather than in sexualities.

No matter how a person identifies—by sexuality, gender, race, religion, level of education, their profession, their social economic status—every American citizen deserves equal protection under the law. Where we seem to be at an impasse, unfortunately, is on how to implement policies that do not infringe on the rights of other groups. In this case, for instance, research shows most females oppose permitting biological males access to biological female spaces.[9] So while transgender females (males who identify as female) should not have to live in fear for their safety, most Americans would assert biological females should not have to compromise their safety or success either.

WHERE IS THE CHURCH?

There appears to be a slow but growing consensus around maintaining biological sex as a binary assigned at birth, particularly among Christians, which is good news. In fact, a Pew Research survey shows the pendulum has swung a bit in favor of defining gender by biology and not postmodern ideologies. Accordingly, the gap between those who believe gender is fluid and constructed from individual identity, and those who believe gender is derived from biological sex, is among those who consider themselves "non-religious" and those who consider themselves Christians. (Evidently, the survey did not include enough Jewish, Muslim, or Mormon participants to parse out those religions.) The 2002 Pew Research Center survey states:

> Growing shares of Americans believe that a person's gender is determined by their sex assigned at birth, which finds major differences by religion on this question and others about transgender issues. For example, a majority of White evangelical Protestants say society has gone too far in accepting people who are transgender, while religiously unaffiliated Americans are far more likely to say society has not gone far enough.

> Among U.S. adults 60% now say that whether a person is a man or a woman is determined by their sex assigned at birth. This figure is even higher among White evangelicals (87%) and Black Protestants (70%). Among Catholics, the share who say a person's gender cannot differ from sex at birth has risen from 52% in 2021 to 62% this year. By contrast, a majority of religiously unaffiliated Americans (58%) say a person's gender can be different from their sex assigned at birth.[10]

Considering the amount of research evidencing inherent biological differences between males and females, given the DSM-5 psychological disorder undergirding transgender identity, bearing in mind the data on how many females prefer separated spaces for their physical safety and emotional wellbeing, it is flat astonishing how controversial this public debate has become.[11] The evidence is overwhelming in favor of upholding sex as a binary and creating policies on this premise. The reality of male-on-female violence exists, and for this reason, sex-segregated spaces remain critically important havens from harm for women and girls. Erasing them requires ignoring biological and statistical realities.

My friend Dr. Katie McCoy wrote an excellent book, *To Be a Woman: How Biblical Womanhood Sets Women Free*, that helps the contemporary church understand how to define womanhood from a biblical framework. It was the book I wish I had read before entering into conversations about gender and sex. McCoy's book was released in 2022 against the cultural tensions around the question "What is a woman?" Her book articulates a biblical vision of womanhood that affirms female dignity and significance. One of McCoy's concerns is that modern secular feminism has distorted views of womanhood and motherhood. She contends that feminism, and other postmodern critical theories of the same ilk, have led to identity confusion. In contrast to culture, McCoy offers Christians a better perspective. She not only offers a biological case for how females differ from males, but even more important for Christians, she underscores a biblical framework for gender distinctions.

LOOKING BACK AND MOVING FORWARD

In retrospect, maybe my tweet was a tad snarky, and perhaps it was a little out of character for me to be so bold, especially for the world to see on full display. Still, in full transparency, I maintain I wasn't aiming for snarky, or cheeky, or pugnacious, or anything along the lines of looking for a fight. I also wasn't directing the rhetorical and hypothetical question at any particular person or even a group, except for perhaps President Biden and his administration. I was impassioned by the injustice occurring to biological women and the complicity of those who stood by silently. Social media has become the contemporary public square, and while I knew that at a subconscious level, I was completely unprepared for the backlash I received from ideologically progressive Christians.

As surprising as it has been to witness the political debate surrounding Title IX, no amount of prior study could have prepared me for experiencing firsthand the level of discord LGTBQ+ narratives have caused in Christian circles. Perhaps I'm naive, but I assumed we, the church body, were on the same page about this. What my 2021 tweet, and the firestorm that ensued as a result, spotlighted was not only the lack of agreement on this cultural issue but also the lack of discipleship younger Millennials and Gen Z have received. There is an apparent deficiency in biblical literacy and Christian apologetics. More than ever, the time has come to address contemporary social justice issues from a Christian worldview perspective.

2

WHAT EVEN IS "SOCIAL JUSTICE"?

Defining Our Terms

Social justice. The very term evokes a visceral response in our hearts. For some, perhaps the connotations are negative. Perhaps what comes to mind are a cadre of young social justice warriors who march, protest, and even commandeer private property for their cause. For others, the term *social justice* likely reflects a deep longing for wrongs to be made right, for evil to be punished, for the vulnerable to be protected. It's much easier to define *social injustice* than *social justice*. We know when our rights have been violated. We see injustice everywhere we look in this fallen world and cry out for someone, anyone, to fix it. Protestors take to the streets, politicians make promises, and philosophers debate the true meaning of a just society. But what does the Bible have to say? How are we as Christians to understand justice, and what role, if any, should we play in pursuing it? Maybe you've wondered about these questions. As I've watched the events of the past five years unfold, these are the questions I have asked myself too.

Many disturbing media images and headlines from the past few years are seared into our collective consciousness. We feel overwhelmed by the injustice and unrest that confronts us at every turn. Our hearts break as we watch the world groaning under the weight of sin and brokenness, longing for the sort of peace and rest that only Christ can bring. Like many friends and colleagues, I began taking a greater interest in the public square not because many of today's social issues are not simply social or political, but even more, because they are biblical. In 2020, we witnessed the tragic deaths of George Floyd, Breonna Taylor, and Ahmaud Arbery, which sparked difficult conversations and riots related to racial injustice in America. The pain and anger were palpable as communities grappled with the ongoing reality of systemic racism and the urgent need for change.

In 2021, we saw another kind of cultural flashpoint with the calls to cancel author J.K. Rowling for her views on gender and biological sex. As you read in chapter one, I experienced similar online defamation and disparagement, but from within pockets of more progressive Christianity. Faith-based circles or otherwise, it was disheartening to see such vitriolic backlash against someone expressing a sincerely held belief. It raised troubling questions about free speech, tolerance, and the direction of our public discourse. And within the Christian community, it challenged where postmodern, progressive theories had come to undermine orthodox, conservative interpretations of biology, sex, and gender. Those concerns only intensified with the redefining of Title IX in America, as new policies regarding gender identity sparked heated debate about fairness, privacy, and the very nature of what it means to be male and female. Navigating these sensitive issues with both truth and grace continues to be a formidable challenge for believers.

On the global stage, we've watched with heavy hearts as violence and suffering continue to devastate communities. The Russian invasion of Ukraine in 2022, for instance, brought shocking destruction and loss of life, forcing millions to flee their homes as refugees. The heartbreaking images of bombed-out buildings and weeping families were a sobering reminder of the brokenness of our world. The unconscionable Hamas terrorist strike on Israel in 2023, and then Israel's defense against Hamas, has gutted a world watching in anguish. The Israel-Palestine conflict has increased the toll of poverty, hunger, and death in the world, and it's all too much to follow. Perhaps, like me, you've grown compassion-weary, fatigued by it all. In the face of such overwhelming need, it's tempting to despair or grow numb.

Yet as followers of Jesus, we have hope. We cling to a defiant hope in the midst of suffering. We know that the pain and injustice we see are not the final word. The gospel tells a different story—one of a God who entered into our brokenness to bring healing and redemption, who will one day wipe away every tear and make all things new (Revelation 21:4-5).

That doesn't mean we passively accept the world as it is. I do not believe we're called to be pacificists. That would be poor stewardship. Instead, we are called to be agents of Christ's truth, love, and justice in accordance with how God defines those concepts in Scripture.

But how? How do we do this?

To be quite honest, I don't have the one definitive silver-bullet answer or the one conclusive golden solution. But may I humbly suggest we start by defining what we mean when we say, "We want justice"? Can we put that phrase in context with how the Bible defines justice? Can we look to examples throughout church history for our social justice methodology? And might we also consider modern-day churches, charities, and ministries that continue to do justice work well? I believe doing so will move us closer to honoring and upholding what God means when He calls us to justice and righteousness.

BIBLICAL JUSTICE: WHEN
CHERRY-PICKING BEARS SOUR FRUIT

Most often when we hear demands for justice in the public square, people are referring to a particular contemporary interpretation that centers primarily on elevating the oppressed. Biblically, that is certainly a facet of God's definition of justice, but it is an incomplete understanding of His holistic design. Christians of all stripes are guilty of choosing scriptures that elevate their particular cause or interests, and I've noticed this is especially true for social justice issues. For example, you've likely noticed both progressives and conservatives are prone to wielding Scripture as a weapon in the battle for social justice, each side cherry-picking verses that support their causes while conveniently overlooking those that do not. The progressive left may point to biblical passages about welcoming the stranger and loving one's neighbor to advocate for more open immigration policies; similarly, the conservative right may highlight verses about the sanctity of life to argue against abortion.

It is not wrong to invoke Scripture in matters of social justice. One is not a woke social justice warrior for caring about the dignity and treatment of those crossing our borders, even if their means of entrance was less than legal. Likewise, one is not a Christian nationalist for believing the Judeo-Christian values on which our country was founded are still the best, most cohesive framework for law, order, justice, and mercy. The trouble arises when we become selective in our application of biblical principles, using them as a cover for our own political agendas rather than submitting to the comprehensive wisdom of God's Word and the totality of the biblical narrative. It is all too easy to fall into the trap of hypocrisy, boldly proclaiming the parts of Scripture that align with our preferred causes while quietly ignoring or even vehemently rejecting the parts of Scripture that challenge our ideologies.

The true test of our Christian witness lies in our willingness to grapple with the entirety of Scripture, even when it confronts our deeply held beliefs and calls us to a higher standard of justice and righteousness. Only by approaching God's Word with humble hearts and attentive minds, through gleaning the wisdom of 2,000 years of church orthodoxy and the engagement of church orthopraxy, can we hope to be faithful advocates for the causes that matter most. The entirety of the Bible speaks to justice; the whole of it points to God's heart for redeeming and restoring what has been broken by the fall in Genesis 3. Before the fall, there was an alignment between the heavens and the earth, between humanity and God. And this alignment and alliance between goodness and righteousness was God's standard for justice.

The whole of Scripture speaks to how God wants us to honor others. In the Old Testament, the prophets spoke out against oppression and injustice, urging the people of Israel to create a society where the poor and marginalized were treated with compassion and equity. In the New Testament, we're called to not only love our neighbors as ourselves by caring for the least among us, but we are also called to do the same for our enemies. Why? Because as Christians, we believe that every human being is created in the image of God and possesses inherent worth and dignity. This belief compels us to work toward a world where at minimum everyone has access to basic life necessities such as food, water, shelter, clothing, safety from harm, and freedom from exploitation or unjust punishment. And in a Western world where those human rights are defined and generally upheld, we work toward a society where all people are treated with respect, dignity, and have an opportunity to flourish toward their full potential.

THE ORIGIN OF SOCIAL JUSTICE

The term *social justice* has become mainstream, but it is not new. It has a complex, multifaceted history, and one strongly connected to Christianity. The phrase is frequently accredited to Luigi Taparelli, an Italian priest and adviser to the Vatican in 1840. Taparelli's term was based on orthodox Catholic teachings and biblical frameworks for social engagement.[1] Taparelli was born into a world of privilege and wealth, and he could have easily turned a blind eye to the suffering of the poor and the marginalized around him. Yet, like the great saints and heroes of church history, he chose a different path. He chose to follow in the footsteps of Christ, to take up the cause of the oppressed and the forgotten, and to work tirelessly for a world where every person is treated with dignity and respect. As a young priest, Taparelli witnessed firsthand the devastating impact of poverty and social inequality. He saw families struggling to survive, children forced to work in dangerous conditions, and entire communities cast aside by a society that valued wealth and status above all else. In the face of such suffering, he could not remain silent.

Taparelli set out to develop a new vision of society, one that would put the needs of the poor and the marginalized at the center of our Christian concern for society. With a heart full of compassion and a mind shaped by rigorous study, he immersed himself in the study of philosophy, theology, and the emerging field of social science, seeking to understand the root causes of poverty and inequality and to develop a framework for a more just and humane world. It was in this context that Taparelli coined the term *social justice* in his writings. For this young man, social justice was not a political slogan or a rallying cry to deconstruct church leadership. Rather, Taparelli believed social justice underscored Christian orthopraxy (practice). It provided a fundamental principle for social engagement that is rooted in the very nature of God's desire to redeem and restore humanity. He argued that every human being, regardless of their social status or economic condition, possessed an inherent worth and dignity endowed by God, and that *imago Dei* (image of God) required a communal respect, protection, and flourishing for all people.

Social justice cannot be achieved through individual action alone; it takes the collective majority working together to impact significant change. Taparelli emphasized the importance of communal solidarity and the need for all members of society to work together in pursuit of the common good. Like the members of a body, each performing its own function yet working together in harmony, Taparelli envisioned a society where every person had a role to play in building a more just and compassionate world. He believed the church is anointed to lead social justice work. Taparelli's vision of social justice was not merely a product of abstract guesswork; rather, his vision of justice was deeply rooted in his faith and his commitment to the teachings of the church. He believed that the gospel message of love and compassion demanded a radical transformation of society, one that would challenge the powers and principalities of this world and establish a new order based on the principles of justice and mercy. As an adviser to the Vatican, he worked tirelessly to promote his vision of social justice within the church and beyond.

Taparelli's ideas about the church and social engagement would go on to influence generations of Catholic leaders. Most directly, Pope Leo XIII, whose groundbreaking encyclical *Rerum novarum* in 1891 drew on Taparelli's efforts and writings. In the Catholic church, encyclical decrees are used by popes to communicate the church's teaching on a particular subject, such as social justice, to address important issues facing the church and the world, or to provide guidance on matters of faith, morals, and social doctrine. Although not considered the infallible Word of God, these documents are authoritative statements and carry significant weight within the Catholic church. *Rerum novarum*, specifically, derives its title from the opening words of the encyclical, which translates to "of revolutionary change" or "of new things" in Latin. At the end of the 19th century, this groundbreaking document was considered the foundational text of modern Catholic social teaching.[2] It was written in response to the growing social and economic challenges of the times, particularly the impact of the Industrial Revolution on the working class. It addressed issues such as the rights and duties of capital and labor, the role of the state in promoting social justice, and the principles of a just economic order.

Taparelli's vision of the church working toward social justice influenced key themes and ideas presented in *Rerum novarum* as well as the Catholic teachings on social justice that followed. Many of the revolutionary ideas presented in these documents now underscore universal and undisputed human rights in most developed countries. For example, the right to fair wages for work, rather than labor exploitation, was an area of reform for which Taparelli advocated. His advocacy is also reflected in *Rerum novarum*'s assertions about balancing private and publicly held property, as well as an economic system that balances against the extremes of socialism and crony capitalism. The papal decree also encouraged more community influence at the local level and less government influence at the state level. Taparelli's vision for social justice had a profound impact on the Catholic church as evidenced by the establishment of policies and lasting impact. Taparelli's work not only laid the foundation for *Rerum novarum*'s statements on the church's engagement with and commitment to social justice, but it also informed future seminal decisions. For example, in the Second Vatican Council, which met from 1962 to 1965, Pope John XXII and Pope Paul VI aimed to renew and modernize the Catholic church's commitment to meeting the needs of our contemporary world. Specifically related to social justice, the Second Vatican Council addressed issues related to religious freedom, pro-life causes, and the role of the church in promoting human flourishing.

SECULAR SOCIAL JUSTICE: THE PATH
MOST TRAVELED LED THE PEOPLE ASTRAY

Although the term *social justice* has deep, undeniable roots to Christianity, the notion of doing common good work to improve society is not exclusive to Christianity or the church. Throughout recorded human history, great thinkers and leaders have grappled with how to create a society that treats people with fairness, dignity, and respect. Principles of cultural and political justice are evident in thousands of years of intellectual thinkers and leaders, particularly in Western culture. It's fair of us to acknowledge the various thought leaders who have made significant contributions to the advancement of social justice, even though they did not ground their ideas in the Christian faith. It's important for us to recognize and learn from these perspectives, as it can help us find common ground to do common good work. We can appreciate their contributions while also acknowledging the unique perspective the gospel brings to our Christian understanding of justice and human flourishing. And perhaps of greater significance to our social justice conversation, considering the contributions of a few non-Christian leaders can help us discern the difference in motivation, purpose, and outcome.

But it's important for Christians to remember that, although we can assert with confidence that Jesus is the only way to eternal salvation and that our lives should be lived for the sake of gospel-minded work, we neither hold the exclusive rights to social justice efforts nor have we cornered the market on them. Throughout global history, men and women of different backgrounds and faiths have contributed to human flourishing and social justice. To cite an early historical example, in a time of political upheaval and moral decay in 500 BC China, the ancient Chinese philosopher Confucius is remembered for his emphasis on the importance of social harmony, moral virtues, and the responsibilities of individuals within society. According to authors C.H. Kang and Ethel R. Nelson in their book *The Discovery of Genesis: How the Truths of Genesis Were Found Hidden in the Chinese Language*, Confucius taught on benevolence, righteousness, and what we've widely come to call the "golden rule." They suggest his teachings laid the foundation for social and ethical thought in East Asia.[3] As most Chinese texts convey, Confucius is remembered for his efforts to restore social harmony and cultivate virtuous character in individuals and society. To illustrate their point, Kang and Nelson share of how Confucius, while serving as a government minister in the state of Lu, implemented policies that reduced crime and poverty by promoting education, meritocracy, and the fair distribution of resources. The authors suggest Confucius's teachings on the "golden rule," which is essentially to "do unto others as you would have them do unto you," resonates with the biblical command to love one's neighbor as oneself (Mark 12:31).

To offer another example of a non-Christian who cared for the wellbeing of society, I am reminded of a book I read in seminary when writing my capstone paper. The paper focused on the church's over 2,000-year engagement with social justice from a biblical justice framework. The lengthy paper not only served as a thesis and application for what I had gleaned in my seminary studies, but it also became the proposal submission for this book. In preparation for the paper, I recall sitting in the quiet corner of the Dallas Theological Seminary library and poring over the pages of Michael Goheen's book *The Gospel and Globalization*. As I read, I couldn't escape the strange feeling—a tension of sorts—burgeoning within myself. Goheen's book, which explores the foundational beliefs shaping globalization from the standpoint of the Christian gospel, challenged my assumptions about the exclusivity I had assumed Christianity held in terms of social justice work. Naively, I imagined the book would further underscore that no other religion has done more for our collective wellbeing than Christianity. After years of study, thought, and conversation on this topic, I would maintain no other religion has done as much good for the world as Christianity. Still, I do not want to imply no other religions or global thought leaders have contributed to human rights or our sense of justice in meaningful, productive ways.

One of the essays in *The Gospel and Globalization* refers to Ibn Khaldun, a 14th-century Muslim philosopher who had developed a theory about the rise and fall of civilizations. The author argues that

Ibn Khaldun's concept of *asabiyyah*, or social solidarity, could offer valuable insights for Christians seeking to navigate the complexities of our globalized world.[4] At first read, I was skeptical. Honestly, what could a medieval Muslim thinker have to say to me, a 21st-century Christian? But as I read and reflected, I began to see the validity in the illustration. Although the Muslim philosopher Ibn Khaldun did not know or follow Jesus, and although we have entirely different worldviews, he, too, recognized the importance of social solidarity and justice in maintaining a thriving civilization. He observed that when rulers prioritize their own interests over the wellbeing of their subjects, they sow the seeds of social discord and eventual decline. In his famous work, the *Muqaddimah*, Ibn Khaldun praises the example of one caliph, a chief Muslim civil and religious ruler, Umar ibn al-Khattab, because he was known for his humility, fairness, and concern for the poor. Accordingly, Umar would walk the streets of Medina at night, ensuring that no one went hungry and that the weak and vulnerable were protected. Ibn Khaldun saw servant leadership in Umar's governance model, one that is just, compassionate, and promotes social cohesion and the common good.

In more recent Western history, British utilitarian thought leaders Jeremy Bentham and John Stuart Mill sought to reform society for the better based on the principle of maximizing happiness for the greatest number of people. Bentham and Mill were both prominent English Enlightenment thinkers at the end of the eighteenth and the turn of nineteenth century. They were widely regarded as the founders of modern utilitarianism, a philosophical theory that emphasizes the "greatest happiness principle," which purports that actions are right if they promote the greatest happiness for the greatest number of people. The happiness notion is the core idea behind utilitarianism, a philosophical theory developed first by Bentham and later expanded upon by Mill. Essentially, the principle states that the most ethical action is the one that maximizes overall happiness or wellbeing for the greatest number of people. In other words, when one is faced with a moral decision, he or she should choose the option that results in the greatest net positive outcome, considering the happiness or suffering of all individuals affected by the action.

By most accounts, Jeremy Bentham and John Stuart Mill were social justice advocates. They advocated for voting rights for women, the abolition of slavery, and the improvement of working conditions for laborers. One story recounts how Bentham, upon learning of the horrors of the slave trade, devoted himself to its abolition and drafted a proposal for the gradual emancipation of slaves in the British colonies.[5] Although his plan was not adopted, it influenced later efforts to end slavery and promote human rights. Proponents of utilitarianism argue that the greatest happiness principle provides a clear and rational basis for making moral decisions and promoting social welfare. Critics, however, point out the myriad of challenges when defining subjective concepts like happiness and morality. Additionally, arguments pertaining to individual rights, such as the life of a baby in utero, for example, may conflict with the purported rights of the mother carrying the baby. And of course, there is the shared idea that some actions may be inherently right or wrong regardless of their social consequences. For example, euthanasia, the act of willfully taking one's life or assisting with another's death, has been and remains a highly controversial practice, even though an individual's death is of little to no concern on the whole of society.

As you might have guessed, although Bentham and Mill believed in "life, liberty, and the pursuit of happiness," neither of these men were professing Christians. In fact, Bentham was a vocal critic of religion, particularly an organized, state implemented religion.[6] Bentham's philosophical views were largely secular. From a Christian perspective, the greatest happiness principle, like other secular social constructs, is an insufficient moral framework for doing social justice work. While the idea of promoting happiness and minimizing suffering may seem an appealing social justice framework on the surface, it fails to account for the inherent value and dignity of human life, the reality of sin and evil, and God as our ultimate source of joy, purpose, and fulfillment. In the upcoming chapters, we'll consider how Christianity presents a vision of justice grounded not in abstract ideals but in the concrete truth of God's moral and just character. Secular frameworks borrow from Christian moral capital, but they resort to human power dynamics for authority. A biblical framework for social justice stands in contrast to the flawed and finite secular approaches; a gospel-centered perspective underscores the redemptive and restorative power of Christ because biblical justice requires not just structural changes but transformed hearts.

3

CHRISTIANITY AND CONTEMPORARY SOCIAL ISSUES

Our Faith in Troubled Times

I f Christianity is the most influential religion for social justice in the world, it's fair to wonder why the world, at least the Western world, has lost sight of its doctrine and good works. The short answer is this: competing worldviews. The longer explanation is the crux of the next section. The impact of various philosophical thought movements on America's relationship with Christianity has been complex. The more I've studied Western thought, the more I've come to understand how complicated the relationship truly is. Initially, in my early academic pursuits, I didn't have a particular interest in history, philosophy, or even theology. In fact, in my undergraduate studies at Texas A&M University, I majored in English and minored in both psychology and education. But it became apparent by my midtwenties, when I enrolled in a master's program in secondary English education, that the intersectionality of history, philosophy, literature, education, sociology—so many various fields of study—cannot be easily untangled. The fabric of American social thought is a tightly woven tapestry, and pulling on one thread inevitably unravels several interrelated threads. By the time I reached my PhD program in education with an emphasis in American literature, I had a fundamental understanding of how the complexity of all this intersectionality could not easily be isolated into small parts. The fields of study have to be considered holistically.

I had a similar revelation with theology. I first noticed gaps in my theology during COVID-19 lockdowns. My faith in the Lord was unmoved and my commitment to church unwavering. But as I witnessed the growing trend of friends and former students deconstructing their faith—some altogether walking away from the church and the Lord—I realized my theological frameworks and cultural apologetics were not nearly as robust as I had hoped they would be at age 40. So I took a highly atypical step away from teaching in higher education, and with nearly ten years of postdoctorate work and college level teaching under my belt, I enrolled as a student in a master's of biblical and theological studies program at Dallas Theological Seminary. I cannot overemphasize how instrumental seminary studies were for helping me understand theological concepts such as soteriology (doctrine of salvation), eschatology (doctrine of end times), ecclesiology (doctrine of the church), hermeneutics (how to interpret the Bible), apologetics, church orthodoxies and heresies, and much more. My time in seminary also provided structure for how to read and study God's Word. And after three years of coursework, I had only just begun to put together all the puzzle pieces that form the whole of my worldview.

Seminary study is expensive and rigorous, so I am not suggesting everyone enroll in it; however, I can attest to how intellectually and spiritually formative it was for me, even after many decades of being faithfully committed to the Lord and a local church. But maybe of even greater significance was how seminary helped me think Christianly about all the spheres the Lord has called me to engage. With greater clarity, I could see our collective drift away from the Bible as the touchstone for American public and private life. It's also apparent how this drift has bred hostility to public expressions of faith in the public square, particularly faith and politics.

WHAT WE'VE LEARNED ABOUT SOCIAL INJUSTICE SINCE 2020

Over the last several years, we've seen an increase of demands for justice in the public square—and for good reasons. Since 2020, we have witnessed more visible contention around complex social and political issues of justice than any period in living history since the tumultuous 1960s. At the beginning of 2020, the world was turned upside down by an unprecedented global pandemic. We were not prepared. But to be charitable to our global leaders, how could we have been? No one foresaw COVID-19, and most of us, whatever our level of influence, were doing our best to navigate a global virus and the mandated lockdowns, vaccines, and masks. The coronavirus erupted from Wuhan, China, in early 2020 and swept the globe with alarming speed. Governments worldwide rapidly implemented strict lockdowns in hopes of containing the virus. While vital for mitigating hospitalizations, particularly among the elderly, these abrupt society-wide restrictions carried steep unintended consequences beyond infectious risks alone. The ramifications were calamitous, and cries for justice across all demographics were ferocious.

Injustices Within Education

In the spring of 2020, schools shuttered overnight and education systems across the world scrambled to convert traditional in-person modes of instruction to an online format. Closing schools revealed major disparities in digital infrastructure and access. In America, we witnessed rural students and disadvantaged communities disproportionately struggle amid the virtual shift, which further exacerbated achievement gaps. Younger learners forfeited critical developmental progress when K-12 education was delivered by way of Zoom classrooms. And distressed parents, many of whom were ill-equipped to homeschool—particularly under the strain of working from home—replaced traditional vibrant, organized, and social classrooms. Emerging research documents historic learning loss between 2020 and 2022, which is especially threatening to marginalized, vulnerable student populations.[1]

Even within my own home, even as an educator, I struggled to adequately homeschool my then kindergartener and second grader while also managing to teach 80 college students as we shifted in-person courses to online learning over spring break. My husband was as helpful as he could be, given his increased workload in healthcare. When the "shelter in place" mandates loosened ever so slightly to allow some semblance of interaction outside of our immediate family, I hired a friend's high school aged daughter to help tutor my kids. But not every parent was so fortunate. And when the fog of it all lifted in May, when kids and parents alike were released from the chaos of balancing virtual work and schooling, we began to see more clearly the educational and professional injustices we experienced those early months of the pandemic.

Injustices for Working Women

The injustice of the pandemic affected everyone differently, but not one of us was unaffected. As a mother, I can attest that homeschooling children was extremely challenging for parents who were also juggling the demands of virtual work. And according to emerging studies, no demographic was hit harder than working mothers with elementary aged children. Even a few years removed, I can still vividly recall the stress of juggling full-time Zoom teaching, full-time homeschooling, and full-time worrying about whether our family was going to survive what at the time seemed apocalyptic. Evidently, I was not the only mother who shouldered this burden. Studies indicate the pandemic had a disproportionate impact on working women around the world. In an analysis by McKinsey and Company, women were nearly twice as vulnerable to job loss than men.[2] Women make up just under half of the global employment, but according to the study, they accounted for 54 percent of overall job losses related to the pandemic.

With widespread school and childcare facility closures, working mothers took on even more childcare work while trying to maintain their paid jobs. A survey across 40 countries found working mothers were three times more likely than fathers to spend an additional three or more hours per day on housework and childcare during the pandemic.[3] This burden has forced many women to scale back their work hours or leave jobs entirely. By one estimate, 80 percent of those dropping out of the labor force in the US during the pandemic were women.[4] Additionally, women are disproportionately employed in sectors like hospitality, retail, education, and healthcare. Those industries were hit hardest by pandemic shutdowns and layoffs. The long-term impact of these job losses on working women could be substantial. Some economists estimate most working women have been set back two to four years in terms of economic parity and equal labor force participation.[5] Working mothers were significantly stymied in their professional efforts, but they were not the only demographic affected by the injustices and inequities of 2020.

Injustices Surrounding Mental Health

Children's learning suffered when they were barred from in-person classrooms, and mothers were exceptionally strained by professional and personal demands, but these were not the only destructive consequences of the pandemic. There was also a significant increase of reported domestic abuse, online child exploitation, and a decrease in mental health. A comprehensive study published in the journal *The Lancet* in 2021 found that the COVID-19 pandemic was associated with highly elevated rates of major depressive disorders and anxiety disorders globally. Researchers found this toll was disproportionately borne by young adults, teen girls, and those with pre-existing mental health conditions.[6] Tragically, as a means of coping, substance abuse and overdose deaths concurrently rose as vulnerable Americans self-medicated distress.[7] CDC data shows there were an estimated 107,622 drug overdose deaths in 2021 in the United States, an increase of nearly 15 percent from 2020.[8]

In the beginning months of the global pandemic, I recall worrying about the impact the lockdowns would have on my children, who were six and eight at the time. But as concerned as I was for the wellbeing of my own boys, I was more distressed thinking about the lives of children in low socioeconomic communities whose already unstable homes would prove that much more volatile. Many nights, I stayed awake crying and praying at the thought of children locked down with unsafe adults. Teachers, pastors, and coaches are most often the sort of mentors who report to the authorities any suspected domestic abuse, but that was not possible when children did not have access to these mentors. It was much more difficult for children or a safe adult to make an outcry.

Injustices with Online Exploitation

When the global pandemic hit, I was serving as a senior thesis adviser for a graduating Baylor student. She wrote her Honors College thesis specifically on the increase of online child exploitation. Advising her research likely increased my anxiety pertaining to children's overall safety. In assisting with her research, I learned that over the past 20 years, the online sexual exploitation of children (OSEC) has increased at an alarming rate. Whereas around 10,000 reports of OSEC per year were made at the turn of the century, 18.4 million reports of new OSEC material, or child sexual exploitation material (CSEM), were made in 2018 alone.[9] These 18.4 million reports included 84 million individual files of online CSEM. Technological development, specifically regarding the internet, has enabled this crime to skyrocket due to increased levels of anonymity and access to children. Today, children are one of the most profitable illegal commodities globally. Since 2019, the online sexual exploitation of children was estimated to be a $20 billion industry.[10] According to my student's nearly 100-page research thesis, there was a 108 percent increase of online child exploitation from the 2019 to the 2020 report.[11] The pandemic and the few years following it had different effects on different children.

To be certain, not every child suffered educational loss, struggled with mental health, or was abused and exploited. But the reports indicate many children did. Child and adolescent psychiatrists cautioned that disrupted routines, education, social connections, and emotional support during crucial developmental windows may have longer term mental health consequences for children that would require sensitive care and intervention. I've worked with youth ages high school to college for just over two decades. Among younger Millennials and Gen Z generations, I have witnessed a slow but steady increase in two areas: (1) professing progressive ideologies and (2) a decline in mental health. This is not to imply that there is a causal relationship, although there might very well be a correlated one. I am thankful, however, that supporting youth mental health continues to be a top priority even after the pandemic. This is an area of social justice with which the church should show concern and is able to assist with the hope of the gospel.

Injustices in Race Relations

The pandemic not only laid bare several pre-pandemic inequities, but it also exacerbated many of them. In addition to educational, economic, and emotional instabilities, America experienced heightened racial tensions in 2020, which further fueled cries for justice. Sparked by a series of tragic deaths of Black Americans, massive protests and cries for justice swept the nation. The brutal, senseless killings of George Floyd, Breonna Taylor, and Ahmaud Arbery, all Black Americans, stirred righteous anger and demands for accountability and reform. As Christians, we're called to speak biblical truth and wisdom to injustices. So I want to unequivocally express this deep lament: That summer, I grieved at the loss of precious human lives created in the image of God. George Floyd suffocated under the knee of a police officer who was supposed to protect and serve. Breonna Taylor was shot in her own home by officers recklessly discharging their weapons without announcing themselves. And Ahmaud Arbery was targeted and hunted down while jogging by vigilantes who assumed the worst of him simply because he toured a home being built in his neighborhood. News reports of racial injustices went viral. By midsummer, nationwide protests called for justice, accountability, and even to defund the police. Following Floyd's tragic death, by midsummer, demonstrations emerged in Minneapolis and rapidly expanded across the United States and globally. Violence broke out during some rallies, prompting more than 40 cities to enforce curfews and many states plus Washington, DC, to activate National Guard troops.[12] The demands for justice were fierce, and the cultural tension surrounding race relations was substantial.

As an aunt to a biracial niece and nephew who have been raised primarily in White, middle-class circles, I have witnessed their lives up close, and they have experienced indirect and even direct racial bias. My niece has shared how when she was younger, curious, well-meaning classmates would ask questions about where her family is from or ask if it is their mom or dad who is Black. On a few occasions, people have been downright insensitive. For instance, years ago, I took my niece to Target for her birthday, and I gave her permission to choose any doll or toy she wanted (within financial reason, of course). Specifically, she wanted to buy a two-foot-tall standing doll of Princess Tiana from the Disney film *The Princess and the Frog*. Perhaps this was the year the film came out, or maybe she desired that toy because she saw herself in the character. I'm not quite sure. When I asked a Target employee if they carried that doll, or any other Tiana toys—or any dolls that were biracial, really—the woman responded rather curtly. She stated, "We don't really sell many toys that look like her in our store. You can try online." And in that moment, my heart sank for my niece. What would that feel like to walk through life not seeing your skin reflected in dolls, Band-Aids, beauty ads, and the like?

This was more than ten years ago, and I'd like to think if Target is willing to sell LGBTQ clothing and toys to children in the name of diversity and inclusivity, which I find reprehensible and indefensible, hopefully they've also improved their selection of ethnic and racial representation for children. I also want to be charitable and assume perhaps the Target employee who was snippy with us was simply having a bad day, that the underlying problem has little to do with racism and is stemming more from a disgruntled personality. I do not want to imply most or even many middle-class White people are inherently racist; they're not. And research indicates this.[13] Most Americans of all races, ethnicities, and faiths are doing their best to live harmoniously with their coworkers and neighbors. But the brokenness of systemic racism and injustices in America could not have been clearer to me than in the summer of 2020.

In 2023, I had the honor of interviewing respected Baylor sociologist and professor Dr. George Yancey about his research on race relations. We hosted the conversation through Dallas Theological Seminary's Hendricks Center on a webinar titled "Faith, Work, and Sociology." Most of my reading, study, and teaching on race has taken place squarely within the context of K-12 and higher education. Yancey's book, *Beyond Racial Division: A Unifying Alternative to Colorblindness and Antiracism*, provides an alternative perspective from most platformed DEI (diversity, equity, and inclusion) voices after 2020. Yancey's book acknowledges where research finds evidence of systemic racism, but it is also honest about how overstated accusations of racism are in America. Yancey's tone departs from the palpable anger seething from other DEI experts, and perhaps this is in no small way correlated to his sincere, integrated faith in Jesus. In his research, Yancey cautions both White and Black Americans against making hurtful racial generalizations about each other that contribute to polarization and misunderstanding. He stresses that notions of White Americans being inherently racist is not empirically supported by data.

In addition to reading Yancey's book, I prepared for our interview by also reading an academic publication he wrote pertaining to race relations in the church. The webinar's aim was to help equip the church body (specifically those in formal ministry) to think about sociology (particularly in terms of race relations). Yancey and his colleague Y.J. Kim published research indicating that interethnic church congregations fostered more positive racial attitudes among attendees across backgrounds.[14] Ultimately, these intentional, faith-based relationships help congregations overcome prejudice. The study analyzed data from more than 2,000 churchgoers across the United States, comparing attitudes of those attending ethnically homogeneous congregations to those attending interethnic churches with diversity across race and ethnicity. People attending interethnic churches were less likely to stereotype racial outgroups and had lower levels of racial resentment. Church participation over time predicted further declines in holding negative outgroup stereotypes.

Injustices of Authority

Since 2020, society has experienced a collective awakening to several social injustices. As previously noted, we've given more attention to mental and emotional health, disparities between those living in wealth and those in poverty, racial biases in multiple spheres of influence, protecting children from online predators and ideological indoctrination, the impossible balance of professional and personal responsibilities for working parents, and educational inequalities pervasive in America's public schools. In the last five to ten years, we've also taken a closer look at systemic abuse embedded within power dynamics. For instance, the Me Too and Church Too movements spotlighted sexual and spiritual abuse occurring within several public and private sectors. The courageous testimonies shared through these movements pulled away the veil covering systemic abuse of power occurring across institutions. As survivors came forward with their stories, it became impossible to ignore the disturbing regularity with which those in positions of influence exploited others for sexual gratification or personal gain. The breadth of accusations spanning Hollywood, media, politics, business, and the church shattered any illusions that systemic abuse was limited to a few isolated incidents. The movements held up a mirror to power and forced leaders to consider their complicity in systems that enabled abuse. Unfortunately, the cultural tolerance for "boys being boys" or "that's just how things are" provided cover for predators. As iconic figures like Bill Cosby and Harvey Weinstein fell from grace, it awakened our society to the reality that enabling systemic abuse inflicts deep trauma with lifelong consequences. The raw pain exposed through Me Too and Church Too testimonies resonated across divides and denominations, uniting people in compassion for victims.

In response to the abuse, many organizations have reevaluated policies, practices, and cultural norms that inadvertently promote systemic abuse. For example, accountability measures, codes of conduct, and abuse prevention training are becoming more commonplace to deter misconduct. External pressure from consumers and congregants refusing to ignore unethical behaviors has also motivated self-examination. Ultimately, the courage of those sharing their stories empowered a social reckoning around systemic abuse of power. While institutions have much work left in preventing abuse, the groundswell from these movements makes it impossible to turn a blind eye ever again. The steep cost of silence has been revealed, and with greater accountability and compassion, we can work toward a society where no one has to choose between speaking out against abuse or self-preservation.

With so many injustices, Christians may find their heads spinning in search of a lasting solution. As we will see, followers of Jesus need not feel overwhelmed. The answer is biblical justice.

4

THE CASE FOR BIBLICAL JUSTICE

Political and Biblical Lessons Learned

In the timeframe from the 2020 election to the 2024 election, we've witnessed a considerable increase in the number of public square thought leaders who—on both the ideological right and left—co-opt biblical narratives to further their political agendas. Both sides of the aisle take biblical principles, obfuscate God's original exhortation to His people, and then use these teachings to wield accusations. Manipulating biblical principles to further political agendas is wrong. But it is equally wrong, and dare I say impossible, to expect people to engage politics through a neutral framework. As we'll consider, our perspective on life is profoundly shaped by our worldview, and it is not a framework we can set aside at will. And even if we could approach public policies and discussions of morality from a completely secular vantage point, it's important to consider that secularism is not neutral; rather, it implies an approach to public engagement that is devoid of God. For people of any faith system, that expectation for public engagement should strike us as offensive and disingenuous.

When a political leader or someone with any level of social influence evokes biblical principles concerning morality, the left commonly denounces their faith-integrated beliefs and labels them "Christian nationalists." Similarly, when more ideologically and politically progressive leaders encourage citizens to engage in justice work because the Bible compels us to, those who have positioned themselves on the far right accuse progressives of being "woke." But the truth of the finger pointing is this: As Christians, we should be accused of being both. Christianity compels followers of Jesus to integrate faith in all spheres of influence; Christianity also compels us do to good in the world as a means of kingdom partnership and stewardship. And we are called to do both unto God's glory. As followers of Christ, we are called to be salt and light in a world desperate for redemptive influence (Matthew 5:13-16). When we integrate our faith into every arena of life, including the public square, we are doing so as ambassadors for Christ. We cannot relegate our faith to a privatized, spiritually isolated space that is insulated from the wider culture. Rather, God commissioned us as ambassadors of reconciliation (2 Corinthians 5:20) to demonstrate kingdom values in our civic engagement, professional conduct, and social interactions. The apostle Paul instructs us, "Whatever you do, work at it with all your heart, as working for the Lord" (Colossians 3:23). This leaves no room for compartmentalizing our faith from our public witness. Whether in the marketplace, government, education, or any other sphere, we should strive for excellence and integrity as an act of worship. By exemplifying honesty, compassion, and sacrificial service in our vocations, we adorn the gospel and point people to the transformative love of Jesus. And in the third section of this book, on justice work, we'll consider Christianity's 2,000-year history of doing good work from a biblical framework. We'll also consider how the contemporary church alleviates social injustices by meeting the needs of our neighbors.

As Christians, we simultaneously hold two conflicting identities: We are citizens of both our country and heaven; we are obliged to obey the law of the land as well as God's law. And often, our earthly, temporal identity conflicts with our heaven-bound, eternal identity. Matthew 6:9-13 encourages us to pray that God's will be done "on earth as it is in heaven." Working toward that can be a difficult mandate in a culture that does not share these aims. As responsible citizens, we have a duty to actively steward our civic privileges and responsibilities in alignment with biblical truth. This includes advocating for policies that protect the vulnerable, uphold human dignity, strengthen families, and foster human flourishing. While no political party perfectly embodies Christian ethics, we cannot abdicate our public engagement to a secular agenda. Through prayerful discernment, we must support leaders and legislation that best reflect biblical values for the common good. In our increasingly post-Christian culture, integrating faith into the public square often incites misunderstanding, criticism, and even hostility. But this shouldn't surprise us. Jesus warned us, "If the world hates you, keep in mind that it hated me first" (John 15:18). Yet even in the face of opposition, we must not shrink back from our prophetic witness. With truth and love, with gentleness and respect, we should be prepared to articulate our Christian worldview and its implications for addressing society's deepest needs (1 Peter 3:15).

By courageously standing on God's truth and exuding His gospel message of grace and salvation, His Holy Spirit works through us and through others to accomplish His kingdom purposes (John 14; Romans 8; Ephesians 1). Ultimately, integrating our faith into the public square is not optional for followers of Christ. It is a biblical mandate to seek the welfare of our communities (Jeremiah 29:7) as we fulfill the Great Commission (Matthew 28:19-20). As the church engages culture with gospel-centered conviction and compassion, we serve as a conscience to the nation and a catalyst for spiritual awakening. So let us embrace our call to be faithful witnesses in every dimension of society, knowing that our labor in the Lord is never in vain (1 Corinthians 15:58). And let us not be afraid of the accusatory labels we may incur because we're walking closely with the Lord and partaking in work He deems good and just.

IS AMERICA A CHRISTIAN COUNTRY OR A COUNTRY FOUNDED BY CHRISTIANS?

America is not a Christian country in that we are not a theocracy. There is no official American church. And unlike England, our founders rejected the establishment of a monarchy, which would grant one person and their lineage supreme authority. America's Founding Fathers built a political foundation upon biblical truths. Specifically, our country was established on the premise that all human beings are made in God's image and endowed with unalienable rights and freedoms. The Declaration of Independence established our nation's humanitarian rights in 1776 when our Founding Fathers stated, "We hold these truths to be self-evident, that all men are created equal, that they are endowed by their Creator with certain unalienable Rights, that among these are Life, Liberty and the pursuit of Happiness."[1] America's Founding Fathers deliberately invoked divine provenance when they penned the iconic words "all men are created equal" in the Declaration of Independence. The clause was a clear and sincere expression of their belief that all human beings possess an innate dignity imparted by God Himself.

The founders rooted the birthright of liberty firmly in the Judeo-Christian conception of the *imago Dei*, the image of God stamped on every human soul. Whether high or low, rich or poor, all people reflect their Creator in His righteousness, creativity, rationality, and compassion. Therefore, as an extension of our biblical understanding of human dignity, no one has the right to deny American citizens the ability to seek life, enjoy liberty, and pursue happiness. Such presuppositions regarding innate, immutable human rights come directly from a Christian worldview. Even the structure of our government stems from insights gleaned from Scripture and Judeo-Christian thinkers throughout history. The concept of covenant and accountability between governed and governors, checks and balances of power, separation of church and state, and natural law theories of resistance to tyranny find their philosophical origins in Reformed theology and Enlightenment thinking, both of which are indebted to Christianity. It is no accident that the Declaration of Independence grounds these "unalienable rights" in humankind's God-given equality. If the government granted rights instead of recognizing them, the government could just as easily revoke them.

Unfortunately, the early American founders did not fully implement these biblical teachings into all facets of public policy and practice. The founders established biblical concepts of liberty, freedom, justice, and flourishing, but for women and people of color, it would take hundreds of years for these demographics to realize the totality of their rights. It would also take the Civil War in the 1860s to abolish slavery and the civil rights movement in the 1960s to establish freedom and equal rights for all men and women. In the third portion of this book, we'll consider ways the church has partnered with civic spaces and worked toward equality and justice. Biblical values were essential cornerstones in America's foundation. It is unreasonable and insufficient to consider American history, law, or culture apart from how Christianity fertilized and nurtured the soil and bore good fruit. Christian historian John Fea pushes back against the claim that America was founded as a secular or even pluralistic nation.[2] He explains how even though the Founding Fathers represented diverse Christian denominations, and though some held some unorthodox views, they nearly unanimously agreed on basic Christian doctrines and biblical principles that shaped their worldviews. So, no, America is not a Christian nation. However, there is ample evidence provided in early American political documents, congressional records, private letters, and public speeches that Christian rhetoric and reasoning were essential touchstones in our nation's foundation.

BIBLICAL JUSTICE OVER SOCIAL JUSTICE

When it comes to social justice ideologies and the people who have adopted them, often their approach to doing good work seems hostile to the church. Well-meaning people, Christians included, want to "fight for social justice," "do better," and "show love to others," which are all noble goals. The problem with social justice narratives is that they are divorced from biblical truisms. They rely on a framework that is fundamentally flawed. Social justice narratives categorize people into a binary of either "good and evil," "right and wrong," "oppressed and oppressor." But the problem, of course, is that the human condition cannot be reduced into two distinct and oppositional categories. Everyone wants to stand on the side of the most vulnerable and the most oppressed. But what do we do when both sides are vulnerable and oppressed? What do we do when on any given day either side is the oppressed and the oppressor—sometimes for thousands of years? That's where it gets extremely complicated. And that's also where the gospel message meets us. In my finite, limited wisdom, I cannot always discern who is my neighbor and who is my enemy. But it doesn't really matter; as Christians, we're called to pray for and extend love to both. Grace in the face of injustice is precisely what's so radical about Jesus.

Typically, when we have conversations about justice, we mean social justice and not legal justice. Legal or punitive justice is impartial, and it entails getting what we deserve. It is a form of justice that is just. It is a distribution of justice not according to grace but one predicated on punishment. When, for example, my younger son comes to me crying because his older brother has hurt him—which unfortunately occurs weekly in our household—I have to discern how to distribute justice. The fairest thing would be to distribute justice according to the same family rules that apply to everyone else. I must discern my older son's heart motive. Did he mean to hurt his younger brother or was it an accident? Was my younger son provoking the older one, and if so, to what extent? And I also need to take into consideration what harm my younger son has incurred. Was it a small scratch? A wound that requires stiches from the ER? It would also be prudent of me to take into consideration how frequently my older son has committed this transgression. According to just systems, there are greater consequences for repeat offenders. To distribute justice fairly, impartially, and justly, I would need to consider all the facts pertaining to the alleged offense.

Imagine if the roles were reversed and my younger son hurt my older son. Imagine, too, if I said to my older son, "Well, you're a whole 20 months older and two inches taller. So, clearly, you are the real aggressor, and your younger brother is the victim." It would be absurd for me to side with my younger son based exclusively on this bias. More than a decade of raising my two boys has already taught me that when there is conflict, rarely is one party completely innocent and the other completely at fault. When my sons were younger, it was much easier to simply lay down the "but you're the older sibling" card. But as they get older, settling conflict and distributing punishment requires greater discernment on my end. If I were to always choose the side of one son over the other without considering all the facts, that would make me partial and an ineffective judge. By God's grace, I am doing my best to remain impartial when dispensing justice as I parent.

Similarly, social justice work outside of God's framework is humanism. It is a form of justice that is partial to our human inclinations and not God's holy standard. Ideologies embedded within social justice frameworks elevate certain demographics and demean others based on social constructs rather than God's sacred context. Within the constructs of social justice, being "oppressed" makes a person less culpable of their crime. The bar for goodness, righteousness, and truth within these ideologies is lowered for those who claim oppression or allege enough intersectionality of diversity to then qualify as a victim.[3] And if one person or party holds more privilege, authority, or influence, that makes them more culpable—not only for their actions, but also for the actions of people like them hundreds of years ago. That is partiality, and it is politically and spiritually dangerous. It's politically dangerous because it inspires harmful policies like defunding the police and being too soft on crime, and it undermines the need for a restorative form of justice that reconciles one back into the community. It's also spiritually dangerous because that's not how God judges people. God looks not at our skin color, or our social economic status, or our ancestry. God looks internally at our hearts. God does not let us off the hook based on our melanin count, or our bank account, or even our evangelism conversion headcount. Thank the Lord! Because we would all come up short against God's standard. He has perfect justice. We are all equally dead in sin apart from Christ. We are all able to be made alive in Christ by grace through faith. So that is the radical equality that the gospel brings. And God is just as concerned about murder and violence and theft and arrogance and pride and deceit.

As followers of Jesus, we should know better. We must stand united against these evils that demean whoever society perceives as the victim or the perpetrator. Because we recognize, without Jesus, we could easily fall into either category on any given day. We must advocate for reforms within our criminal justice systems and the betterment of community relations. But more importantly, we must look inward at our own prejudices that diminish the *imago Dei* in every human heart, regardless of color or background. Only by God's grace can we build a more just, equitable, and loving society that sees, honors, and protects the inherent worth endowed by our Creator to people of all races, ethnicities, countries, social classes, and educational achievements. Biblical justice flows from the heart of God and the teachings of Scripture, whereas social justice originates from human ideologies and shifting cultural norms. The prophet Isaiah declared, "Learn to do right; seek justice. Defend the oppressed" (Isaiah 1:17). This divine mandate for justice is rooted in the character of God, who "loves righteousness and justice" (Psalm 33:5). Biblical justice seeks to uphold the inherent dignity of every person as an image-bearer of God (Genesis 1:27). It recognizes that true justice requires both individual righteousness and societal transformation. The gospel calls us to embody Jesus's sacrificial love, which breaks down dividing walls of hostility and reconciles people to God and each other (Ephesians 2:14-16).

Social justice, by contrast, often champions causes based on identity politics, intersectionality, and a secular understanding of equity. While these frameworks can illuminate societal disparities, they lack the transcendent moral authority and redemptive power found in biblical revelation. Apart from God's Word, human notions of justice inevitably reflect our fallen biases and limitations. Social justice often politicizes human identities and fosters an "us versus them" mentality. It can breed self-righteousness, resentment, and a pursuit of power rather than humble service. Divorced from the grace of the gospel, social justice activism risks perpetuating cycles of brokenness and alienation. In other words, social justice and biblical justice often have similar outcomes, but the heart motives are compelled by different narratives. While Christians should affirm the noble aims of social justice to rectify societal wrongs, we must anchor our pursuit of justice in biblical truth. Only by aligning our hearts with God's redemptive purposes can we be agents of lasting transformation in a hurting world. Biblical justice, fueled by the gospel, offers hope for true reconciliation and human flourishing.

THE BATTLE IS REAL, SO HOW DO WE ENGAGE IT?

In terms of the accusations we dismissively throw at one another, I'm not sure if I will ever understand how the right's allegation that the left are "social justice warriors" and the left's indictment that the right are "culture warriors" are actual insults. Generally speaking, both charges are true. The left typically values mercy, compassion, and justice; the right frequently values upholding truth, tradition, and pragmatism. But we fail to recognize how both accusations are good and necessary. We need a church body holistically upholding orthodoxy and orthopraxy. We need Christians on each side of the thought line to work for justice against evil as well as fight cultural battles against what stands in opposition to things that are "good and worthy of praise. Think about the things that are true and honorable and right and pure and beautiful and respected" (Philippians 4:8-9 NCV). We forget that the battle is indeed real, but it is not against one another; it is not against flesh and blood (Ephesians 6). The Bible encourages us to put on the appropriate armor needed for war, but it is not to fight one another. The battle is spiritual, and it is against the spirit of darkness—Satan, our real Enemy, who comes to distort, destroy, steal, and kill what God has deemed good (John 10:10). What a win for Satan and a loss for the church body when we allow the Enemy to manipulate and trick us into fighting the wrong battles, or far worse, fighting among ourselves.

Typically, when Christians are accused of being culture warriors, it's almost always in the context of Christians partaking in conflicts between orthodox Christian beliefs and cultural shifts toward progressive practices. For instance, just in my lifetime, I've witnesses an increasingly aggressive clash of ideological, political, and theological beliefs on issues such as religious freedom, abortion, LGBTQ curriculum in public schools, gender transitioning for children, gender roles in the church, racial tensions, and now a wave of antisemitism in the throes of the Israeli and Palestine war. And this just scratches the surface of what's boiling underneath our social tensions.

As a conservative-leaning, orthodox-revering Christian, I fully understand why like-minded folks want to hold the line. I understand why we're compelled to enact public policies that resemble God's morality more than culture's shifting, relative standards. I count myself among those with growing concern for our culture's ostensible moral decline. The rapid changes present challenges to longstanding social norms and religious traditions, even in the most pluralistic and tolerant cultures. The shift in cultural positions often contradicts deeply held religious convictions and teachings. For instance, issues related to gender identity, abortion rights, same-sex marriage, or the separation of church and state clash with Christian beliefs about the sanctity of life, traditional marriage, and faith integration.

The theological and moral slip aren't simply conjecture. Several Christian scholars have written on the decline of our collective morality. They've expressed concerns about the drift in sexual ethics, the rise of pornography, the decline in spiritual health, the breakdown of the family, the rampant addiction to technology, drugs, violence, and other variables leading to an overall decline in societal health. Recently, I read Dr. David Aikman's *The Delusion of Disbelief: Why the New Atheism is a Threat to Your Life, Liberty, and Pursuit of Happiness* on a plane ride with my husband to celebrate our 20th wedding anniversary. I knew the book would make a poor beach read in Cabo, that I'd likely regret not selecting something more lighthearted, so I read it instead on the plane rides to and from the trip. (Full disclosure: I'm quite terrible at choosing fun, fictional reads for vacations, so I welcome any suggestions!) The book is nearly two decades old, and yet it examines a century-old question: *How much has Christianity influenced what we value in America?* In preparation for writing this book, I wanted a more holistic understanding of the socio-historical scope of America's declining morality and whether that decline was in fact related to a decline in Americans professing Christianity.

Aikman contends that the rise of atheism has destructively affected America's traditional values, ethics, and societal wellbeing. He expresses concerns about shifts in morality, ethics, and societal norms that he sees directly correlated to the decline of an American Christian worldview and a rise in atheism and secularism. Specifically, Aikman critiques how, in the last few decades, prominent figures such as Richard Dawkins, Sam Harris, Daniel Dennett, and Christopher Hitchens have affected public opinion. Aikman argues that these "Four Horsemen" of New Atheist thinkers challenge religious beliefs, especially Christianity, while promoting a worldview that relies solely on scientific reasoning and secularism.[4] Aikman asks a question few of us are brave enough to ask in a cancel-culture climate; he questions whether American liberties survive in the absence of widespread belief in God on the part of the nation's people. In short, he maintains we cannot. Aikman suggests the rise of New Atheist thinking threatens traditional biblical values, arguing secularism undermines foundational Christian principles that have historically guided societal norms and ethical conduct. He contends that New Atheism's dismissal of religious faith could have detrimental consequences for individual freedoms and the pursuit of meaning and purpose in life. Aikman challenges the philosophical foundations of atheistic worldviews. In his book *The Delusion of Disbelief*, he argues secularism erodes the rock of Judeo-Christian values and suggests it becomes difficult to make a case for values like justice, mercy, peace, equality, and the value of human life without a biblical touchtone.

EQUIPPING THE NEXT GENERATION FOR BIBLICAL JUSTICE

Jesus, Justice, and Why We Should All Care

A few years ago, I led a workshop titled "How the Church Can Combat Human Trafficking" at a large annual Christian missions conference held in Oregon. When I finished, about half a dozen attendees lingered to ask follow-up questions. In retrospect, I couldn't tell you anything particularly unique about these attendees or their questions. They struck me as a common group of evangelicals with a heart for reaching the lost with the gospel. But I did meet one young lady who I think about often and likely won't soon forget.

Unlike the other attendees who were in their thirties and forties, well out of college and into their ministry or professional work, this young lady was still in college. Her age alone set her apart from the group, but mostly I was taken aback by her follow-up question and the resolve she exuded when asking it. When the line dwindled and she reached me, she got straight to the point and, with confidence beyond her years, stated, "I feel called to do justice work. When I finish college, I want to do justice for Jesus. How can I find a job doing that?" What struck me most about her question wasn't just the astute theological juxtaposition of doing good work for kingdom purposes, which alone was impressive at her age. Rather, I was most surprised by the phrase "justice for Jesus." Maybe it was the punch-packing alliteration, but I really liked the sound of that. As it turns out, this young lady is not so unique for her age demographic. Holistically speaking, Millennials and Gen Z generations have a strong inclination to engage social justice issues, and that is a genuinely admirable attribute.

EQUIPPING A JUSTICE-ORIENTED GENERATION

At Dallas Seminary, I worked with their Hendricks Center, writing a grant for a project on the possible correlations between college students who deconstruct their faith and their involvement—or lack thereof—in church and parachurch ministries. Through my research for the grant, I came across fascinating research tangentially related to how younger generations think about the world and justice. Recent studies by Christian research organizations indicate that Gen Z and younger Millennials are much more motivated toward social justice activism compared to previous generations. And I've witnessed this sociological trend firsthand. In my 15 years of teaching college students, I have seen this passion for engaging the common good work exemplified time and again in my classroom.

According to research, social activism is more prevalent in those under age 40 than other generations in living history.[1] Barna Group finds 86 percent of Gen Z believes that "loving your neighbor as yourself" means caring for the marginalized; this compares to just 65 percent agreement among Americans in older generations.[2] Nearly 60 percent of Gen Z says fighting for justice and equality defines living out your faith. One non-faith-based study as quoted in the Barna article found over half of Gen Z view their purpose in life as fighting social injustice, and 71 percent of those participants reported that fighting injustice will create more equity and inclusion.[3] About 50 percent say they withdrew support from companies not aligned with social justice values—twice the percentage of Gen X.[4] Generally, researchers agree this social justice perspective reflects this generation's upbringing in a more diverse, politically polarized, post-Christian society. Youth are growing up with instant digital access to global issues, which has made social injustice more visible. Social media has galvanized youth toward action. Research consistently demonstrates Gen Z and younger Millennials feel called to confront injustice, but channeling this zeal toward spiritually grounded, biblically rooted activism remains an opportunity for further discipleship.

A passion for social justice arises from genuine compassion. I don't think one needs to be of a younger generation to find solidarity with those who value mercy, justice, and compassion. Those are biblical values that can be traced throughout the Old and New Testaments. But increasingly, it has become challenging to distinguish the difference between younger Christians whose activism is derived from humanism and those whose social ethics are rooted in Christianity. Like their nonreligious counterparts, Christians in the Gen Z and Millennial generations are passionate about engaging in good work, but there is a lack of cohesion between their efforts to combat injustices and a recognition of the spiritual roots of injustice. In short, younger Christians have lost the biblical narrative of being created in God's image, the fall of humanity because of original sin, Jesus's redemption through salvation, and God's ultimate plan of restoration. Without this holistic perspective, Christians engaging justice work are doing so apart from God's plan to save humanity from itself. Social activism alone cannot heal broken hearts or broken social structures. Lasting justice requires personal transformation through Christ.

It's apparent these generations value working toward the common good, which should be applauded and encouraged. But as followers of Christ, our resolve for doing social justice is found in Jesus, rather than purely in hopes that our contribution will somehow yield a better, more just society. Our impetus for feeding the hungry, clothing the poor, caring for orphans and widows, and freeing those enslaved in human trafficking is not rooted in humanist, socialist frameworks. We certainly have enough in common through common grace to partner with those efforts. But if the Bible is our touchstone for truth and our motivation for loving others well, our reasons for doing good unto our neighbors will be vastly different from someone engaging similar efforts from a secular framework. The whole of the Bible's narrative, Jesus's ministry, and church history offer a framework for how and why Christians are called to engage social justice from a biblical worldview.

Despite what the contemporary cultural narrative may lead us to believe, social justice work is not actually an invention of postmodern ideology, nor is it unique to progressive Christianity. In the Gospels and throughout the New Testament, we witness Jesus and His followers' concern for the spiritual and social welfare of all people, particularly the marginalized, disenfranchised, and victimized. Early church leaders understood the importance of orthodoxy and orthopraxy and integrated these values into church doctrines and creeds. Let's consider some principles to help tether justice to Jesus. Applying a biblical framework to justice requires that we understand how our worldview influences every facet of our being. In brief, a worldview is a person's core set of beliefs and values. It is an integrated framework of learned and shared beliefs and behaviors that help give meaning and purpose to life and death. It is a framework for how to consider and engage life through this lens. It encompasses values, customs, principles, and actions—all of which bind a society together and establish a sense of identity, purpose, and solidarity within a community. A person's worldview is profoundly important, since it determines how the entirety of his or her life is lived. As one can imagine, the more worldview cohesion shared between people, families, groups, and organizations and the micro level of community, the more commonality shared within the macro cultural ethos.

In the following sections, we'll consider why a Christian worldview approach to social justice—and all of life—matters for our Christian witness and for God's glory. In the briefest of words, I want to offer a succinct definition here. A Christian or biblical worldview means to "think Christianly" about life. A Christian worldview is derived from Scripture and provides answers to existential life questions such as: Where did we come from? Who are we? What has gone wrong with the world? What solution can be offered to fix it?

BIBLICAL APPLICATION ON CULTURAL TENSIONS

Church family, the battle is real. But it is not against flesh and blood. The battle that seems like it's against culture is really one that's against the Enemy and the lies he convinces others to believe. Clad yourself in the armor of God. Make no mistake: There is a war. Since humanity's fall in the garden (Genesis 3), Satan has waged war against God's people. The Enemy and his legions seek to kill, steal, and destroy all that God has created in His image, deemed good, and designed to point us to eternal life. But in Jesus's name, you have power to overcome evil. God's armor is purposed to withstand the spiritual battle (Ephesians 6). Though the war is real, may we remember it is not against our neighbor. Let us be clear with the truth and compassionate with our engagement. We are called to love, and love does not lie (1 Corinthians 13). In fact, affirming a lie is a win for the Enemy—the father of lies—and a deep loss for those who believe it and for those who propagate it. You are equipped to see straight through the Enemy's oldest "did God really say?" trick.

1. In a Culture Constantly Pulling Us Left and Right, Let's Choose Up Instead

Test the voices coming at you (including mine) against the truth of God's enduring Word. Hold fast to God's Word. Anchor yourself to it; let the Bible be your touchstone and your compass. Resist being swayed by cultural winds across a shifting, relative landscape. Those drifts lead to dry, rootless deserts. Others have wandered there, but no one thrives without living water (John 7:37-39). The Bible is living and active, sharper than a double-edged sword (Hebrews 4:12). And God's Word can be trusted above all over worldviews and narratives. God's timeless truth endures forever, while human cultures are fleeting. Isaiah 40:8 states, "The grass withers, the flower fades, but the word of our God will stand forever" (ESV). Likewise, while cultures invent ever-new ideologies, the church is called to preserve and profess orthodox doctrine revealed in Scripture across generations. As Jude verse 3 urges, "Contend for the faith that was once for all delivered to the saints" (ESV). This faith, grounded in sound doctrine, serves as true north while fleeting human philosophies spin wildly. Cultural narratives may appear enlightened for a season, yet often regress into destructive lies.

One of my favorite contemporary Christian authors is Os Guinness. (My husband and I had the opportunity to meet him when Os and I both spoke at a retreat for Museum of the Bible. My husband and I lost all sense of polish as we fanned over him and rapid-fire asked cultural engagement questions. We had no chill!) In several of Guinness's books, he encourages Christians not to blindly follow shifting cultural values. In *Dining with the Devil*, specifically, Guinness asserts that discerning cultural currents requires measuring them against God's Word, illuminated by the Spirit and time-tested church teaching. We must uphold the supremacy of biblical truth amid tempting cultural sirens calling the church to radically revise ancient foundations to suit modern sensibilities. Clarity comes through prayerful study of Scripture and the tested wisdom of orthodox church tradition, not adherence to fashionable theories. God's Word stands sure.

2. Tether Yourself to Jesus. Meet with Him Daily. Walk by the Holy Spirit

Jesus, not humanity or social justice narratives, is our foundation for discerning whatever is true, whatever is honorable, whatever is just, whatever is pure, whatever is lovely, whatever is commendable, whatever holds moral excellence, and whatever is praiseworthy (Philippians 4:8). Which is why the Lord tells us to dwell on Him. Among the spiritual disciplines essential for Christian formation, developing a daily practice of meeting with Christ in prayer, reading and meditating on Scripture, and humble listening is foundational. As a student at Dallas Theological Seminary, I read Dallas Willard's books *The Spirit of Discipline* and *The Divine Conspiracy* in a spiritual formation course. Both were helpful for sharpening my understanding of why the Lord wants us to daily encounter Him. Scripturally, Christ's own example of frequently withdrawing to solitary places for communion with the Father demonstrates the priority of solitude with the Lord (Luke 5:16). Psalms extol the blessings of meditating on God's Word day and night (Psalm 1:2).

The early church devoted themselves to prayer and time in the apostles' teaching (Acts 2:42). Such habits keep the flame of faith alive. As theologian J.I. Packer wrote, "Bible study and prayer are inseparable...we study our Bibles in order that we may pray, and we pray because we have studied our Bibles."[5] In addition to reading Scripture, listening for the inner witness of the Holy Spirit is also part of essential daily time with Christ. As Jesus promised, the Spirit guides believers into all truth (John 16:13). Paul continually exhorted early Christians to walk by the Spirit's wisdom (Galatians 5:16). When believers begin each day waiting on the Lord (Psalm 5:3; Isaiah 40:31), the Spirit floods their inner being with kingdom perspectives and purposes that transcend human limitations. Whether through devotional classics, meditative prayer, journaling, or other disciplines, setting aside time to meet with Jesus daily in His Word and by the Spirit is essential to living fully into Christ's purposes. This practice centers all of life in loving relationship with the Lord.

3. Partner with the Body of Christ. The Church Needs You and You Need Her

The church has more than a 2,000-year history of seeking the Lord and doing good for His glory. She's an imperfect bride, alas. But she is wed to Jesus for all her earthly days and into eternity (Ephesians 5:22-33). Throughout the New Testament, Scripture consistently emphasizes the importance of believers participating in the collective body of Christ. At salvation, one is "baptized by one Spirit so as to form one body" (1 Corinthians 12:13). This unity of the Spirit is what holds together humanity's diversity. As Paul elaborates in 1 Corinthians 12, God designed the interdependent diversity of spiritual gifts to strengthen the unified organism of the church. For this reason, isolation from the nurture and accountability of the church body severely hinders Christian maturity. Every believer has a vital role to play in building up the church.

Years ago, when I was taking a doctoral literature course on God and theodicy (suffering), we read several books by Christian heroes who have experienced deep grief, like C.S. Lewis's *A Grief Observed*. But of all the works we read on trying to find God through the cloud of unknowing, theologian Dietrich Bonhoeffer's classic work *Life Together* provided my greatest takeaway. In this work he wrote, "The physical presence of other Christians is a source of incomparable joy and strength to the believer."[6] Through this I learned that Christians cannot reap the full spiritual benefits of sanctification apart from committed fellowship. Amid even the most trying times, we must cling to the body of Christ.

4. Engage Justice Work from a Biblical Framework

As Christians, why we engage social justice matters just as much—if not more—than how we do it. There are varying definitions of what constitutes social justice, but I especially like how Timothy Keller distinguishes the differences between social and biblical justice. In his book *Generous Justice*, Keller notes a distinguishing difference is that social justice deconstructs traditional systems and structures considered to be oppressive (as determined by culture) and then redistributes power, resources, and finances in ways that better ensure the equality of outcomes. Biblical justice, on the other hand, is conformity to God's moral standard, obedience to His commands, and the pursuit of what He deems right, just, and holy.[7] In brief, social justice is common good work done unto society, but biblical justice is more than that. Biblical justice engages broken, fallen places from a profound understanding of God's grace. And the work is done unto His glory, not merely for the improvement of society. The social justice narrative relies on ideologies and language that can further divide along lines of politics and foster resentment. Biblical justice seeks unity and equality in the Lord and not humanity. As Galatians 3:28 declares, "There is neither Jew nor Greek, slave nor free, male nor female, for you are all one in Christ Jesus" (ESV). Believers carry on Christ's ministry as agents of biblical justice and reconciliation. Micah 6:8 summarizes this calling: "He has told you, O man, what is good; and what does the LORD require of you but to do justice, and to love kindness, and to walk humbly with your God?" (ESV). Christians witness God's restorative justice by confronting dehumanizing practices, caring for the vulnerable, and sharing the hope of the gospel that transforms hearts.

PART ONE: REFLECTION QUESTIONS

1. In what ways do you see evidence of a spiritual battle raging around us? How do you also see people wage war against each other rather than directing their fight against the spirit of darkness? Why is it easier for people, even Christians, to be angry with each other than to acknowledge Satan's attacks and fight back with spiritual weapons?

2. Culture has co-opted many of the Bible's teachings. For example, quips like "Love your neighbor; do not judge; God loves everyone." Often and unfortunately, these verses become excuses to sin or they're weaponized against one another. In what other ways do you see culture lying about Christ? What does it say about humanity that we want truth, even if we package it and sell it as half-truths? What is the danger in the half-truths?

3. Why is it essential for us to spend time alone with the Lord? If we know the importance of walking by the Spirit, why do we frequently try to do so apart from the Lord? Can you discern a difference in your life when you are trying to do good work with the Lord from when you are doing it through your own strength?

4. In addition to needing strength from the Lord, we also need the body of Christ. We are designed to work within a holistic structure rather than in isolation. How has the church made a difference in your life? In what ways has the Lord used the church to bless you? And in what ways have you been able to contribute to the church?

5. Even outside of the church, people want to do good work. How might this show that we are all made in God's image? Younger generations have a measurable desire to do good work. Why is it problematic to try to do this apart from a biblical framework? Why, as Christians, do we need a relationship with the Lord and a church body to engage justice work?

YOUR WORLDVIEW MATTERS

HOW IN THE WORLDVIEW DID WE GET HERE?

A Roadmap Back to Christ

In all my years of teaching writing courses for high school and college students, I have consistently told my students that these two truisms are most important when writing a persuasive piece: First, your argument does not have to be perfect; but it must be supported. Second, keep reminding your readers and yourself of the thesis. This book required a year's worth of writing (and arguably a decade of thinking, researching, and learning), and it is still far from perfect. That's okay. And I have not lost sight of the thesis: It matters what we believe because that will impact all we do. In short, our worldview matters. This is the sub-thesis we'll unpack here in part two. Ultimately, the way we see the world influences the way we engage it. As Christians, our conversations about how to best participate in social justice efforts aren't nearly as fruitful if they are detached from a biblical worldview. Before we consider *how* to do great work in the world, it's helpful for Christians to understand *why* we're called to do it. As professor and scholar Richard Weaver famously stated in 1948, "Our ideas have consequences."[1] Understanding the epistemology (study of knowledge) and the origin of our ideas gives greater meaning and purpose to our work in the world. We want to ground our ideologies in a biblical worldview. The soil in which we root our beliefs affects the fruit we produce. And the Bible's teachings provide the soil we need to bear good fruit in the world. Examining what the Bible states about social justice efforts and how church history has enacted these teachings provides a framework for our contemporary social justice work.

The fundamental bedrock to doing social justice work begins with recognizing how essential it is to be rooted in Christ. Scripture offers several agricultural and horticultural metaphors aimed at helping us better understand what it means to follow Christ and flourish through Him. Admittedly, I have little interest in or knowledge of nature. Aside from the occasional trip to Colorado to escape the harsh, hot Texas summers or our family's annual two-night camping trip with a group of friends and our gaggle of children, I can confidently say I don't intentionally spend time in nature. I am decidedly more of an indoor girl. Other than lounging on the beach with a good book and ocean waves as my soundtrack, I try to avoid the wilderness as a vacation option. But I have wondered a time or two if certain parables in the Bible would resonate deeper if I had more of a proclivity for outdoor adventure or appreciation for nature. Generally speaking, our modern Western society has far less in common with the Middle Eastern agrarian culture described in the Bible, and yet, the analogies Scripture uses to help us understand the importance of staying tethered to God's Word and in relationship with Christ are apt and timeless.

In John 15, for example, Jesus employs a powerful illustration that explains the life-giving relationship between Himself and His followers. As the true vine, Jesus is the source of spiritual nourishment and vitality, while we, the branches, must abide in Him to bear fruit and fulfill our God-given purpose. This abiding in Jesus is not a passive or abstract concept but a dynamic and transformative relationship that requires our active participation. We must daily choose to remain connected to Christ through prayer, meditation on His Word, and obedience to His commands. Apart from Him, we can do nothing of eternal significance, but when we abide in Him, we draw from His strength and wisdom to navigate life's challenges and bear witness to His love (John 15:5). Moreover, as we abide in Christ, we invite the pruning work of the Father, who lovingly removes the unfruitful and distracting elements in our lives. This process, though sometimes painful, is ultimately for our good and God's glory, as it enables us to bear more abundant and lasting fruit. By surrendering to the Father's pruning and remaining firmly grafted into the true vine, we experience the joy and purpose of a life rooted in Christ.

Jeremiah 17:7-8 compares people who trust in the Lord to trees planted by the water, which have roots that reach deep into the river. These trees are not bothered by heat or drought, their leaves stay green, and they never stop producing fruit. Just as a tree draws nourishment from the rich soil in which it is planted, so, too, do our lives draw spiritual sustenance from the truth of God's Word. The deeper our roots grow into the fertile ground of God's Word and the living water we experience through relationship with Him, the more our faith flourishes and bears fruit in the form of God-honoring beliefs and actions. A tree planted in shallow or rocky soil may appear healthy for a season, but when drought or storms arise, its weak roots fail to support it. When we plant ourselves firmly in the soil of God's Word, allowing its truth to permeate every aspect of our lives, we develop a robust and resilient faith. Our faith, which is nourished by the living water of the Holy Spirit, produces a bountiful harvest of love, joy, peace, patience, kindness, goodness, faithfulness, gentleness, and self-control—the fruit of a life rooted in Christ (Galatians 5:22-23).

THE BIBLE INFORMS OUR
PERSPECTIVES AND DEFINITIONS

A few years ago, I had the honor of attending the William Wilber-force Conference hosted by the Chuck Colson Center. My panel was asked a question regarding how Christians might discuss and engage justice in a way that is similar to nonbelievers. Essentially, the attendee wanted to know how Christians can find common ground to undertake good work alongside those who do not share our reasons or motivations for doing that work. I appreciated John Stonestreet's answer. He replied, "It's no good having the same vocabulary if we're using different dictionaries."[2] It was a simple answer, but it provided a profound perspective shift. John was right. If the Bible is our dictionary and our touchstone for truth and life, it should define how we interpret the world. And in the case of social justice, our biblical reasons for doing good should be vastly different from those of someone doing similar work from a non-Christian framework. In other words, yes, there is room for common language and goals in the context of doing social justice. But for Christians, our reasons for doing justice should be radically different from the reasons of those who do not follow Christ or His teachings.

Rapid cultural changes across the American landscape have made the work of Christian leaders especially complex. The sharp shift from a collectively held Judeo-Christian worldview coupled with the mounting challenges of pluralism and secularism create a cultural tension for faith integration in the public square. From legal shifts in government sectors, to domestic and global economic pressures, to developments in technology, to ideological chasms between older and younger demographics, for the first time in her history, America is navigating her way through a post-Christian Western society. We've experienced social fragmentation, cultural polarization, family dysfunction, and social isolation. These changes yield challenges, particularly for Christians engaged in common good work in the public square.

Before we can fully understand how to engage our world, we need to understand our worldview. We must face cultural challenges from a biblical perspective. We must also come equipped with the wisdom of over 2,000 years of historic Christian orthodoxy (doctrine or beliefs) and orthopraxy (practice). Section one of this book aimed to spotlight the problem: *What* is the contemporary cultural tension between a Judeo-Christian worldview and competing narratives and worldviews? Section two aspires to make a case for biblically informed thinking. Here, we consider *why* our Christian worldview matters when we engage our spheres of influence, specifically social justice work. Section three will highlight the distinction between social justice and biblical justice. Even more, we will examine *how* the historical church engaged good work in society. We also consider leaders, ministries, and institutions *who* are currently leading and serving well in various areas of contemporary justice work.

ARE WE SEEING THE WORLD RIGHTLY?

I didn't know I needed eyeglasses until my third semester of college when seated in a large lecture hall with about 300 classmates. I had managed to go through 20 years of my life without knowing I was nearsighted until I enrolled in an introductory level geology course with what felt like half of Texas A&M University's student body. Prior to college, my classes had less than two dozen students, and the classroom sizes were proportional to student enrollment. In that confined context, I could see the board or screen just fine. But in college, when I was assigned a seat several dozen rows from the front of the classroom, I had difficulty discerning words in the lecturer's PowerPoint presentation. On the first day of the course, I noticed my adjacent classmates appeared to have no difficulties taking notes. I looked up and down my row. I lifted myself slightly to catch a glimpse of students seated in front of me too. I probably even did one of those awkward faux stretches and yawns characters do in movies to catch a glance of classmates behind me. As best I could tell, everyone else deciphered the PowerPoint without any trouble.

Genuinely confused, I whispered to the new classmate beside me, "Can you see that? Can you read the bullet points?" He looked over as if to notice me for the first time. He glanced up at the screen and then back to me, and returned the whisper, "Yes. But not without my glasses." That was it! That was precisely the problem. Why had I not noticed his glasses earlier? Why had I not noticed nearly a third of the students seated near me were wearing glasses too? And I imagine several others had contact lenses instead. It had not occurred to me until that moment that when my environment changed, it also altered my perspective. In my circumstance, I could see clearly only when seated a few feet away from the screen or board, but when my proximity was yards away, it all became blurry. My view was distorted, and I could no longer discern what was accurate and what was false. For the next few weeks, until I was able to make an eye exam appointment and receive prescription glasses, I photocopied the notes of the guy next to me. Each Monday, Wednesday, and Friday, we'd head straight from class to the copy machine in the building's foyer. And that's how I made it through studying for the first round of geology quizzes and a test. In retrospect, I'm not sure if my classmate had pity or a crush on me. But either way, I thank the Lord for his charity. For weeks, I relied on his interpretation of what was being presented until I was able to clearly see it for myself. Thank goodness he was a smart kid double majoring in engineering and math; who we depend on for an interpretation will ultimately influence our own. (Had I sat next to a fellow English major, I might have been at an academic disadvantage!)

Our worldview is akin to a pair of glasses through which we perceive and interpret reality. But not all glasses accurately help us see the world. Some perspectives distort truth, like a flawed lens prescription. Like sunglasses, some views frame reality in a certain hue without necessarily distorting it. Cracked, smudged, or ill-fitting worldview lenses also obstruct us from accurately seeing what's truly there. Everyone has a worldview lens shaping how they define and judge the world. Often we unconsciously see through our ingrained perspectives without examining them. We must intentionally analyze our worldview glasses to assess whether they align with truth instead of distorting reality. No neutral position exists; even a "secular perspective" has an inherent bias. We all bring interpretive frameworks, whether conscious or subconscious. Careful introspection can help us recognize the ways our underlying assumptions filter how we see the world, rather than taking reality at face value. Evaluating worldviews requires looking at the lens itself, not just gazing through it. The goal is aligning our perspective with a biblical worldview that sees and interprets the world as it truly is in light of God's Word. This provides an undistorted vision of reality. So it's essential for Christians to recognize we need God's glasses to see the world according to His design. It's also important for Christians to develop biblical apologetics by examining the lenses used for discerning purpose and meaning for life.

How we see and think about the world also influences how we engage it. Our worldview also informs the *why* behind the justice work we do. In the church and academic circles to which I contribute, I've noticed an unfortunate pattern in the last decade or so. Increasingly, Christian leaders (pastors, professors, podcasters, and so forth) encourage their audience to think critically about the faults of the American church, but there is little consideration given to the disintegration of our once majority-held Christian worldview. In other words, we're looking at the troubling fruit culture has produced without examining the social changes in the soil. Collectively, we've put on a cultural perspective, but we have failed to ask ourselves if the perspective aligns with God's.

As part of my work as a research associate with Dallas Theological

Seminary's Hendricks Center, I had the opportunity to delve into research pertaining to Christians' mental health and their relationships with the church and faith as part of a grant proposal. Since 2020, data indicates there has been a sharp decline in our overall mental health, a mass exodus from churches, an increase of once churched kids becoming faith-deconstructing adults, and a 33 percent decrease of self-professing Christians who are able to answer questions about faith according to a biblical worldview.[3] Christian researchers correlate the acute decline in mental health and de-churching to COVID lockdowns in 2020 and 2021. And though COVID certainly contributed to our collective mental and spiritual crises, research suggests that the global pandemic merely accelerated or unmasked what was already occurring.[4] It's impossible to isolate every societal variable and claim any definitive causation, and yet, there is a correlation between these disheartening societal trends and our collective waning from a long-held Christian worldview. Society as a whole, and most of us, unwittingly, has adopted a postmodern, post-Christian worldview. That paradigm has led us away from thinking about and engaging our world from a distinctly biblical perspective. Seeing the world through a Christian lens is no longer our culture's default assessment. To consider the world according to Christ now requires great intentionality, particularly for those engaged in social justice work.

DISTORTED WORLDVIEWS DISTORT TRUTH

I first began thinking about worldview philosophies and their implications during my PhD studies. Even a decade later, I can still recall the precise moment I realized the impact a person's worldview has on the ways he or she navigates life. I had this epiphany while I was teaching undergraduate students in a social issues and education course. One young lady in my class—I'll refer to her as Jane—helped me see how her worldview deeply affected the ways she engaged the course. I was teaching a course titled "Social Issues in Education" to a class of about 20 students, most of whom were education majors. It was my second time teaching the course at a private, Christian university in Texas. The course's official catalog description states, "The course will explore social and cultural issues that influence education." This description certainly left room for a broad interpretation regarding which issues I would select and how they would be addressed.

The first semester I taught the course, I relied heavily on the resources and thoughts of instructors who had come before me. There was no shortage of respectable, reliable PowerPoints, notes, books, and resources made available. These resources included topics surrounding race, class, poverty, and gender. I covered these selected topics thoroughly, engaged students in lively, dynamic discussions, applied the social issues to realistic classroom scenarios, and received positive feedback from students. Overall, I had every reason to be pleased with the way the course had transpired. Yet, I could not shake the feeling that something integral was missing from the way the course was structured and taught, and I used much of winter break considering what might be modified for the upcoming spring semester.

In my second semester teaching the course, I selected a more holistic social issues textbook and expanded the syllabus to include topics such as religion, disabilities, and even sexuality. Even with these changes, however, it was not until the second day of class that a student's unexpected candidness helped me recognize what the course was lacking. I had given an outside assignment with the purpose of helping students get to know themselves and one another better. After studying micro, meso, and macro socialization, which considers the multiple layers of culture's influence on individuals, I challenged students to reflect on some of their values, attitudes, and actions that they believed—for better or worse—they had been socialized to accept as true. Then, they were to gather three items that best reflected their core beliefs and values at each of these levels, place the items in a decorated bag or box, and present the items to the class with a brief explanation. After approximately ten students had presented, a theme was evident. Male and female students at this university proudly displayed token Christian items such as Bibles, crosses, and photos from church camps. There was the occasional fraternity or sorority item and some sports paraphernalia, but by and large, it was apparent their Christian faith had shaped their identities.

But then Jane broke the mold. The items she chose were curious, and that was evident even before she explained their significance. The first item she pulled out of her psychedelically decorated bag was a feather; this, she said, represented her sexual orientation: bisexual. The feather represented her ability to "float back and forth" between male and female relationships. The next item was a DVD on Pagan religion, which she credited as shaping her faith system. The third and final item pulled out of her bag was a rock. The class held a collective breath. The room was tense. No one stirred or took their eyes off Jane. The rock, she informed us, represented her solidarity with polyamory. Did we know what "polyamory" meant? she inquired. The class remained silent, but we politely and collectively shook our heads "no."

"Does it mean you believe in multiple gods?" I offered, genuinely unsure and hesitant. A flash of excitement ran across her previously stoic face. "Close! It means I believe in multiple lovers." she then proceeded to explain her polyamorous beliefs and how sexual relationships are meant to take place outside the context of marriage and with multiple, simultaneously consenting partners. The rock signified the necessity of a "strong belief in self" to maintain multiple relationships.

When she finished, the class looked to me, as the instructor and voice of authority, for a reaction—words that would appease the awkwardness in the room. Except, I was just as taken aback by Jane's outlier presentation as they were, and I lacked an adequate response. It was evident to the class that her presentation was genuine; it was not a prank or a joke but rather an honest reflection of her values. With all the sincerity I could muster, I thanked Jane for her vulnerability. The nine or so remaining students stumbled through their presentations and delivered them to a dumbfounded audience. After class that day, when there was a moment to process the gravity of what had taken place, I realized that Jane's bag, much like other students' bags, represented her worldview. The contents in her bag made up the lens through which Jane saw life, and, ultimately, her bag was the lens through which she would examine the K-12 social issues covered in the social issues course. It occurred to me that day precisely what was missing from the course: an intentionally integrated and clearly communicated Christian worldview.

It was also apparent to me in that moment that I had been poorly equipped as both a doctoral student and faculty to think Christianly about what I was teaching. After Jane's presentation, it was evident the course would need some minor restructuring of content and desired outcomes to reflect an integrated Christian worldview in ways that stood in contrast to the secular one she was presenting. At the time, I knew a Christian worldview draws from Old Testament and New Testament narratives, and together these narratives contain references to the origin, fall, and redemption of human life. Beyond this, I was uncertain what a Christian worldview entailed, and, as the instructor, I was tentative about how to integrate this worldview into the course or how to encourage my students to engage it. My attempts were tenuous, at best. I included liberal, secular voices and balanced them with conservative, Christian perspectives when covering issues such as racism, classism, religion, gender identity, and disabilities. This approach provided enough space between the contrasts to generate meaningful conversation about how Christians and non-Christians might approach these issues in K-12 classrooms. Even in doing so, I recognized this method was slightly disingenuous.

The dichotomy between secular and sacred spheres was not a holistic approach to contrasting *the world* against the Christian worldview.

While teaching the course I often wondered—sometimes aloud to colleagues—how might other instructors interpret what is meant by a Christian worldview? How might they approach structuring their course through this lens? How do professors at other Christian universities encourage their students to engage social issues from a Christian worldview? These questions would become the catalyst for my dissertation. But ultimately, they would also inform my professional, personal, and ministry engagement from that moment forward. I could no longer, in good faith, claim our worldview didn't matter. Even at a very rudimentary level, I realized from that experience that our worldview shapes and informs the whole of our lives. In this section, we'll consider how our worldview affects the ways we engage the world.

WHAT IS A WORLDVIEW?

To look back on that teaching moment after nearly 15 years of studying, writing, and teaching on the significance of our Christian worldview, it is a bit perplexing to consider how little I knew about faith integration when I rounded out my twenties. To think how infrequently conversations on faith and work were broached in Christian circles is confounding. By that time in my life, I had seven years of experience in the K-12 and higher education classroom, nine years of commitment to following Christ, and I was only one year away from earning a PhD from a Christian tier-one research university. And in all this exposure to Christianity and educational pedagogy, I had never seriously considered how my faith informed my professional praxis. Moreover, I had not given much thought to how Christianity compels us to do good work through all our spheres of influence. Perhaps I am not alone here; maybe most of us have not given serious reflection to how our Christian faith should animate the ways we engage our work, our family, our community, our ministry—all of life, really.

We don't usually pause to "think about our thinking," a concept we refer to as metacognition in education. But our thinking and our worldview are inextricably related, and both very much influence what we believe and what we do. Every person, in every culture and throughout time, has held a worldview. As I briefly stated earlier, a person's worldview is the lens through which a person sees life, and it is the touchstone for their judgments, decisions, and interactions with the world. It consists of frameworks, and comprehensively, these frameworks form a cohesive narrative that gives meaning and purpose for life. It encompasses a person's fundamental beliefs, values, and assumptions about reality, the nature of existence, knowledge, morality, and the purpose of life. A worldview serves as a mental filter and a lens through which people make sense of their experiences and the world around them, influencing their perspectives on a wide range of issues, including religion, ethics, politics, culture, and science. Worldviews can be shaped by various factors, including cultural, religious, philosophical, and personal influences, and they often play a significant role in shaping a person's attitudes and behaviors. A worldview also encompasses values, customs, principles, and actions—all of which binds a society together and establishes a sense of identity, purpose, and solidarity within a community.

Essentially, our worldview is what shapes our lives and gives meaning to them. It is our belief system for morality, our compass for navigating the world, and our touchstone for discerning what is true. Our worldview is also the basis for why and how we engage social justice work because it determines how we view humanity and why we believe humanity is worth sacrificing our time, energy, and finances. Whether from a religious or an a-religious (not religious) worldview, throughout history and across cultures, people have sought answers to what it means to be human, how we should engage the world, and what happens to us when we pass away.

Good research always begins with great questions. Only, when I began my dissertation over a decade ago, I had no idea what to even ask, much less how to wrestle the research process. A professor of mine at the time, Dr. Perry Glanzer, was an instrumental catalyst when I began my worldview research. After class one day, I spontaneously swung by his office with a list of potential topics all aimed at answering this fundamental question: "What makes a Christian educator different from a non-Christian educator?" His thought-provoking retort was something along the lines of "Well, what makes a Christian *anyone* different from a non-Christian *anyone*?" Are there measurable or even discernible differences between, say, a Christian football coach and a non-Christian one? Business owners? What about businesses themselves? Can an entity like a corporation or a college even be Christian? I wasn't aware at the time, but these were worldview questions.

As a starting point for studying how our worldview impacts our engagement with the world, Dr. Glanzer recommended Dr. James Sire's seminal book *The Universe Next Door*. The book was highly acclaimed in Christian academic circles when it was released in 1976, and today it is in its sixth edition. I would imagine it would be the most beneficial edition for understanding the major contemporary worldviews and how those influence our culture. What I found particularly insightful in Sire's books was learning the core, essential life questions humanity has asked throughout history. Although it's not an exhaustive list, to summarize pages of notes from Sire's books, all of humanity longs for answers to the following worldview questions:

1. Where do I come from? What is the meaning of my existence and who is my Creator? A question of design, identity, and worth.

2. Is there purpose or meaning to life beyond the material world? A question pertaining to purpose.

3. How do we determine truth and knowledge? This is a question that seeks to understand the basis of reality and how our beliefs are constructed.

4. Why is there injustice, suffering, and evil in the world? How do we explain and deal with human pain? Or asked another way, if there is a God, and He claims to be good, why does evil exist?

5. What ethical values or obligations should guide how we live and act? This is a question of morals and ethics. People are looking for a plumb line for what constitutes truth, beauty, and goodness.

6. What happens after we die? Is there life beyond the grave? Throughout history and crossculturally, people have sought to explain how we arrived on earth and what happens when we leave it.

7. How do we explain human consciousness, or our souls, or the supernatural? How do we rationalize the intangible facets of humanity? When science, technology, and medicine cannot answer our transcendental nature, how do we make sense of it?

8. How should we live together in community? What social systems best facilitate human flourishing? And then of course, we would have to define what we mean by community, social systems, and flourishing.

To reiterate, this is not an exhaustive list of soul-searching, faith-seeking questions, but it does highlight the longing in human hearts to know truth and be known by our Creator. Theologians and philosophers of varied ideological persuasions agree all major worldviews are an attempt to answer a common set of core questions about human existence, albeit in different ways.

After reading Sire's books, I had even more questions. I wondered, for example, does a worldview change or morph when one is presented with new information? For instance, when scientific discoveries conflict with a person's belief system, how does a person reconcile this? If we discover, for example, extra-terrestrial life in space is real, how do we reconcile that discovery with the biblical narrative? I also questioned if our worldview becomes cemented at a certain age, or if it changes as we read and learn and grow. I wondered whether a worldview is socially constructed, or divinely given, or some combination of the two. But as interested as I was in how these frameworks are constructed, as a Christian, I was even more concerned with how my worldview helps me navigate engaging a world so vastly different and sometimes outright antagonistic to a biblical framework. In this section on Christian worldview, we'll consider how the Bible provides answers to these philosophical questions.

A SECULAR WORLDVIEW AND A CHRISTIAN WORLDVIEW

What's the Difference?

Just after my husband and I married, we moved from Dallas, Texas, to Boston, Massachusetts. I spent those newlywed years in culture shock. The New England region is quite different from the South. The South doesn't have Ivy League colleges, or great public transportation, and the weather is far milder (until you hit a Texas summer). What was probably the greatest adjustment, though, was the lack of evangelical church influence in Boston. In Texas, we have an abundance of robust, thriving churches that influence our culture. Boston, on the other hand, has a culture of its own, and, interestingly, it has a much longer history of Christian influence. Unlike in the South, there is a strong Catholic presence: universities, hospitals, museums, charities, and so forth. And yet curiously, given its hundreds of years of Protestant and Catholic Christian influence, the region lags behind the South in church membership and participation. In my Boston spheres of work, church, and friends, it was highly common to be drawn into intellectual musings about education, politics, or religion. Religion was valued in that it helped keep the social fabric woven together, akin to how most of us would think about the traditional family unit. Rarely, though, was I pulled into an even remotely spiritually edifying conversation unless it was with someone from my church. That was a striking difference from my Texas childhood where Christianese flowed from radio stations, billboards, bumper stickers, and conversations. At 23, I had not yet begun to think about how greatly our culture affects our worldview or how our worldview likewise influences culture. But it was also the first time in my adult life I realized people who were so similar to me in many ways could think so differently.

In those early years of marriage, my husband and I explored all the excitement Boston offered: authentic Italian restaurants, symphonies, Fenway Park, and those beautiful cobblestone streets lined with historic brownstone homes. Exploring helped ease the sting of being homesick for Texas. When I wasn't playing, I was teaching eighth-grade English at a private Christian school, and I also took a few evening courses at Harvard University. The opportunity to take a few courses at Harvard was too enticing to decline, and I wanted to have the quintessential Boston academic experience. I knew we weren't staying forever, so like a new, dry sponge, I soaked up what the city had to offer in hopes that I could later squeeze out the best Boston memories when I was someday living back in Texas.

One of these beautiful experiences entailed taking the T (the public subway system) from my apartment in Newton, Massachusetts, to Harvard square in Cambridge, Massachusetts. In my mind's eye, it was almost always snowing and cold, so I was bundled up in my down J. Crew peacoat, gloves, and snow boots. I crunched my way through the snow from the subway station to Harvard University's campus. It was such a treat to arrive early, walk into Harvard's bookstore, and get a warm latte before class. I loved glancing up at the enshrinements of great scholars who had walked the campus long before I had the opportunity to learn from them. Walking through the gates of one of the world's most prestigious universities, settling into my lecture hall seat, and sipping my coffee felt like living an academic dream.

In one of my courses, which was on the British Romantics, I became acquaintances with a slightly older classmate, Linda, who worked for Harvard in the admissions office. We would chat before and after class and on breaks. She was curious to learn more about my "Why we left Texas" story, and I was fascinated by her "I've always wanted a graduate degree from Harvard" ambition. She wasn't a professing Christian. She was born and raised just outside of Boston, and her family was Catholic; however, she considered herself non-religious. I recall sharing with Linda one late afternoon before class about my student, a young girl at the school where I was teaching, who had Lyme disease. She contracted it from a tick, doctors believe, and her symptoms were so severe that she was wheelchair bound, chronically tired, and sometimes in pain. She missed school frequently. I shared with Linda that when my student first fell ill, the doctors did a battery of tests and discovered that she had a very serious, life-threatening condition. But at first, they couldn't figure out the cause of it. They did everything they could with all the medical technologies available to them, but initially it wasn't enough to determine her ailment. The doctors said this girl could die.

So our Christian school prayed daily. Each morning in assembly, at lunch, and before faculty meetings or sporting events. Her church prayed too. One woman even came up to the school to pray over my student's desk, believing she would once again sit there in school. We prayed fervently with like-minded, Jesus-loving people. In the weeks following, there was no medical diagnosis or treatment, but my student's condition started to improve. She rapidly recovered. In fact, it started to turn around; within a few weeks, she was out of critical condition and on the road to recovery. The doctors were absolutely baffled. They couldn't explain it. Even after discerning she had Lyme disease, they had never seen a patient with this condition rebound so quickly and fully. Some of the doctors even reluctantly admitted: "It's a miracle."

How would most Christians interpret that course of events? If a young girl became critically ill, and the doctors were unable to attribute her healing to medicine, most of us would likely interpret that as a divine intervention from God. We would, at least in part, consider the healing an answer to our prayers. Naively, I thought Linda would interpret the story the same way and share my enthusiasm for the good report. But Linda was an atheist, or agnostic at least. She was the sort of person who read Richard Dawkins books to combat Christian apologetics. When I shared with her about my student's miraculous road to recovery, I suppose I expected her to at least be open to the possibility. That wasn't the case. She insisted the doctors must have been mistaken about the severity of the girl's condition, that there must have been a medical explanation for her rapid recovery. Perhaps the girl was just an outlier case, Linda suggested. When I asked whether she thought prayer played a role in helping the girl recover, Linda insisted prayer helped only in that it offered (false) hope to those petitioning God. She agreed the occurrence was surprising, but it was not supernatural. How had Linda and I come to interpret these events so differently? Our worldviews were vastly different.

WHAT ARE THE MAJOR MODERN WORLDVIEWS?

As I've continued to study worldviews, I've learned our frameworks are not developed through individual contemplation alone, and are certainly not nurtured in isolation. Rather, a worldview is fostered through a collective endeavor. Worldviews are socially constructed through a complex relationship between culture, doctrines, and individual experiences. A worldview is also constructed through relationships with family, friends, and community. The concept of a socially constructed worldview is a central theme in disciplines like sociology, anthropology, philosophy, and religious studies. These fields approach worldview study from various angles, but they all seek to understand how our beliefs, values, and perceptions are profoundly influenced by the society we are born into.

To be clear, a person's worldview is not the same as their personality or disposition. Plenty of cheery people hold a secular worldview. Numerous peaceful, reserved people hold a Christian, a Muslim, or a Jewish (theistic) worldview. Likewise, many people hold a postmodern worldview, most of them in the younger Millennial and Gen Z generations. Although our worldviews undoubtedly influence our identities and loves, our personalities and means of self-expression are not the same as our worldviews. Our temperaments are distinct from our belief systems. The lens through which people look at life tends to be quite similar when their worldview is constructed within the same eco-system. As Christians, we know Scripture is, or at least should be, our touchstone for truth, and my aim for this portion of the conversation is to highlight why worldview matters and how the Bible is a compass for navigating life. Before we consider what constitutes a biblical worldview and how we should apply it, particularly within the context of social justice issues, it's helpful to consider a few frameworks that comprise a worldview. Examining these facets not only helps believers understand how those outside the body of Christ are being influenced, but it also illuminates the ways we might be influenced by the world too.

Depending on which scholar you read, you'll receive varied responses to the question, "But how many contemporary worldviews are there?" For instance, Biola University professors J.P. Moreland and William Lane Craig have written on four major worldviews.[1] They summarize all worldviews into the categories of theism, naturalism, nihilism, and postmodernism. They suggest these worldviews are how people approach key philosophical issues related to the nature of God, truth, knowledge, ethics, and purpose.[2] According to David Dockery, president of Southwestern Seminary and a renowned Christian worldview scholar, there are five major worldviews. To Moreland and Craig's list, Dockery adds deism.[3] In James Sire's book *The Universe Next Door*, he identifies seven contemporary worldviews in his fifth edition. Here, Sire adds existentialism, pantheism, and New Age to Moreland's list, and he considers deism an extension of theism. In Sire's sixth and latest edition, he distinguishes pantheism from New Age.[4]

Some academics may disagree with this assertion, but I'd suggest the average person—Christian or otherwise—doesn't need to know all the nuances of each of these worldviews. Copiously comparing and contrasting these worldviews likely isn't helpful for developing a Christian or biblical worldview. But for the sake of underscoring how the Christian worldview stands apart from others, it is beneficial to consider an overarching meta-narrative. A brief consideration of the most influential worldviews and how those ideologies stand in opposition to the biblical narrative can help us see how the biblical worldview answers questions pertaining to life and eternity that other worldviews cannot. Looking at the scope of other worldviews is particularly beneficial for discerning *why* and *how* we should do social justice work. To provide a macro-level perspective of worldviews that contest the Christian worldview, we'll use three divisions of Sire's categories as the foundation for our scope: (1) theism and deism, (2) naturalism, and (3) modernism and postmodernism.

As Christians, we want to discern biblical justice from social justice. Biblical justice is rooted to God's moral standards. Social justice is influenced by cultural ideologies. Social justice is primarily focused on human systems, power dynamics, and redistributing resources. But it does not seek to address the deeper spiritual realities that lead to injustice in the first place. Social justice narratives often co-opt

Judeo-Christian values and virtues. For instance, "love your neighbor" is a phrase commonly used outside of a Christian context. And sometimes this co-opting of language and values offers common ground to engage in common good work. But fundamentally, social justice ideology does not offer God's redemption and restoration. And that is because only God's moral standard for justice can redeem and restore us. Biblical justice is an invitation to partake in God's plan for humanity's salvation and sanctification. When we embrace biblical justice, we're not just adopting a moral standard, but we're also participating in God's redemptive story.

ONE OF THESE THINGS IS NOT LIKE THE OTHER

Theism, Deism, and Christianity

The Christian worldview is centered around the biblical narrative. It maintains the existence of one eternal, transcendent God who created the universe and sustains it through His power and sovereignty. Humanity was created in God's image but fell into sin. God intervenes in human history ultimately through the incarnation, death, and resurrection of Jesus Christ who saves people by grace. The Bible is God's authoritative Word and source of knowledge and ethics for life. After death, humans face eternal judgment to heaven or hell based on accepting or rejecting Christ. Ethics and meaning derive from God's nature and commands.

Deism shares with Christian theism in that this worldview also believes in a Creator who designed the universe. But unlike Christian theism, deists believe that a Creator does not directly intervene in the world. This distant God does not involve Himself in human affairs or suspend natural laws through miracles. One of the best metaphors I've heard to explain deism is to liken God to a clock-maker. A clockmaker designs, creates, and sets a clock in motion, and then he walks away. Similarly, according to deism, God designed the world and humanity, but then He took a hands-off approach to inter-acting with His creation. Every metaphor falls apart at some level, but I imagine within this context, when the clock runs out, when the battery expires or the clock needs to be rewound, the world just simply ends. Deism presents a distant and absent God, which is a bleak and heretical description.

Theism itself is not actually a biblical worldview; it's the "Christian" qualifier that defines it as such. Any religion that claims to believe in one God is theistic. For instance, Christianity, Islam, and Judaism all have the monotheistic belief in a God, which is a belief in one God. A polytheistic religion, such as Hinduism, holds a belief in many gods.[1] Theism is centered around belief in an omniscient, supernat-ural, and transcendent God who actively sustains and is involved in the universe. Within this worldview, God is infinite, eternal, imma-terial, omnipotent, omniscient, omnipresent, omnibenevolent, and perfect. Humans are God's special creation, made in God's image with intrinsic value. Morality and meaning derive from God's nature and divine commands. There is an essential distinction to be made, how-ever, in where these worldviews derive their authority from. Christi-anity claims the Bible; Islam claims the Koran; and Judaism claims only the Old Testament.

A BIBLICAL PERSPECTIVE

In one of the first theology classes I took in my seminary studies, I was required to write a lengthy doctrinal statement. The assignment asked us to support our doctrinal beliefs with passages from the Bible. It was a valuable research exercise. For many years, I had written and spoken on defining a Christian worldview and integrating it into all spheres of our vocation. But if I am being honest, until that point in my academic work, my research was primarily dependent on other scholars' interpretation of Scripture. In other words, I was relying on someone else's eyesight to determine my own perspective. I was using their glasses to develop my own framework for what the Bible teaches on worldview. Thankfully, I relied on trustworthy scholars. But spending a semester seeking scriptures to support my doctrinal assertions was a gift. The course helped me understand how the Bible was canonized and organized. But even more, the assignment helped me discern the trustworthiness of Scripture. To summarize the reliability of the Bible in shaping our worldviews, here is a summary paragraph from the 20-page doctrinal evidence research paper:

> A Christian, or biblical worldview, begins by acknowledging Scripture is the inspired, inerrant, God-breathed Word of the Lord. As 2 Timothy 3:16-17 reads, the Bible was "breathed" by God. Accordingly, the Lord gave life to a living and active Word for our human flourishing. The Bible was composed by man, but according to 2 Peter 1:20, it is not by man but by the Holy Spirit that Scripture was written. The Holy Spirit directed the Bible's authors (Luke 24:27; Acts 1:16). For this reason, Scripture is not attributed to the wisdom of the men who wrote it but instead to the Holy Spirit who inspired it (1 Corinthians 14:37), to God who ordained it (Psalm 119:142), and to Jesus who became flesh (John 1:14) and brought us the gospel (Matthew 28:18-20). Since God is the author of Scripture, and because the Trinity partakes in the fruition of it, we can trust it to be authoritative. Scripture is historical, but it is also prophetic and polemic. The Bible is sufficient for teaching us about how salvation is by faith alone (Ephesians 2:8-9) through Christ (John 5:24; Acts 16:30-31). The Bible also provides followers of Jesus with a dependable guide

(Psalm 119:128) for how we ought to live life and engage the world (Psalm 19:7-11; Romans 15:4; Isaiah 40:8).

Foremost, what I gleaned from the seminary assignment is that a Christian worldview begins with trusting that the Bible is God's authoritative Word. A Christian worldview is also rooted in four essential aspects of the biblical narrative: creation, fall, redemption, and restoration. The Bible evidences God's redemptive and restorative plan for humanity. Dockery writes that a Christian worldview speaks to core questions such as "Where did we come from? Who are we? What has gone wrong with the world? What solution can be offered to deal with these challenges?"[2] When we look at the Bible holistically from Genesis to Revelation, all 66 books speak to the creation of humanity, our fall into sin, God's redemption through Jesus, and the restoration of what has been broken. A biblical or Christian worldview is predicated on the whole of the Bible's narrative, and this worldview is distinctly different from all other major worldviews.

Creation

As Christians, we can answer worldview questions about our origin, identity, and purpose with confidence. Genesis 1 and 2 are an outline of God's perfect, peaceful plan for His creation. The Hebrew word *shalom*, meaning peace, paints the backdrop for the creation of the world and humanity. The beginning of the Bible tells the story of the beginning of creation: The world was made peaceful, for human flourishing, and for kinship with God. From the very beginning of the Bible, we learn all of creation was made by God and for His glory, but humanity was formed in His image. Genesis 1:26-28, along with a more intricate narrative in Genesis 2:5-25, recounts the scriptural account of the direct formation of man and woman.

I cannot recall exactly where I first learned about an important distinction between the creation of the earth and the creation of man, but it gave even more gravity to the significance of the theology of the *imago Dei*, which explains how and why we are made in God's image. The creation account in Genesis 1 repeats how God said, "Let there be." Concerning the creation of humanity he uniquely asserts, "God said, 'Let Us make man in Our image, according to Our likeness'" (NKJV). God has fashioned humans in His image and likeness, distinct from the image of anything He had previously created. Initially, one might interpret this notion to pertain to our physical resemblance to God. But it is more our spiritual nature that resembles our Creator. Men and women, being created in the image of God, possess rationality, morality, spirituality, and personality. They can engage in relationships with God and fellow humans. In Genesis 1:26-28, we learn we have also been tasked with exercising dominion over the earth and its creatures. In the beginning, there was oneness between God and man.

Fall

Adam and Eve defied God's authority by choosing to eat forbidden fruit. We know, of course, that the tree and the fruit itself were not the concern; it was Adam and Eve's willful disobedience. It was their desire to be more like God, to share in His ultimate power and authority. It was the same sin committed by Satan before the world's creation (Ezekiel 28:12-17; Revelation 12:7-9). As a result of Adam and Eve's sin, their rebellious choices led to the downfall of all humanity. Despite being created in God's image, the introduction of sin into the world significantly and negatively affected God's creation, particularly humans who were made in His image.

Initially, God had established ideal conditions for humanity, and everything in this created world was deemed good, with the creation of men and women labeled as very good (Genesis 1:31). Due to sin, the image of God was not obliterated (Genesis 9:6; James 3:9) but rather tainted by sin. The task of exercising dominion (Genesis 1:28) was severely disrupted by the consequences of sin on humans and the curse on nature (Genesis 3). Harmony, peace, and shalom with God, others, nature, and humanity was broken. All efforts at righteousness fall short in God's eyes (Isaiah 64:6; Romans 3:23). Ultimately, humans are spiritually dead and estranged from God (Ephesians 2:1-3), rendering us incapable of properly reflecting the divine image and likeness as originally designed and created (Romans 1:18–3:20). The fall resulted in a separation or spiritual death, disrupting communion with God.

In Genesis 3, we read of the consequences of sin but also of God's mercy concerning our disobedience. The fall resulted in disunity with God and enmity between Satan and all of humanity. As a consequence of the fall, women would experience pain in childbirth, and there would be marital strife. For men, work that was once experienced as a co-laboring, life-giving endeavor would become difficult and arduous. The soil was cursed with thorns and thistles; the labor to produce fruit was agonizing. Yes, there is struggle, and there is physical death; and yet, there is also grace.

Redemption

Though there are consequences to our sin, God promises they will not lead to our spiritual death. The Lord also promises that through Eve's descendants, Mary, the mother of Jesus, would birth a Savior for humanity who will crush the head of the Serpent (Genesis 3:15). It is evident from the beginning, God's design for humanity was always union with Him. Even when our sin separates us from the Lord, He offers grace and a means of salvation. In the Old Testament, God offers redemption through sacrifices and obedience. Where the Old Testament law and covenantal relationship required animal sacrifices to atone for sins or circumcision to evidence a contrite heart, the new covenant requires full submission to a Savior, the circumcision of the heart, and a life of sanctification. In the New Testament,

God offers redemption through the death of His Son, Jesus Christ. In Christ, God's people are both justified and sanctified. Christianity holds justification and sanctification as two distinct but closely related theological concepts. Justification is the declaration of salvation and righteousness; it is a set-apartness. Justification recognizes that all have sinned and fall short of God's glory and need a Savior (Romans 3:23-24). In Christ, we are justified by His death, resurrection, grace, and redemption. Sanctification and justification are concentric and yet distinct. Sanctification is the process of becoming transformed, renewed, and made holy according to God's plan and purposes (Hebrews 2:11). We are being redeemed from glory to glory (2 Corinthians 3:18).

Restoration

There is arguably no theologian who has influenced my faith as profoundly as Tim Keller. When he passed away from cancer in 2023, I joined the global church as we mourned the loss of one of our generation's greatest Christian scholars. I imagine several others share my sentiments when I say that losing Keller felt like losing my own local pastor. He wasn't just a scholar; he was also the contemporary church's pastor. He was both a modern-day C.S. Lewis and Billy Graham. I had the honor of meeting him briefly in 2019 when he was the headline speaker for the Hendricks Center's Faith and Work conference at Dallas Seminary. Keller was just as witty, intellectual, humble, faithful, and in love with the Lord as he appears in his books.

I've read nearly all of Keller's books, and *Generous Justice* ranks among my favorites. In his book, Keller contends that the concept of restoration is essential for a holistic Christian perspective. The restoration principle assures humankind that it's not God's intention to leave the world in the chaos that people created. Rather, God is working to restore "on earth as it is in heaven" (Matthew 6:10). When Jesus returns to earth, He will restore the created order finally and fully to the way

He intended it to be (the key point of restoration). Keller reminds us that as followers of Christ, we are called to partner with a holy calling, to walk not pursuing the things of this world but following after the Spirit (Galatians 5:25). Each of us is born with a sin nature, which in our efforts cannot be eliminated. But as we seek Christ, walk by the Holy Spirit, and remain in fellowship with the body of Christ, the Lord guides our lives.[3] When I was in seminary, I read M.G. Kline's book *Images of the Spirit*, which speaks to how we are endowed with certain spiritual gifts meant for the edification of the church body, the furthering of His kingdom on earth, and ultimately to bring Him glory.[4] Kline underscores that we have been saved, by faith and through grace in Christ, and we are then called to live out the Great Commission. We are in this world but not of the world. We are called to be sojourners, ambassadors, and witnesses for Christ.[5] We were created for partnership with God, but we have been separated by sin and brokenness. But God still longs to reconcile us back to Him. That is the restoration principle. This is God's plan for humanity.

SCRIPTURE SHAPES OUR WORLDVIEW

The greatest warfare the Enemy wages against us is a lie about our identity. This is not a contemporary method of spiritual warfare. Satan has been lying to us about who we are and to whom we belong since the garden of Eden. Satan wants us to find our identity in anything other than God. But as the whole of Scripture validates, God fashioned humanity to bear His image and partner with Him in creation's flourishing. To bear God's likeness constitutes our identity and worth. His image in us and purpose for us transcends all worldly narratives for human merit. God's standard for righteousness and justice, His design for humanity and creation, did not cease because of the fall. In fact, in His abundant love, God paved a way for our redemption and reconciliation through Jesus. This is the *imago Dei* in us; this is a biblical worldview for humanity that undergirds God's vision for social justice. Christ alone repairs fractures from this catastrophic fall that distorted all human relations and institutions. Through His atoning sacrifice, Jesus regenerates our hearts and provides a model for Christlike love, identity, inclusion, and equity that is both countercultural and transcendental. This model for social justice is based on God's truth and not the world's distortion of it.

God's biblical worldview provides a framework for doing good in the world because we are Christ's ambassadors. We are called to build just societies because the cross has made us just. Our renewed humanity in Christ supersedes cultural divisions. Our justification in Jesus equips us to confront inequities and dehumanization with Scripture's truth pertaining to both human dignity and depravity. For Christians, doing justice is not pointing fingers at perceived oppressors and shouting "do better!" Nor is it turning a blind eye to others' suffering and labeling those who care "social justice warriors." Instead, the Bible teaches that following Christ entails stepping into broken, hurting, and depraved spaces with God's unchanging Word and radical love. The whole of the Bible espouses a creation, fall, redemption, and restoration framework; that is the biblical worldview. And the biblical worldview orients Christians to advocate for social justice efforts that are rooted in God's Word, in human dignity, and in the gospel's redemptive power.

As you read about other contemporary—and arguably competing—worldviews, I encourage you to overlay those with a biblical worldview. Ask yourself where you see alignment and misalignment. Where do you discern opportunities for Christians to partner with those who hold a different worldview? Partnership is essential for common good work. But more importantly, where do you discern differences in other worldviews' beliefs, doctrines, motives, and goals? In what ways do they lead us further from, rather than closer to, God's plans and purposes for His people?

DIVINE DESIGN OR COSMIC CHANCE?

Christianity and Naturalism

When we were in our mid to late twenties, my husband and I struggled to start a family for five years. I'm inclined to say our struggle to conceive a baby occurred coincidentally in the same season I began reading Christian worldview books in preparation for writing my dissertation. In retrospect, though, I can see how those simultaneous experiences were providential and not at all coincidental. I sought the Lord throughout our infertility process and treatment. Each step of the way, with each decision that needed to be made, I searched Scripture, stayed connected to our church community, and opened my heart before the Lord. But it was the heavy, defeating agony of miscarrying my first pregnancy that shed light on how distinctly different my philosophical framework was from that of my atheist doctor's.

Over a decade later, I can still vividly recall the day we went in for our eight-week ultrasound. That moment was a culmination of years of medical specialists, examinations, medicines, procedures, tens of thousands of dollars in financial investment, countless prayers, and immeasurable tears. So when the radiologist failed to find my baby's heartbeat, my heart broke too. I rolled away from him on the narrow examination table and curled toward the wall. The stark white sanitary paper crinkled and crunched beneath me as I pulled my knees up to my chest and allowed hot, heavy tears to flow down my cheeks. My defiant recoil coupled with that hard, dry lump in my throat halted the conversation. I pulled my legs tighter to my chest and formed a protective cocoon in a feeble effort to find some semblance of solace, some comfort from within. There was but a brief pause in conversation to acknowledge grief's looming presence before my doctor resumed our discourse, this time a little slower, a little lower, and more emphatically.

"Christina, you don't want this baby. Trust me. There's something wrong with it. It's human tendency to nurture life, but sometimes our bodies take control and tell us to let go through…natural selection. Again, I'm sorry."

I clasped my husband's hand tighter to brace myself against the anguish of acknowledging life's fragility and finality. How wrong that doctor was. I would have given anything to hold my baby—then and now. It was apparent how very differently we were looking at the value of human life.

For years we worked with a team of doctors and medical professionals to conceive. Through tests, surgeries, medicines, invasive procedures, financial sacrifices, tears, and prayers, we hoped against hope with each new step and each new day. And then to finally conceive a little one, whose heart stopped beating just as mine was beginning to beat again, was nothing short of devastating. It simply didn't make sense or seem plausible. Yet here we were. Crestfallen. Broken. Devastated. The months following my miscarriage were laden with grief.

After a year of working with this particular doctor, and walking through a miscarriage under his supervision, I had come to realize he held a very different worldview than mine. He had shared in previous conversations about his Jewish upbringing and how studying Jewish hereditary diseases in college led him on a path to practicing endocrinology and eventually infertility treatment. And although I can't recall precisely how the divine or supernatural became part of our doctor-patient exchanges—perhaps those were a natural extension of existential musings on life and fertility—in a few appointments, he relayed his disbelief in God and any semblance of an afterlife. He had developed a perspective on life rooted in a scientific, naturalistic, and secular worldview. With those predominant lenses, there was little room for a biblical interpretation. I want to be as charitable as possible in interpreting my doctor's worldview; I can only attest to what he shared about his own faith and his reaction to my miscarriage. But I would imagine, through this worldview lens, a miscarriage is merely part of some biological, evolutionary process, not an isolated tragedy. Devoid of any religious narrative that frames life and death as part of a divine plan, my doctor likely perceived miscarriage—and perhaps infertility in general—as part of a natural selection process dictated more by the intricacies of genetic variability than God's sovereignty.

This isn't to imply that he wasn't sympathetic or that he wasn't trying to comfort me in my loss. I would suppose the absence of a religious worldview allowed him to engage his work free from the constraints of moral judgment or existential questioning. My doctor couldn't help ease my distress; he wasn't able to provide spiritual comfort because his frameworks for understanding human experiences like life, death, hope, and disappointment weren't developed from a Christian worldview. He held a worldview that most resembled naturalism.

In the briefest of explanations, naturalism holds there is nothing supernatural or transcendent in life, that every material event or tangible item has a naturalistic explanation. Within a naturalistic worldview, several branches stem from this tree: scientific materialism, evolution, humanism, atheism, environmentalism, and various similar frameworks that rely on a materialistic explanation for constructing meaning and reality. Much of my understanding of naturalism has been informed by J.P. Moreland's book *Kingdom Triangle: Recover the Christian Mind, Renovate the Soul, Restore the Spirit's Power*.[1] In this worldview, the world and humanity are composed of matter and energy operating through natural forces in space and time. The material universe—what is tangible—is all that exists in life. Supernatural or spiritual realities are rejected because they are unverifiable. Human consciousness or the soul, therefore, emerges merely from physical brain complexity, not spirituality. And morality and ethics are defined primarily by human rationality. This worldview asserts there is no supernatural realm or divine being. All phenomena can be explained through natural causes and scientific observation. Human life is purely material with no inherent meaning except what humans make of it.

To be certain, a Christian worldview is in opposition to a naturalistic worldview, but it is not in opposition to medicine or science in general. In fact, I attended a brilliant lecture touching on this at Baylor University in 2017, delivered by Christian scholar Alvin Plantinga. In his talk, Plantinga discussed the tensions and harmonies between science and faith. In his book *Where the Conflict Really Lies: Science, Religion, and Naturalism*, he explores the relationship between science, religion, and naturalism from a Christian perspective. And that lecture aside, I have several medically trained friends—doctors, nurses, scientists, and so forth—who love Jesus. It is possible to approach science from a biblical worldview.

A BIBLICAL PERSPECTIVE

It would have been such a gift to have had a fertility doctor who held a Christian worldview. After that agonizing doctor's appointment, everything in me wanted to retreat from the world. The pain of miscarriage can be all-consuming. I wanted to shrug off all responsibility, hide under my bed covers, and emerge when all physical and emotional pain subsided. But my anguish was not wasted on God, of course. He longs for us to bring our hurt to the foot of the cross. The tragedy of our miscarriage in the throes of infertility encouraged me to think biblically about the sanctity of life, pain, suffering, and grief. And those years of infertility taught me valuable lessons about living through pain by leaning into my marriage, my friendships, and my faith. My heart broke when my baby's heartbeat stopped. And yet, in the quiet chambers of my heart, the truth of Scripture's most profound lessons reverberated. Even through the cloud of unknowing, as I sought the Lord in His Word and worship, I found a deeper, biblically rooted understanding of the sanctity of life. As a follower of Jesus, He has been an unwavering cornerstone in my life, but my faith was solidified even more through the crucible of losing a baby. In the lengthy, agonizing, and broken journey to motherhood, my hope was deferred, and my heart was sick. The future felt painfully precarious in that moment as I looked for hope through a thick cloud of unknowing.

It wasn't that I hadn't known heartache before. I had. Yet, there was something distinctly different about the pain associated with a miscarriage. Until my late twenties, my heartache was primarily the result of sin wreaking havoc on my life—sometimes other people's, sometimes my own sin. When I started walking with the Lord in college and began maturing in my relationship with Him, I learned to take the sort of pain that comes from imperfect people living in an imperfect world to the Lord. I rightly understood when someone hurts you, when someone leaves you with a gaping, bleeding wound, you don't ask the person who inflicted the wound to heal you. Instead, you go to the Great Physician. You allow Him to heal you, to fill you, and to make you whole again. And once you are healed, you are then able to go back to the aggressor and bestow forgiveness.

In this particular trial, however, there was no one at whom I could point my finger as the cause of my pain. The loss of this child wasn't my doctor's fault, or my husband's, or even mine. My heartache was not the result of feeling disappointed in someone; rather, my heartache was the result of feeling disappointed in God. This revelation was a much deeper place of theological struggle than any pain I had ever known. It's one thing to feel let down by man; it's wholly another to feel let down by the Lord. The months following my miscarriage were laden with grief and a nebulous understanding that my heavenly Father would somehow bring beauty from ashes, as He promised He would. Walking through the years of infertility treatment and a miscarriage taught me three valuable lessons about leaning into the Lord when in the throes of pain. No other worldview would have led me closer to Christ than a Christian worldview.

Pain Produces Fruit If You Walk Through the Trial with the Lord

Trials are an opportunity for the refiner's fire to purify our hearts, draw us closer to the Lord, and solidify our identities in Him. The greatest hindrance to tasting the goodness of God is the lingering taste of bitterness. Bitterness deprives us of delight. If you give bitterness a day, it will take a year; if you give bitterness a year, it will take your life. Disappointment produces bitterness and distorts our identity if disappointment is not laid before the throne. Trials are also an invitation for deeper intimacy with Him. God walks beside us in our victories, but He carries us in our trials. He carries His sheep through the pain because He longs to be near. For it is in this nearness, this intimacy with Him, where we find a joy and fulfillment nothing else on earth can satisfy—not even bearing children.

The Enemy is out to kill, steal, and destroy our identity and joy in the Lord. He wants us to feel ashamed, abandoned, and isolated in our disappointment. Satan's rebellion in the kingdom consequentially made him history's first orphan, and he wants God's children to feel the same way. But the Lord calls us His children (John 1:12). We are given a new identity (Romans 6:6) and a double portion of inheritance (Isaiah 61:7). Brennan Manning articulates this well when he writes, "Define yourself radically as one beloved by God. This is the true self. Every other identity is illusion."[2] When we embrace our trials and fall on the cross, we come out the other end refined and more secure in our identities.

We Need the Lord and the Body of Christ to Flourish

In the weeks and months after our miscarriage, we experienced an outpour of love from friends and family. They helped us through the pain and over the finish line when we didn't even have the strength to lift our heads. I was losing my baby, and in the process, I was also losing a substantial piece of my heart. Friends came over to contend before God on our behalf. They brought cards, flowers, meals, Scripture, and one dear friend even wrote and recorded a song of empathy on my behalf. With our friends, we believed for children in faith, but we also echoed Shadrach, Meshach, and Abednego's proclamation in Daniel 3:18 when we, too, declared, "but even if he does not," He is still worthy of our praise! It was in this trial that we learned how to better walk out the biblical charge in Acts 2:42-47 by living a life of faith with the body of Christ. Community alone cannot give what God intends us to find in Him, but community can carry you to the feet of Jesus when you've lost strength to go unaided.

The Gospel Is a Testimony of Hope Renewed

Six months after grieving and processing the pain of our miscarriage with the Lord, each other, and our church community, we felt ready to try IVF a second time as a means of conceiving. We implanted every remaining embryo. We went on to have a beautiful, joyful son named Christopher, which means "bearer of Christ."

Doctors told us we had less than a 1 percent chance of conceiving on our own, not because they could find anything wrong but based upon the statistics of how many years we'd been trying. So you can imagine our surprise and joy when on Christopher's first birthday what I thought was a case of flu was actually the pregnancy with my second son, Corban. We named him "a gift from God dedicated back to Him," because our trial through infertility and miscarriage taught us our hearts were the sacrifice He was after all along. And in return, God not only made beauty out of our ashes, but He also gave us a double portion of inheritance. Through our suffering, we learned trials are not purposed to punish us; they are purposed to refine us. The Lord uses our pain to purify us, which is precisely why 1 Peter 4:13 encourages us to rejoice in our sufferings, so that we might be "overjoyed when His glory is revealed." When we embrace the trial and fall on the cross, we come out the other end changed for the better by the refiner's fire.

Over the last few years, I've had the honor of sharing my story with different women in small-group and large-group settings as a testimony of God's goodness. Recently, a colleague of mine asked me to come share with her undergraduate students in her child and family studies course. I've also had the honor of sharing this testimony at women's conferences and even on the Dallas Theological Seminary podcast *The Table*.[3] I count it joy to share how I submitted my greatest place of pain to the Lord, and in His goodness, He restored my hope and strengthened my identity in Him. Perhaps the greatest lesson I learned through our infertility trial is where to look for eternal hope. Christ, who is the foundation of the Christian worldview, provided hope beyond temporal circumstances.

A Christian worldview approach to social justice differs from a naturalistic worldview. A naturalistic or scientific worldview tends to view life as having only subjective value determined by human preference, with death representing the complete end of personal existence.

But the Christian worldview holds that human life possesses inherent, God-given worth that transcends utility or circumstance, and teaches that physical death marks not an ending but a transition to eternal existence. We are either eternally in communion with God or separated from Him. This fundamental difference profoundly shapes how adherents of each worldview approach questions of human dignity, purpose, and moral responsibility.

Someone with a naturalistic worldview might approach social justice work primarily as correcting material inequities within our finite existence, focusing on structural changes and equitable distribution of resources as the ultimate goal. In contrast, a Christian worldview approaches social justice as participation in God's redemptive plan, seeing human flourishing not just in material terms but as spiritual restoration—advocating for justice while recognizing that perfect justice will only be fully realized in God's kingdom. Christians might emphasize both addressing immediate suffering and pointing toward transcendent hope, seeing each person they serve not merely as a victim of terrible systems but as an eternal being made in God's image whose ultimate needs include but also exceed material wellbeing.

10

MODERNISM AND POSTMODERNISM

Reconstructing Truth in Deconstructing Times

I f in reading the worldview section of this book you've skipped around, I won't hold that against you. You are among respected, loved company; even my husband does this when I ask him to read anything I write. I'll also refrain from a lengthy exposé on how postmodernism has conditioned us to do just that—to personally tailor our consumption according to our likings. I do it too. We all do it. But that lighthearted caveat given, I humbly suggest this section is worth your full attention. There are three forms of modernism that compete with a biblical worldview, and most of us are wholly unaware of how these worldviews have co-opted and distorted what the Bible and church history have to say about the pursuit of holiness and a life well lived. It is precisely for this reason that we should consider how three expressions of modernism have appropriated biblical teachings but led people further from the truth.

In the Christian worldview research I've read, very few scholars consider modernity a worldview. It is, or rather it was, considered more of a literary and historical era (circa 1900-1960). The values and views held in the late 19th and early 20th centuries during modernity align closely with naturalism. And perhaps this is why scholars parse those worldviews separately from modernity as a worldview. But when evaluating the cultural evolution to postmodernism, which most scholars do consider a worldview unto itself, I find it helps to contrast the collective shift in thinking. Within modernity, hyperspecialization, bureaucratization, and pursuit of value-neutral objectivation resulted in parceling out what was once broadly integrated under a shared Judeo-Christian worldview. For example, within modernity, government, education, faith, and other spheres grew increasingly siloed, disconnected, and less concentric.

In the previous section on cultural tensions, we considered the Western shift away from a once predominately held Christian worldview. In the devastating aftermath of two World Wars, faith in God—particularly His goodness and sovereignty—declined. Amid the wars' rubble, beliefs that had withstood centuries of Western thought were crumbling too. Some intellectuals asserted God was altogether dead. Among those scholars stood German philosopher Friedrich Nietzsche who famously proclaimed, "God is dead! And we have killed him."[1] By the 1960s, the quote notoriously captured the disillusioned sentiments of both Nietzsche and modernity regarding Christianity. In response to the cultural moment, *TIME* magazine ran an Easter cover story in 1966 provocatively titled "Is God Dead?"[2] Exploring philosophical and popular debates, author John Elson noted how for the modern person raised on materialist assumptions, it had become "hard...to give a convincing answer" for God's apparent absence amid immense suffering.[3] What Elson articulated in his inflammatory article was that secularism, scientism, and urbanization posed new challenges to religious belief.

MODERNISM'S INFLUENCE

Modernism emerged not just as a response to a waning Western belief in God but also as a response to the radical changes brought about by industrialization, urbanization, and technological advancements. As a worldview, modernism is characterized by a belief in progress, a confidence in reason and science, and a commitment to objective truth. Modernist thinkers often gravitated toward universal principles and sought to create a cohesive, ordered worldview. Modernism places a high value on the idea of objective truth and the ability of reason and science to reveal that truth. Its proponents believe in the possibility of discovering universal principles that can be applied across different disciplines. From the 1900s to the 1950s, many spheres of American society saw great systemization. The onset of modernity onward catalyzed trends toward ordering areas of human activity and knowledge into compartmentalized domains of specialized expertise and institutional control. This reflected emerging philosophical assumptions and political reforms shifting away from integrated worldviews toward bureaucratic rationalization. In other words, much of life became systematized and organized. To offer a few examples, we can see modernity's influence in fields like the government, education, and theology, just to name a few.

Government

Regarding governance, modern democratic theories advocated separating church and state authority into secular government versus private religion to avoid imposed Christian orthodoxy and to uphold both a freedom *of* and a freedom *from* religion. This differentiated separation removed state power from enforcing religious practice. Though some scholars argue later distortions corroded religious freedom. In fact, several Christian scholars argue for more faith integration in the public square, advocating for the inclusion of religious perspectives in public discourse. Former theologian and priest

John Neuhaus was a strong advocate for the engagement of religious voices, particularly Christian perspectives, in the public square. He founded the journal *First Things*, which provides a platform for discussing the intersection of religion and public life. And in 1981, he founded the Institute on Religion and Democracy.[4]

Other respected theologians have also expressed concern over modernity's attempts to wash religion from the public square. For instance, author and speaker Os Guinness. In Guinness's books *The Case for Civility* and *The Global Public Square*, he emphasizes the importance of religious freedom and the need for faith to play a significant role in the public sphere. Guinness is a committed, faithful follower of Christ, and he recognizes our Western and American liberties were derived from a Judeo-Christian worldview. And yet, he advocates for space and civility for all religions to have a voice in our democracy. Specifically, in his book *The Case for Civility*, Guinness strongly criticizes a Christian defense of religious freedom that privileges a Christian theocracy; he maintains that "is not only counterproductive but egregiously wrong and hypocritical."[5] Guinness writes frequently about Christianity's contribution to American civics while also upholding pluralism in the public square.

Education

Much like the government, public education grew increasingly standardized and detached from the church during the modernist era. Religion became individualized rather than a potency for public formation. We also see a deliberate cultivation of tightly run school days. The class to class by bells, the standardized testing, even organized sports were all birthed from modernity's heavy classifications and taxonomies. Modernity significantly influenced K-12 schools in America in various ways, affecting the educational system's structure, curriculum, and pedagogical approaches. Several key changes can be identified: Focus increased on measurement and accountability, particularly in math and science. Standardized testing became a tool for assessing student performance and, over time, influenced curriculum design and teaching methods. Educational philosophy also shifted from a traditional, teacher-centered approach to a more progressive, student-centered approach. Modernity's emphasis on efficiency and organization led to the development of bureaucratic structures within school systems. For example, students were now placed by age and grade in separate classrooms and buildings. These changes included the establishment of school districts, standardized administrative procedures, and a hierarchical organizational model.

Theology

Theology during modernity also witnessed a growing divide between academic theology and practical theology. The trend toward systemizing the Bible was cultivated in universities and seminaries that used critical historical methods and analyzing texts instead of relying on communities to nurture spiritual formation. When I was in seminary, I once grumbled to a friend about how many "systematic theology charts" I was required to create for courses. It was quite the systematizing learning curve. My friend was puzzled, since she did not have to create a single chart during her MDiv course work at another seminary. I have wondered if there is a correlation between when the seminary I attended was founded during modernity and how they've designed their courses. My seminary experience was far more systematic and lecture based than her dialogical and Socratic method experience.

POSTMODERNISM

We would not have *post*modern thought if we did not first have modern thought. Typically, postmodernism is where Christian worldview scholars focus their attention because the impact of it on our contemporary ideologies cannot be overstated. Postmodern thought is a response to modernism. I've touched on how in the early 1900s and in subsequent decades, many spheres of public interest in America were influenced by the philosophies of modernity, including our government, public schools, and even the organization of theology. By the late 1960s, across most fields of study, a shift in the American mind cultivated new ways of thinking and ultimately a new worldview: postmodernism. It's difficult to assert specifically when Western thought shifted from modernism to postmodernism. Typically, scholars correlate shifts according to major world events such as wars, rulers, or the turn of centuries. And perhaps that shift in American thought occurred during the social unrest of the civil rights movements, the death of President John F. Kennedy and the loss of Camelot, the Vietnam War protests, and the tidal wave of the sexual revolution, feminism, and *Roe v. Wade*. What is clear, however, is that dramatic changes occurred in the 1960s, and those changes had significant ramifications for American culture and the church. The shift also had a profound impact on the ways Christians engaged social justice.

Several Christian scholars foresaw what these changes would mean for Western Christianity and our social fabric. During the God Is Dead Movement in the 1960s, renowned theologian and professor Peter Berger wrote extensively in opposition to public accusations that God is no longer needed in the public square. Berger wrote on the existence of God and the value of faith in shaping policy and praxis. He was a scholar on the sociology of knowledge, which is, essentially, how we collectively construct meaning in life. One of his most acclaimed books, *The Social Construction of Reality: A Treatise in the Sociology of Knowledge*, explores the process of constructing a worldview and our worldviews' implications for society. In this work, and throughout his scholarship, Berger argued that a faith-based worldview, rather than a secular or a nonreligious one, is best for the flourishing of an individual and the whole of society. He suggests faith helps people make sense of the world as well as connect the supernatural and transcendent to the ordinary and material aspects of life. Berger's worldview scholarship not only informed how culture shapes our worldviews, but it also made a cogent argument for why a Christian worldview, not a modernist or postmodernist one, is essential for navigating a culture.

What Is Postmodernism and How Has It Influenced Culture?

A few years ago, some dear fellow Wacoan friends of ours, Josh and Jill, were featured on the then wildly popular HGTV television show *Fixer Upper*. As the show goes, my friends purchased an older, run-down home in Waco, Texas, in need of a great deal of renovation and restoration. The couple then entrusted the home's makeover to Chip and Joanna Gaines, the show's nationally acclaimed hosts. Our friends bought an eyesore of a home, and they affectionately called it a "postmodern mix-match." After years of studying postmodern theories in literature and the social sciences during graduate school, I was familiar with the term *postmodern*, but until this conversation, I had not heard it used in reference to architecture.

"What is a postmodern home?" I inquired. Over lunch one day, my friend Jill explained, "It's a home with no real rhyme or reason. Anything goes. Decades of various designs and styles are all merged together. It's very mixed-matched." Her 1970s home had weathered nearly five decades of additions, demolitions, carpet, paint, and wallpaper. Whatever its original design, it was difficult to discern upon their purchase. The episode's title calls the home "mid-century modern," but when I walked through it prior to renovation, it was evident the 1980s and 1990s had left their marks too.

Much like Josh and Jill's mixed-matched, mid-century, postmodern home, postmodernism as a worldview is quite similar. Postmodernism builds on the foundation of modernism in that it moves away from the supernatural and transcendental as plausible explanations for anything material in life and relies quite heavily on human rationale. Unlike modernism, however, postmodernism posits that there is little objective or measurable truth in the world, and for this reason, truth is determined by an individual's interpretation of what is true for him or her. Perhaps this ideology is best evidenced in the popular "my truth, your truth" phrases we use to encourage tolerance and describe how people arrive at such different conclusions. Postmodernism emerged in the mid-20th century as a reaction against the certainties of modernism. It is frequently characterized by skepticism toward grand narratives, a rejection of absolute truths, and an emphasis on the subjectivity of experience. Postmodernism challenges the notion that there is a single, objective reality and encourages an exploration of diverse perspectives.

The *Fixer Upper* conversation with my friends a few years ago gave me reason to think not only on the home's design, redesign, and purpose but also about its foundation and bones. Living in Waco, Texas, I've had the opportunity of walking through several before-and-after homes renovated by Chip and Joanna Gaines. In fact, many of the clients on the show have been friends and acquaintances. I have seen the transformations firsthand, and they are stunning! Even as I write this book, I am doing so from their newly renovated Hotel 1928. It's breathtaking, especially in light of what the hotel looked like sitting empty for decades. But in all my Waco-based *Fixer Upper* transformation discussions, I've often wondered about the aspects we cannot see, like the foundation. What about the support beams in the walls? Were the studs up to code? Was the roof replaced? Was the structure itself solid? That these houses, restaurants, and hotels have experienced a beautiful transformation is apparent, but I am even more curious to know the reliability of the frameworks. In a number of ways, remodeling a home is analogous to reevaluating a worldview in that we want to consider more than just the surface ascetics; we must also consider the strength and dependability of the structure holding it all together.

DECONSTRUCTION

In 2020, I witnessed several friends in my social circle publicly denounce and "deconstruct" their faith. Maybe you did too. Deconstruction, the initial act of tearing down systems and beliefs, isn't new. In fact, deconstruction and its processes—critical theories—were formally developed through the Frankfurt School in Germany in the early 20th century during modernism. But interestingly, the theories were not popularized outside of academic circles until postmodernism. Where modernism relied heavily on systemizing and streamlining based on measurable evidence, postmodern critical theories are far broader, more abstract, and more based upon the critique of tradition as a method of investigation. The primary characteristic of this school of thought is that social and critical theories—whether applied to educational research, art, philosophy, literature, or business—should play a significant role in changing the world, not just recording information. The first generation of critical theorists working in Frankfurt between WWI and WWII rejected rationalism, and this became a cornerstone framework for postmodernism. These philosophies were established by the works of scholars such as Kant, Hegel, and Marx. These philosophers rejected realism and tradition of the past to embrace theories from postmodernism. Postmodernism employs deconstruction as a method of analyzing and challenging traditional structures of thought. Its proponents seek to uncover hidden power dynamics and question established norms.

From studying and teaching the history of Western education's theory and praxis, I see a notable shift from modernity to postmodernity in higher education in the 1960s and 1970s. By the 1980s and 1990s, postmodernist critical theories began making their way from the ivory towers to the public square. Curriculum study in the United States has progressed from the critical theory of the early Frankfurt school to academics who now attempt to become actively engaged in promoting social change within the education system and the culture itself. They seek to promote change by "becoming part of the self-consciousness of oppressed social groups."[6] These researchers have rejected the realism of the past (namely Enlightenment and modernity) to embrace theories from postmodernism, which are derived overwhelmingly from relative ideologies.

ARE RELATIVISM AND POSTMODERNISM ONE AND THE SAME?

You've likely heard someone use the rhetorical phrase, "Well, that's relative." Perhaps when you have, you've wondered, *Well, relative to what?* The tricky aspect to postmodern thought is that the answer is, essentially, it's "relative to relative." If that line of thought seems circular, it's because it is. There is no absolute standard by which to judge the arbitrary. Relativism and postmodernism may not be precisely the same ideology, but they are both philosophies branching from a tree firmly rooted in the soil of secularism. Unlike relativism, postmodernism is an entire worldview, according to James Sire in his book *The Universe Next Door*. It's a worldview complete with its own set of beliefs and praxis. We are all immersed in the sea of postmodernism whether we know it or not, and its presuppositions are rooted so deeply in our thinking, even those who are Christians often reveal postmodern attitudes. Postmodernism can be challenging to define, and I find it particularly challenging to differentiate postmodern thought from relative creeds. Generally, though, historians, academics, and theologians agree that postmodern theory rejects the supposition of a meta-narrative. During my seminary coursework, when I was writing a required paper on postmodernism, I referred to Gene Edward Veith's book *Postmodern Times*. In it, he describes postmodernism as the time period after modernism, defined by its three major rejections: (a) that there are no universal and eternal truths and values; (b) rejection of Enlightenment claims of one method and approach to rationality; (c) claims of an irresistible social and economic force of the future. It is a relativistic arrangement and structure of thinking and viewing that refutes absolute truth and objectivity.[7] According to pastor and writer Erroll Hulse, it is often difficult to find a satisfying universal definition of postmodernism, but most agree that it is composed of four aspects: deconstructionism, relativism, pluralism, and existentialism.[8]

Relativism, on the other hand, is not an entire worldview, but it is a philosophical belief rooted primarily in secularism. Within relativism, ethical truths and even reality all depend on the beliefs and values of the individuals and groups holding them. And absolute truth, particularly "truths" that cannot be validated through the scientific method, are instead relative to one's interpretation, particularly interpretation derived from experience. In other words, morality, theology, goodness, beauty, and even science and medicine are all relative in truth and worth according to the society that gives meaning to these sorts of values and ethics. Interest in relativism as a philosophical doctrine goes back to ancient Greece. In more recent decades, however, relativism has also proven popular not only as a philosophical position but also as an idea underwriting a normative ethical and political outlook. A number of philosophical considerations, as well as socio-historical developments, explain the enduring interest in and the more recent popularity of relativism. And in the last 50 to 75 years, relativism has become affixed to postmodernism.

Specifically on the feasibility of relativism, literary critics and philosophers Richard Rorty and Stanley Fish have asserted that no one is truly a relativist, and I think I mostly agree.[9] No reasonable, rational, intellectual person believes two competing and opposing beliefs can be simultaneously true. As Rorty infers, either something is or it is not, but it cannot be both. And yet, how often does our postmodern culture attempt to defy Rorty's claim? As an undergraduate college professor, I've watched long-held, orthodox truth bulldozed by the word *tolerance*. Even worse, on a Christian campus, I watch fellow believers badger others into thought submission with the misuse of the biblical command to "love our neighbor." For example, when I publicly asserted on social media that biological males should not occupy biological female spaces—such as sports and changing areas—ideologically humanist-leaning people accused me of not loving my trans neighbor well. I was charged in the court of progressive public opinion of "espousing TERF rhetoric," to quote one student majoring in social work, referring to "trans-exclusionary radical feminism."

Foremost, from a Christian worldview, we can make the case that God's love never compromises truth (Isaiah 40:8; Matthew 24:35; Hebrews 13:8; James 1:17). When Scripture speaks on a cultural issue, such as the difference between males and females, or the sanctity of life, or honoring the Lord by upholding His commands, the issue is biblical and not merely political. And if God is love and His Word is truth, we can also surmise that His truth is far more loving than anything humanity could define apart from God. Second, from any worldview, how is it more loving to protect biological males who struggle with gender dysphoria than it is to protect biological females who are far more vulnerable to abuse and exploitation? It's not. To even attempt to make an argument along these lines would require us to not only deny biological and biblical truths, but we would also have to adopt a relativist perspective as well as adapt several postmodern critical theories to fit that oppressor-versus-the-oppressed narrative.

Isolated from an event, person, or specific demographic, assertions like "Men can become women" or "Your truth is your truth" or "A baby in the womb is a fetus unless the pregnancy is wanted, and then it is a baby" likely seem absurd to most reasonable folks. Mostly, I think these false narratives are subconsciously derived from postmodern thought, and people are unaware of how relative they sound when they espouse them. But the ramifications of postmodern ideologies often present as quite relative. For instance, postmodernism challenges traditional, historical, and biblical interpretations of marriage and family structure, but relativism altogether redefines gender and sexuality according to individualistic preference. Stanley Fish posits that "While relativism is a position one can entertain, it is not a position one can occupy. No one can *be* a relativist."[10] Similarly, Richard Rorty maintains, "Relativism is the view that every belief on a certain topic, or perhaps about any topic, is as good as every other. No one holds this view. Except for the occasional cooperative freshman, one cannot find anyone who says that two incompatible opinions on an important topic are equally good. The philosophers who get called relativist are those who say that the grounds for choosing between such options are less algorithmic than had been previously thought."[11] I'm not sure I agree that our Western culture isn't trying with all their might to be relativistic. Yes, in theory, no one can muster enough cognitive dissonance from reality to hold a consistently relativist perspective no matter how pluralistic, humanistic, secular, or tolerant culture attempts to become. And yet, it strikes me how much more relative Western culture is now than when Rorty and Fish made these assertions decades ago.

A BIBLICAL WORLDVIEW PERSPECTIVE ON POSTMODERNISM AND SOCIAL ACTIVISM

What postmodernism and relativism share is that they are incompatible with a biblical worldview because these ideologies contradict what Scripture says to be true. In theologian Nicholas Wolterstorff's essay "True Words," he suggests that while we should accept God's Word as true, to ask if every single verse in the Bible is "true or false" is to miss the story and heart of God completely. That is an important question, he writes, but it is secondary to asking, "What is God saying here?"[12] He notes that we can whimsically make up our own definitions of truth, but that does not (a) in any way change reality or (b) give us any authority. In fact, in defining reality according to our own terms, we are doing so on our own authority and not God's.

Can we trust ourselves as the authority? Scripture and church history would argue we cannot. Wolterstorff insightfully defines truth as that which "measures up" to a particular standard or facts pertinent to the context.[13] Rather than ill-defined subjectivity, truth entails accurately corresponding to relevant reality.

This aligns with how Scripture frames truth's essential nature. For example, even Jesus affirms His words in accordance with the whole of Scripture. He states in John 5:31 that His lone testimony "is not true," and then references the Torah to establish truth in legal disputes. Jesus affirms a greater authority beyond Himself attests to His identity (verse 39). So biblical truth-claims appeal to appropriate benchmarks for evaluation, not personal preference. As orthodox Christians, our assertions carry no inherent certainty apart from measuring our claims against permanent standards. And for Christians, the Bible is our unchanging standard for discernment. This grounds truth in God's reality, not human relativism. Scripture underscores imperatives based on God's authority alongside divine revelation, making empirical statements about the world.

Postmodernism is not easily reconcilable with a biblical worldview. Holistically speaking, this worldview discards Christian doctrines such as absolute truth, doctrinal orthodoxy, and church hierarchy—particularly in the form of patriarchy. Postmodernism questions tradition and is deeply suspicious of authority. The critical theories embedded in postmodernism argue against forms of spiritual authority and instead believe in giving voice and power to more oppressed and marginalized people groups. According to postmodernism and its critical theories, those who have traditionally held power and influence cannot be trusted because they have not wielded their power and influence equitably.

Postmodernism as a worldview does not acknowledge the existence of God the Creator. Therefore, there is no origin story, no account of the human condition, and no transcendental purpose to life. Postmodernism shares a great deal of concentric philosophical theories with relativism, which is the belief that truths are contingent and incapable of objective reasoning. As scholar D.A. Carson notes, both relativism and postmodernism insist all values, morals, and ethics are cultural and therefore temporary; they are merely social constructs.[14] The Christian worldview, however, does not share in the shifting nature of relativism or the deconstructionism required in postmodernism. The Christian worldview stands apart from both.

Polls indicate that when asked about their faith or even worldview, most Americans identify as Christians, not postmodernists.[15] But across all faiths, studies also indicate how much postmodern thought has influenced our worldviews. Within Christianity, for instance, a Barna study suggested the respondents' views, comprised of Protestant pastors, were strongly influenced by postmodernist thought.[16] Barna found that for many, especially those in the millennial generation, their core beliefs do not align with a close interpretation of the Bible, and they share more in common with postmodern narratives than a gospel narrative. Barna has conducted a nationwide survey every five years since 1994, and the results indicate that a growing number of individuals who attend churches, whether Protestant or Catholic, have accepted beliefs that clash with the teachings of the Bible and those espoused by the church they attend. For example, a large number of Americans believe differently from biblical teaching on a number of issues including the sinless life of Jesus Christ. While the Bible teaches Jesus never sinned, less than half of confessing Christians (42 percent) embrace this view.[17] People under the age of 38 make up the majority of this group with 49 percent of the total number of those who disagree.[18] In this study, Barna concluded people are willing to pull from an assortment of conflicting and even opposing theological resources. Surprisingly, just under half of the respondents (42 percent), challenge the idea of the Bible being the primary source of truth and consider the Bible, the Book of Mormon, and the Koran to be different statements of the same spiritual truths. Further, the same Barna study found 54 percent of Americans hold to the belief that personal experiences, feelings, and reasoning are the only way to discover truth—not through a book—which is inconsistent with the traditional Protestant belief that the Bible is the source of truth. [19]

Barna's research suggests, even among professing Christians, a slow shift of theological views away from the Bible as the touchstone for truth. The study's findings surmise that the handing down of Christian heritage from generation to generation is quickly diminishing, and it is being replaced by a fusion of culture-based theology. The research shows that Americans still respect the Bible and consider themselves to be Bible believers, but the data indicates that they do not believe the Bible is exclusively or even primarily a source for Christian truth. Recent Barna studies suggest Christians, particularly those currently under 40 years of age, continue to adopt spiritual beliefs from various religions, critical theories, and their own personal experience to frame "their own truth," which has become a popular phrase in contemporary vernacular. What Barna and other researchers have noticed among the 70 percent of Americans who identify as Christian is a rise in postmodern thought and a decline in a Christian worldview forged primarily through a biblical lens. [20]

Tensions are evident between Christianity and postmodern ideologies for Christian educators, but this is true for all followers of Christ working in every sphere of influence, even in places of formal church ministry. Understanding where Christians may find conflict with some of the underlying assumptions and teachings of postmodernism—especially with regards to culturally sensitive topics such as social justice, multicultural education, racial reconciliation, and gender identity—could help inform them how to better prepare younger followers of Christ to engage theses narratives in the public square and from a biblical worldview. Christians should consider the intersections between their faith and justice. In fact, much of what is appealing to Millennials and Gen Z about postmodern thought, and its varied critical theories, is its emphasis on lived experience for truth and social justice for the common good. But without a robust biblical framework for doing social justice work, often our reasons and efforts assume a form of postmodern relativism. Christian values and biblical truths become subjective in light of what culture espouses, and God's standard is eclipsed.

The result of relativism is suspicion toward claims of truth, history, leadership, and even objectivity. But we cannot continue to drift from the touchstone of a biblical social justice and assume culture will not co-opt and distort God's Word. The biblical worldview buffers the body of Christ against false narratives in a postmodern culture constantly grappling to redefine what God proclaims is true, noble, right, pure, lovely, admirable, excellent, and praiseworthy.

FOUNDATIONS OF FAITH

Standing on a Biblical Worldview in an Ever-Shifting Culture

When I was a little girl, I can distinctly remember singing the Sunday school song "The Wise Man Built His House Upon the Rock." If you frequently attended church as a kid, particularly in Southern Baptist and nondenominational churches, you likely sang it too. Unlike the song "Father Abraham," which I mistakenly thought was about Abraham Lincoln until circa the fourth or fifth grade, or the song "In the Lord's Army," which I erroneously thought was about joining America's actual armed forces, I could understand the song about the wise man and his house. Even in elementary school, I understood the rock and sand metaphor. The importance of building a solid foundation on God's Word was not lost on me. The simple Sunday school song carries a profound truth that even young children can grasp: The foundation upon which we build our lives matters immensely. As the parable teaches, the wise person anchors their life on the solid rock of God's Word, while the foolish one builds on the shifting sands of anything the world has to offer apart from God's truth.

The lyrics for this song were taken from Jesus's parable in the Sermon on the Mount. The parable of the wise and foolish builders, found in Matthew 7:24-27 and Luke 6:46-49, effectively summarizes the importance of living life from a biblical worldview. In this parable, Jesus compares two builders: one who builds his house on a solid foundation of rock and another who builds on a weak foundation of sand. The wise builder represents those who hear Jesus's words and put them into practice, building their lives on the solid foundation of biblical principles and obedience to God. When storms and trials come, their lives remain stable because they have rooted themselves in the truth of God's Word. The foolish builder, in contrast, represents those who hear Jesus's teachings but fail to apply them to their lives. They build their lives on the shifting sands of worldly values, man's opinions, and their own interpretation of what is good, true, and beautiful. When the storms of difficulty and trial arise, those who built upon the sand watch their homes crumble because they lack the firm foundation of biblical truth.

The parable of building our lives on the rock of God's truth underscores the significance of building upon a biblical worldview. Our worldview is not only our lens for life; it is also our foundation for withstanding life's storms when the "rains come down and the floods come up." Building upon a biblical framework is not merely about hearing or knowing God's Word, but it also entails actively applying it to every aspect of life. It emphasizes the importance of aligning one's thoughts, actions, and decisions with biblical principles. Or, as Saint Augustine describes in his famed work, *Confessions*, a life submitted to God requires us to "rightly order our lives" in accordance to God's Word and will, as this is the only way to build a life that can withstand the challenges and uncertainties of the world.[1] The parable underscores the necessity of obedience to Christ's teachings.

In a culture that increasingly celebrates self-determination, hyper-individualism, and postmodern relativism, the temptation to construct our identities and purpose apart from biblical truth is ever-present. But as the children's worship song "The Wise Man Built His House Upon the Rock" reminds us, only by aligning our lives with the unchanging wisdom of Scripture can we hope to weather the storms and trials that inevitably come our way. Building our lives on the rock of God's Word involves more than merely hearing or acknowledging biblical principles; it requires the hard work of daily obedience and the humility to submit our desires and plans to the authority of Christ. In Matthew 7:21, just before the parable, Jesus states, "Not everyone who says to me, 'Lord, Lord,' will enter the kingdom of heaven, but only the one who does the will of my Father who is in heaven." This reinforces that a biblical worldview is not merely an intellectual assent to a set of beliefs or even simply a profession of faith; rather, it is a holistic, transformative, lifelong commitment to living out God's Word in our daily lives. As we do so, we discover the unshakable peace and joy that comes from living in partnership with God and seeking His purpose for our lives.

THE ESSENTIALS OF A BIBLICAL WORLDVIEW: WHY IT MATTERS FOR SOCIAL JUSTICE WORK

As Christians, we find ourselves navigating a postmodern, post-Christian Western world, one with competing and inconsistent ideas and worldviews. In an era marked by unprecedented technological advancements, vast globalization, and a synthetic sense of interconnectedness, we are more exposed to and influenced by these disparate perspectives than ever before. Given these competing frameworks, it's essential for followers of Jesus to consider how profoundly these worldviews have penetrated the minds and hearts of Christians. Since 1995, Barna Research has studied various modern worldviews and the sociological impact these vastly different ideologies have on the American people. Several other respected research groups and think tanks study the relationship between faith and culture. Pew, Gallup, and The Barna Research Group are particularly interested in how self-professed Christians embrace or reject facets of a biblical worldview.

If it seems both the public square and private church-influenced spaces feel less Christian, it's because, according to research, they are. In a 2023 worldview study with 2,000 participants, Barna conducted research that sheds light on the decline of shared orthodox, biblical values. The research reveals a startling reality: The percentage of professing Christians who holistically hold a biblical worldview has fallen to 4 percent—a significant drop from the 6 percent in the 2017 study.[2] The same study also found the following:

- Most Americans (68 percent) still consider themselves to be Christians. But less than half of the self-identified Christians can be classified as born-again, defined as believing that they will go to heaven after they die but only because they have confessed their sins and accepted Jesus Christ as their Savior. Within the born-again population (just 33 percent of the adult population), a shockingly small proportion (13 percent) hold a biblical worldview.

- Age has a consistent correlation with biblical worldview incidence. The younger a person, the less likely they are to be an Integrated Disciple (i.e., have a biblical worldview). Among adults under 30, just 1 percent have a biblical worldview. The incidence rises to 3 percent among people in their thirties and forties; 5 percent among those ages 50 to 64; and peaks at 8 percent among adults 65-plus.

- Adults without children under the age of 13 living in their household were slightly more likely to have a biblical worldview than those adults who do have preteen children (5 percent compared to 3 percent).

- People from the highest-income households were more likely than other adults to qualify as Integrated Disciples. Overall, 6 percent of people in homes earning beyond $100,000 were Integrated Disciples, compared to 4 percent among people in the $60,000-$100,000 category and also 4 percent among people from households with a pre-tax combined income below $60,000.

- People living in regions of the country considered to be more religiously active had slightly higher levels of biblical worldview. Six percent of residents of the South and 5 percent of those living in the Midwest had a biblical worldview, compared to just 3 percent in the West and 1 percent in the Northeast.

- Formal education shows little correlation with having a biblical worldview. The incidence of biblical worldview among those who never attended college is 3 percent; among those who attended college but do not have a 4-year degree is 4 percent; and among those with a bachelor's degree or more, it is 5 percent.

- Among adults who are consistently conservative on political issues, 12 percent are Integrated Disciples. In contrast, just 2 percent who are consistently moderate on political issues and 1 percent of political liberals and progressives have a biblical worldview.

Barna's decades of benchmark studies also delve into the extent to which the central tenets of other prominent worldviews—including new spirituality, secularism, postmodernism, and Marxism—have shaped Christians' beliefs about the nature of reality and the way the world ought to be. Astonishingly, the findings reveal a strong agreement with ideas rooted in nonbiblical worldviews among practicing Christians. The pervasive influence of these competing worldviews upon Christian thinking extends beyond mere philosophical frameworks; it even encompasses religious beliefs. As followers of Christ, we must grapple with the implications of these findings. In a world where truth is increasingly relativized and the lines between worldviews are blurred, it is more critical than ever that we anchor ourselves firmly in the timeless truths of Scripture. Only by immersing ourselves in God's Word and prayerfully seeking His guidance can we hope to navigate the complexities of our age with discernment, wisdom, and unwavering faith. In Barna's 2023 American Worldview Inventory, the report identifies the "seven cornerstones of the biblical worldview." They are:

1. An orthodox, biblical understanding of God.

2. All human beings are sinful by nature; every choice we make has moral considerations and consequences.

3. Knowing Jesus Christ is the only means to salvation, through our confession of sin and reliance on His forgiveness.

4. The entire Bible is true, reliable, and relevant, making it the best moral guide for every person, in all situations.

5. Absolute moral truth exists—and those truths are defined by God, described in the Bible, and are unchanging across time and cultures.

6. The ultimate purpose of human life is to know, love, and serve God with all your heart, mind, strength, and soul.

7. Success on earth is best understood as consistent obedience to God—in thoughts, words, and actions.[3]

In his insightful analysis of the American Worldview Inventory 2023, George Barna, the center's namesake and lead researcher, notes a startling discovery about the state of Christian belief in America. The study reveals that a mere 3 percent of the population ascribes to all seven cornerstones of a biblical worldview. These cornerstones, which Barna describes as "basic Christian tenets, not advanced or sophisticated theological constructs," serve as the foundation for a life that brings glory to God and offers a sense of purpose and direction. Barna emphasizes the importance of not only understanding these principles but also passionately embracing them as a guiding force in one's life. He explains, "Statistically, we see that if this base is not solid, a person's worldview will be an inconsistent and unpredictable mess. Since worldview is our decision-making filter, a person who has a weak foundation will be characterized by a life that is a constant struggle."[4]

The study also reveals a stark generational divide, with younger adults being less likely to embrace the seven cornerstones. Among those aged 18 to 29, only 1 percent agree with all seven principles, while a mere 10 percent accept four, five, or six of them as valid. This trend highlights the urgent need for the church to engage with younger generations and effectively communicate the truth and relevance of biblical principles. Perhaps the most striking finding of the study is the correlation between embracing the seven cornerstones and possessing a biblical worldview. According to the study's findings, an overwhelming 83 percent of adults who accept all seven principles have a biblical worldview, while only 2 percent of those who reject one or more of the cornerstones exhibit such a perspective. When examining each cornerstone individually, the numbers paint a sobering picture. Only 50 percent of American adults embrace the true nature of God, 35 percent believe Jesus is the only way for salvation, 27 percent recognize humans as sinful, 46 percent accept the Bible as true and reliable, 25 percent believe in absolute truth rooted in the Bible,

36 percent see their purpose as serving God, and a mere 23 percent define success as obedience to God.[5]

Despite these discouraging statistics, the study also offers a glimmer of hope. From 2020 to 2023, there were significant shifts in certain measurements, including increases in recognizing human sinfulness, viewing the Bible as the true and reliable words of God, and defining life's purpose as serving God with all one's heart, soul, mind, and strength. As Barna notes, "We don't often see adults initiating large shifts in their life philosophy, but these statistics remind us that such change is possible, especially in times of social instability and uncertainty, such as we have today."[6] The 2023 American Worldview Inventory serves as a clarion call for the church to increase its efforts in discipleship and evangelism. By faithfully proclaiming the truth of God's Word and demonstrating its transformative power in our own lives, we can help others build a solid foundation on the seven cornerstones of a biblical worldview. As we navigate an increasingly complex and divided world, it is more crucial than ever that we anchor ourselves in the timeless truths of Scripture and invite others to experience the abundant life that comes from knowing and serving Christ.

A BIBLICAL WORLDVIEW IS NOT WHITENESS, POLITICS, OR CULTURE WARRING

The aim of part two of this book is to underscore the significance of a biblical worldview as well as highlight how other contemporary worldviews compete with and co-opt biblical teachings. My hope is that this section not only helps followers of Christ see the difference in the multitude of worldview narratives, but even more, to highlight why the Bible's narrative is reliable, trustworthy, and sufficient. Primarily, I hope to emphasize why rightly aligning ourselves with Scripture is essential if we want to rightly engage the world for Christ. But I would be remiss to ignore some of the critiques on biblical worldview scholarship.

One of the primary contemporary critiques of Christian worldview scholarship comes from Jacob Alan Cook. In the *Baptist Standard*, an online and decidedly more progressive publication, Cook has written a series of shorter articles arguing against Christians posturing "their" worldview above others' worldviews. He has also written a lengthy, dense academic book, *Worldview Theory, Whiteness, and the Future of Evangelical Faith,* with the same objective. In both publications, Cook alleges that the Christian worldview framework, the history informing it, and the contemporary movement around it is all rooted in *Evangelical Whiteness.* Cook asks readers to reconcile ugly parts of church history, like the historical validation of slavery from prominent Christian leaders. He contends that evangelicals' adoption of worldview theory has inadvertently led them to embrace culture wars rather than living out a compelling and faithful alternative. He argues that using world-viewing as a theological framework compels evangelicals to narrate humanity in ways that distort Christian identity as a personal, social, and theological reality. This distortion, Cook suggests, is rooted less in the Bible and more in an unacknowledged, subconscious concept of "Whiteness." He gives detailed examinations of influential White evangelical leaders who employed the worldview concept for political engagement and cultural transformation. It's worth noting, however ironic, that Cook is an educated, White, Christian male—the very demographic he's calling to the carpet. And though he is skeptical of Christians who claim a biblical worldview is a cohesive framework stemming from one definitive source, he scarcely uses the Bible to make his points, which is a problematic theological approach. Instead of Scripture, Cook relies heavily on sociology, social commentary, and a few case studies.

Cook is not alone in his critique. Other scholars and commentators have alleged a political motivation behind Christian worldview scholarship. Some critics, like Cook, have questioned the coherency of a biblical worldview. Others have directly or indirectly challenged aspects of Western church values such as purity culture, patriarchal leadership, or Christian nationalism. Recently books like *Jesus and John Wayne*, *The Making of Biblical Womanhood*, and *Taking America Back for God* have raised fair questions about whether certain characteristics of evangelical expressions are actually biblical, and which are extra-biblical, meaning they have become customary more because of culture's influence rather than Christ's teachings.

To address the valid concerns, this needs to be stated plainly and simply: A biblical worldview is not Western White privilege, Christian nationalism, or culture warring. It is not a product of Western White privilege; rather, it is a comprehensive understanding of reality that is rooted in the timeless truths revealed in God's Word. This framework is derived from Scripture and transcends all cultural, ethnic, and socioeconomic boundaries, as it is grounded in the universal narrative of creation, fall, redemption, and restoration that encompasses all of humanity. To suggest a biblical worldview is merely an expression of White privilege is to ignore the vast, diverse tapestry of believers who have been woven into the church body throughout history and across the globe. From the early church in the Middle East and North Africa to the vibrant faith communities in Asia, Latin America, and Sub-Saharan Africa, the biblical worldview has resonated with and transformed people from all walks of life.

A biblical worldview consists of biblical principles shared by the global church, not just a Western, American expression of the body of Christ. And for this reason, a biblical worldview is not Christian nationalism nor any sentiment that intimates "making America great again" in Jesus's name. This is not to imply that a biblical worldview will not influence a person's political view. Consciously or subconsciously, every adult holds a worldview, and that worldview will influence a person's political views. In fact, a holistic, fully integrated biblical worldview should lead us to vote for leaders who share our values. Dignifying life from womb to tomb, supporting restorative justice initiatives, caring for the homeless, protecting vulnerable demographics such as women and children, elevating marginalized voices, and working toward racial reconciliation are not Republican or Democratic talking points. They do not belong exclusively to conservative or progressive ideologies; they cannot be co-opted by the far right or far left.

Working to ensure human flourishing is a profoundly biblical value rooted in the *imago Dei*. No other worldview can lay claim to this truth. Much of what our country professes to embody—the call to love one's neighbor, the mandate to seek justice and mercy, the right to worship publicly, freely, and without persecution—these notions of human rights are derived from Scripture. These principles, when properly understood and applied, should compel Christians to combat injustice, stand in opposition to racism, and alleviate oppression, rather than perpetuate or benefit from them. Yes, it is unfortunately true that Western Christianity has historically been complicit in colonialism, crusades, and slavery. Historically, Christianity has been manipulated and abused to justify oppression. But those expressions and applications were distortions of God's Word and character. A true biblical worldview calls us to humility, not hubris. To repentance, not revenge. And when we engage in what some critics consider "culture warring," we fight not against flesh and blood. Our wrestling is against Satan's principalities, "against powers, against the rulers of the darkness of this world, against spiritual wickedness in high places" (Ephesians 6:12 KJV). A biblical worldview reminds us that our real Enemy is the one who has come to "steal, kill, and destroy" all that God has made (John 10:10). Ultimately, a biblical worldview recognizes the transformative power of the gospel to heal broken hearts and systems, lead the lost to salvation, transcend human divisions, and unite people in the name of Jesus. And as we seek to bring the Lord glory and honor, we become sanctified by His grace in the process.

LOVING GOD MOST SO WE CAN
LOVE OUR NEIGHBORS WELL

For the last five or six years, nearly each night when I tuck my boys into bed, I ask them the same fundamental worldview question: "What are the two most important things we should do in this life?" And I've taught them to respond with the verses from Matthew 22:37-40, which states that we should love the Lord with all our heart, soul, and mind and love our neighbor as ourselves. As morbid as this might seem, I ask my boys this question because if—heaven forbid—anything tragic should happen to me, I want these words from the Lord to be the primary theological apologetics I impart to them. On one of the evenings when I was lying in bed with my younger son, Corban, who was about eight at the time, he dutifully answered the anticipated question, but his response was in reversed order. He replied along the lines of "Love other people and love God."

"That's close, buddy," I responded cheerfully, "but it's actually the other way around; it's 'love God and then love others.'"

"Oh, what does it matter?" His reply had an undertone of annoyance. I didn't want to exasperate him with a lecture, so I chose a brief, succinct explanation.

"Well, it matters because we can't love others well unless we first love God most."

If I were to summarize a Christian or biblical worldview in the briefest of words, the response I gave my son would encapsulate my explanation. The order of loving God first and then loving our neighbors matters significantly because it aligns with the foundational teachings of Jesus and reflects the priorities of the Christian faith. Section two of this book has sought to underscore the importance of our worldview and rightly ordering our loves according to God's desires for our lives. Loving God above all else fulfills the greatest commandment as, Jesus taught. Loving God with all one's heart, soul, and mind is the foundation of the Christian life (Matthew 22:37). It acknowledges God's supreme authority, sovereignty, and worthiness of worship. Prioritizing love for God involves devotion, obedience, and submission to His will, which ultimately leads to a transformed heart and a life that glorifies Him.

Loving the Lord is paramount to building a biblical worldview and living a God-honoring life. In doing so, the grace we receive from the Lord empowers us to love others well. In the same passage, Jesus also commands His followers to love their neighbors as themselves (Matthew 22:39). Christians understand that genuine love for God naturally overflows into love for their neighbors. I can recall the first time I ever paused to think on not only how much the Lord loves the world but also how He orders His love for all He has created. I was in a graduate English course on Christian literature, and our class was discussing C.S. Lewis's *The Weight of Glory*. Specifically, this passage was the crux of our discussion:

> It is a serious thing to live in a society of possible gods and goddesses, to remember that the dullest most uninteresting person you can talk to may one day be a creature which, if you saw it now, you would be strongly tempted to worship, or else a horror and a corruption such as you now meet, if at all, only in a nightmare. All day long we are, in some degree helping each other to one or the other of these destinations. It is in the light of these overwhelming possibilities, it is with the awe and the circumspection proper to them, that we should conduct all of our dealings with one another, all friendships, all loves, all play, all politics. There are no ordinary people. You have never talked to a mere mortal. Nations, cultures, arts, civilizations—these are mortal, and their life is to ours as the life of a gnat. But it is immortals whom we joke with, work with, marry, snub, and exploit—immortal horrors or everlasting splendors.[7]

It occurred to me that day in our class conversation that when Jesus says, "God so loved the world," He did not mean the material, tangible world such as the trees, the sea, the stars, and so forth; although, I would contend, like humanity, those elements of the world are created to reflect His glory. But God's love for people—both those who follow Him and those who reject Him—holds far greater affection in His heart than anything else He has created. God has created all of heaven and earth, but only people are made in His image.

C.S. Lewis borrows his title, *Weight of Glory*, from a verse in 2 Corinthians that assures followers of Christ that heaven will surpass anything the world can offer, and that the weight of glory outweighs whatever burdens the world puts upon us (4:17). We often settle for worldly pleasures when, in reality, we are designed to seek heavenly joy. God delights in us just as a father delights in his son. There is an order to why and how God loves. And it is for this reason that the order of our love matters too. Our love for our neighbors should be rooted in an overflow of our love for the Lord. When we prioritize our relationship with the Lord, the Holy Spirit compels us to love others sacrificially, compassionately, and selflessly in accordance with what God deems good, beautiful, right, and holy. By prioritizing our love for God first and then extending that love to our neighbors, we offer a supernatural, transformative expression of love that honors God and blesses others. This order aligns with Jesus's teachings and underscores the centrality of God in the Christian life while also emphasizing the importance of loving relationships within the community of believers and beyond. In part three of this book, we will frame our efforts to do good work in the world on Jesus's commandment to His followers that we should express God's love through tangible actions toward others.

PART TWO: REFLECTION QUESTIONS

1. If a biblical worldview is rooted in the narrative of creation, fall, redemption, and restoration, how does this framework shape the way Christians should engage with the world, particularly in the context of social justice? How is a biblical worldview different from other major worldviews?

2. If a biblical worldview transcends cultural, ethnic, and socioeconomic boundaries, how might the global church better display this truth? How can the church effectively communicate universal biblical principles to younger generations who have been influenced by postmodern and relativistic thinking and other competing worldviews?

3. Barna offers seven cornerstones of a biblical worldview. In doing so, their research underscores the significance of not only intellectually understanding the cornerstones of a biblical worldview but also deeply integrating them into our lives. What practical steps can Christians take to embody these foundational truths more fully in our daily thoughts, decisions, and actions?

4. How might Christians respond to biblical worldview criticism and demonstrate that this framework is grounded in Scripture rather than advancing cultural or political agendas? In what ways are the distinction between church and state, sacred and secular, human thinking and divine wisdom important distinctions? In what ways do these distinctions make it challenging for Christians in our current cultural climate?

5. The Bible calls us to love God first and then love others as an overflow of that primary love. How does this order of priorities shape the way Christians approach social justice work? And how might we engage in good work with those who hold different worldviews?

PART THREE

DOING GOOD FOR GOD'S GLORY

12

LOST AND FOUND

God's Relentless Pursuit of Prodigal Justice

My son Christopher was born a runner. He is naturally athletic and incredibly fast. Without much training, he wins 5K races and school track meets when competing against his peers. And even in the womb, he was unbelievably active. When he came out of the womb, he began crawling, walking, and running unusually early. We moved into a new house shortly after he turned two. A month into living in our new home, my husband and I still had not yet grown accustomed to closing our driveway gate. And this bad habit proved to be a real problem one early March morning when I allowed my dog and toddler to play in the backyard. On an otherwise ordinary early morning, our six-month-old was still asleep in his crib, and my husband was in the shower getting ready for work. My plan was the same as many mornings before: I'd pour myself a second cup of coffee, grab my journal and Bible, and head outside to join my older son and the dog in the backyard. I envisioned squeezing in some quiet time while Christopher chased our dog around the yard and the dog frantically tried to escape my son's unforgiving toddler grip.

But that morning, in the mere minute it took me to pour coffee and gather my items, my dog and two-year-old had vanished. I opened the back door to an eerie silence instead of my son's delighted giggles. I calmly called out both their names, but there was no response. I set down my quiet time items, then I sprinted to the front yard and scanned the street. They were nowhere in sight. I rushed back inside, crying out "Christopher!" as I desperately searched each room. But the house was quiet except for the baby monitor emitting soft sleepy sounds from my infant's room and my husband's shower running in the master bathroom. Tears welled up as my heart flooded with fear. I sprinted to the other side of our house, out to the driveway, and my fears were confirmed: We had failed to shut the driveway gate the night before, and the dog and Christopher had escaped. I tried to reassure myself: Surely my 28-month-old couldn't have gone far in just a diaper and his bare feet. Still, he could be in real danger out there alone.

I burst into the master bathroom and flung open the shower door. "They're gone!" I shouted. "We left the gate open and they've escaped!" My husband, Craig, stood stunned under the running water trying to process my words. But there was no time for confusion. "You have to go look for them now!" I clarified urgently. "Christopher and the dog are missing somewhere in our neighborhood!"

Craig sprang from the shower, leaving shampoo still lathered in his hair. He grabbed the first pair of shorts he saw and took off out the front door barefoot, shirtless, and suds dripping down his face. On instinct, he turned left down the street. I snatched my keys and headed for the car, speeding right in the opposite direction. Rounding the corner, I saw an elderly neighbor sitting outside reading his newspaper. I quickly rolled down the window, hoping my pajamas and disheveled hair weren't too obvious. "Sorry to bother you," I blurted out. "But have you seen a dog or a little boy run by here?"

The man peered up, clearly irritated by the interruption. "They went that way," he muttered with a dismissive hand wave to the right. Later, it occurred to me how odd it was he hadn't intervened upon seeing a naked toddler chasing a dog. But in the moment, recovering my son was all that mattered.

To my relief, I turned down the next street just in time to see Christopher cheerfully ambling along, our dog trotting beside him without a care in the world. Gratitude washed over me as my shirtless, dripping wet husband came running toward them from the other direction. We scooped up our son, weeping grateful tears. I specifically remember shoving my transmission into park, leaping from the car, and dropping to my knees to embrace him right there on the curb in front of a neighbor's home. We didn't care who saw us in this disheveled state, elated to hold our precious boy close again. In those agonizing minutes of separation, our minds had spiraled to unfathomable worst-case scenarios. We were profoundly humbled by gratitude that our greatest fears weren't realized. By God's grace, we only had to go a street over to find our son safe and sound. We were more than relieved; we were overjoyed!

After that frightful experience, we ensured we shut the gate each night before bed. We also invested in a toddler leash backpack—something we had sworn we'd never use before becoming parents. But Christopher's tendency to explore compelled us to take extra precautions. But more than how to better baby proof our home, that incident gave me a tiny glimpse into our heavenly Father's heart for his lost children. Like any parent, I was willing to search to the ends of the earth for my son. That early parenting moment gave me a glimpse into the father heart of God. If I, as a fallible and sinful human parent, felt compelled to search for my lost son at all costs, how much more does God actively and continuously pursue those of us who stray from Him?

Jesus speaks often about finding the lost and reconciling them to the Father. In Luke 15, Jesus shares three parables about reclaiming what was once lost and now found. In the parable of the lost sheep, the lost coin, and the lost son, all that was once thought lost become celebrated when found. Jesus juxtaposes these parables to emphasize how much He rejoices when valuable possessions are returned to their owner, their caretaker. In Luke 15:3-7, Jesus begins by asking His listeners to imagine they have 100 sheep and one goes missing. The shepherd leaves the 99 in the open country to search for the lost one. When he finds it, he joyfully puts it on his shoulders and returns home. He then calls his friends and neighbors together, saying, "Rejoice with me; I have found my lost sheep" (verse 6). Jesus concludes the parable by explaining its meaning: "I tell you that in the same way there will be more rejoicing in heaven over one sinner who repents than over ninety-nine righteous persons who do not need to repent" (verse 7). This parable illustrates God's relentless love for every person, His active pursuit of those who have strayed, and the great joy in heaven when a lost person returns to God. It emphasizes the value God places on every single soul and His willingness to go to great lengths to bring people back into relationship with Him.

In Luke 15:8-10, Jesus tells the parable of the lost coin. He describes a woman who has ten silver coins and loses one. She lights a lamp, sweeps the house, and searches carefully until she finds it. When she does, she calls her friends and neighbors together, saying, "Rejoice with me; I have found my lost coin" (verse 9). Jesus then explains the parable's meaning: "In the same way, I tell you, there is rejoicing in the presence of the angels of God over one sinner who repents" (verse 10). This parable, like the lost sheep before it, emphasizes God's diligence in seeking those who are lost. The woman's thorough search represents God's careful and persistent effort to find those who have strayed. The celebration upon finding the coin illustrates the joy in heaven when a sinner repents. The parable underscores the value God places on each individual and the happiness that comes with spiritual restoration. It also shows that God's love is active, not passive, in seeking out the lost.

Finally, in Luke 15:11-32, we come to the parable of the prodigal son. This parable tells of a father with two sons. The younger son asks for his inheritance early, then leaves home and wastes it on wild living. Facing poverty and famine, he decides to return home, hoping to work as his father's servant. The son is humiliated, dejected, and disgraced. He knows his actions have also shamed his family's honor. The son believes he has forfeited his rights as a son, but he hopes his father will allow him to work among his servants. To his surprise, his father sees him from afar, runs to embrace him, and celebrates his return with a feast. The father says, "This son of mine was dead and is alive again; he was lost and is found!" (verse 24). The older son, angry at this reception, refuses to join the celebration. The father reassures him of his love and inheritance, urging him to rejoice in his brother's return. This parable illustrates God's unconditional love and forgiveness. The prodigal son represents sinners who stray but repent, while the father symbolizes God's eager welcome and celebration of their return. The older brother, whose hardened heart makes him a prodigal too, reflects those who struggle with God's grace toward others. The parable emphasizes themes of repentance, forgiveness, and the joy of restoration, highlighting God's boundless love for all His children when they repent and seek restoration.

And if Jesus can rejoice with us over reclaiming a lost sheep, coin, or wayward son, how much more must the Lord rejoice when one of His children is reclaimed for eternity? The Lord affirms His love through the progression of Luke 15. He begins with a sheep (a precious possession but still an animal), to a coin (a possession of monetary value), to a son (infinitely more loved than any possession). Each story crescendos with a celebration, a rejoicing that echoes through heaven itself. And in the final parable of the chapter, a father welcomes home his lost son with a magnificent banquet. Jesus illustrates how much more joy there is in heaven with redemption of a human soul. The joy described here isn't just happiness; it's a deep, exultant gladness that permeates heaven itself.

If God rejoices this much over temporal reconciliations, how much more does He celebrate the eternal reconciliation of His children? In essence, Jesus is inviting us to glimpse the Father's heart. He's showing us that our redemption isn't just a transaction or a duty God performs. It's the source of divine celebration. Our return to Him doesn't just make Him content; it fills Him with incomparable joy. This truth should both humble and exhilarate us. We are loved beyond measure, sought after with unrelenting passion, and our redemption is the cause of heavenly exultation. In our moments of doubt or wandering, may we remember, we are the sheep worth leaving the 99 for, the coin worth turning the house upside down to find, the child whose return prompts a feast. We are that loved, that valued, that missed when we're lost, and that celebrated when we're found. God waits expectantly for His wayward children to turn their steps back home, running to meet us as soon as we do. He looks upon us with tenderness and mercy, not anger at our rebellion.

My fleeting experience of panic and longing for my son gave me just a small glimpse of the Father's constant, faithful love for His precious children. He never stops searching for the lost. We may foolishly chase after empty things that promise happiness but in truth only leave us destitute. Our own sinful nature compels us to rebel and run far from our secure place in the Father's house. But no matter how waywardly we wander, God's arms remain open wide to joyfully welcome back every repentant child who returns. This amazing grace humbles me. I am profoundly thankful that in God's family, there is always room for the repentant prodigal, and God never stops seeking or awaiting our return.

As Christians, we are called to reflect God's character and priorities in our own lives and actions. If God places such high value on seeking and restoring the lost, we, too, should be actively engaged in this work. This means not only sharing the gospel but also addressing the physical, emotional, and social needs of those around us. Biblical justice isn't just about punishing wrongdoing; it's about restoring right relationships—with God, with others, and with creation. The joy described in these parables at the recovery of what was lost should be our joy too. When we see lives transformed, injustices corrected, and the marginalized uplifted, we should celebrate just as heaven celebrates over a repentant sinner. This joy can be a powerful motivator in our pursuit of justice and good works, reminding us of the eternal significance of our earthly actions.

The parable of the prodigal son also challenges us to examine our own hearts. The older brother's resentment at his father's celebration reminds us that sometimes our sense of justice can become warped by self-righteousness or envy. True biblical justice, like the father's love, should be characterized by grace, forgiveness, and a genuine desire for restoration, not by a punitive spirit or a desire for personal vindication. God's care for biblical justice and good works stems from His profound love for all people, especially those who are lost, marginalized, or suffering. As Christians, we are called to share this concern and actively work toward justice and restoration in our communities and the world at large. Our efforts in this regard are not just moral obligations but opportunities to participate in God's redemptive work in the world. By engaging in biblical justice and good works, we demonstrate God's love, contribute to the restoration of individuals and communities, and participate in the joy of heaven over every life that is transformed. This work is not always easy, but it is deeply meaningful and aligns us with the heart of God Himself.

SHEPHERDING JUSTICE: WHEN SEEKING THE LOST REQUIRES TOUGH LOVE

Earlier, I mentioned walking through a very public and painful trial in 2021 when I asserted Biden's redefining of Title IX was unsafe and unfair for women. A small but raucous group of undergraduate students started an online petition to have me fired. Essentially, their claim was that if I did not accept the transgender narrative wholesale—that biological males are females too—I was unsafe for students to be around. For the sake of my soul, I didn't give the petition more than one passing glance. But my husband read every comment, most which he found so absurd he laughed when conveying some of them to me. One of the comments wielded the biblical parable of the lost sheep against me. The college-aged young lady claimed that "Jesus would leave the 99 for the 1," and so I should too. As a side note, the young lady later applied for a professional position for which a friend of ours was hiring. And since he, too, read her public comment, I can't say her comment did her any favors. Upon hearing this, it was a profound reminder that we are held accountable in the real world for our online words and actions. This young lady had a point; although, I don't think she realized the greater argument she was actually making.

The parable of the lost sheep is a metaphor for God's care for His people. While it emphasizes God's relentless pursuit of the lost, it also illustrates important aspects of His shepherding that involve protection, discipline, and boundaries. In the parable, the shepherd left the remaining sheep in each other's company. He did not place the 99 in grave danger or require them to follow the one who had wandered off from the shepherd's good, safe, and loving care. This detail is significant because it shows that God's concern for the lost doesn't come at the expense of those who remain faithful. Jesus, our Good Shepherd, cares for the safety and wellbeing of His flock. While there is certainly an inherit risk that comes from the shepherd leaving the flock "in open country," Jesus doesn't suggest we recklessly endanger the many for the sake of finding the few. This isn't to say the Lord doesn't ever call us to dangerous places for the sake of sharing the good news. The greatest commandment asks us to love others (John 13:34-35), and the Great Commission asks us to share the gospel to the ends of the earth

(Matthew 28:16-20); fulfilling both may require physical and emotional risks and sacrifices. But it's worth noting that in the parable of the lost sheep, it is Jesus who assumes the risk, not the entire flock of sheep.

The shepherd's joy upon finding his lost sheep is abundant. That is evident in both Matthew 18 and Luke 15. But this joy doesn't preclude the use of corrective measures. Shepherds were known to use their rods not just for protection against predators but also to guide and discipline wayward sheep. The rod and staff in Psalm 23 are said to "comfort" the psalmist, indicating that godly discipline, while potentially uncomfortable, is ultimately for our benefit and security. What's even more possible, given that the shepherd "joyfully puts [the lamb] on his shoulders" (Luke 15:5), was that the sheep was wounded. Perhaps he was wounded from his own infliction, a probable outcome of wandering from safety. Or perhaps the sheep was not wounded, but the good shepherd chose to carry the lamb back to safety to prevent it from wandering off again.

This fuller picture of shepherding and reclaiming the lost reminds us that God's love is not just gentle and accommodating, but also includes discipline, consequences, and boundaries—all meant for our good. Hebrews 12:6 tells us, "The Lord disciplines the one he loves, and chastises every son whom he receives" (ESV). God's discipline is always rooted in love and aimed at our growth and protection. In our pursuit of biblical justice and good works, we should reflect this balanced approach. While we should eagerly seek to restore the lost and heal the broken, we must also recognize the place for godly discipline, clear boundaries, and sometimes even hard consequences. True love and justice often require difficult choices and actions. Loving others well and engaging social justice does not mean we must always affirm someone's poor choices or false beliefs, especially when those choices and beliefs lead us farther away from the Lord and farther from His truth. But even when we have drifted, God's heart is always for restoration and reconciliation. He brings beauty from our ashes as only He can.

13

THE BRIDE OF CHRIST AS THE CATALYST FOR SOCIAL JUSTICE

Doing Justice with the Church

The body of Christ has saved my life. That's not a hyperbole or figurative speech. Quite literally, being in church and knowing Jesus has saved me not only from the maltreatment of others but also even more from my own destructive tendencies. Not just once, or twice, or in a specific moment in my life. But over and again, I have found my identity in the Lord and community in His church. In seasons of my life when I have been at my lowest, feeling utterly broken and alone, it was the church that welcomed me with open arms. It was in the embrace of fellow believers that I found the strength to keep going, to believe that my life had purpose and meaning beyond the pain I had endured. In the darkest moments of my childhood and adolescence, when I felt like giving up, it was the light of Christ, shining through His people, that guided me back to hope. The church is not just a building or a weekly gathering; it is a living, breathing testament to the transformative power of God's love. It is a place where the broken can find healing, the lost can find direction, and the weary can find rest. When we come together as the body of Christ, united in our faith and our commitment to one another, we create a force for good that can move mountains and change lives. I know this because I have experienced it firsthand.

But the church is not just a source of personal healing and growth; it is also a powerful agent of change in the world. When we come together in the name of Jesus, we have the capacity to transform communities, to bring light into the darkest corners of society, and to offer hope to those who are suffering. We are called to be the hands and feet of Christ, to love our neighbors as ourselves, and to work tirelessly for justice and righteousness in the world. This is the true power of the church, the power that has saved my life and countless others throughout history. It is the power of a love that knows no bounds, a grace that extends to all, and a hope that endures through every trial and tribulation. As followers of Christ, may we never take for granted the gift that is the church, the gift of a community that reflects the heart of God and the love of Christ. Let us cherish it, nurture it, and allow it to continue transforming lives, one soul at a time.

C.S. Lewis, in his book *Mere Christianity*, writes about the role of the church in guiding those who are lost or searching for meaning. He states,

> The Church exists for nothing else but to draw men into Christ, to make them little Christs. If they are not doing that, all the cathedrals, clergy, missions, sermons, even the Bible itself, are simply a waste of time. God became Man for no other purpose. It is even doubtful, you know, whether the whole universe was created for any other purpose.[1]

Here, Lewis emphasizes the central purpose of the church: to lead people to Christ and to help them become more like Him. He suggests all the outward manifestations of the church, such as its buildings, clergy, and even the Bible itself, are meaningless if they do not serve this primary goal. And Lewis is right. But I would add a more contemporary caveat to what constitutes the church's purpose: to engage in justice work for Jesus for the sake of leading people to Him. If we fail to care for the poor and disadvantaged, if we fail to pick up the mantle of ending sexual abuse or child exploitation, if we fail to enact policies that support life from womb to tomb, then we have failed to be the church. Likewise, if we engage these efforts but fail to lead those we serve closer to Christ, we have also failed in our witness and purpose. The church plays a crucial role in providing guidance, support, and a sense of belonging to those who are lost or struggling. By pointing people toward Christ and nurturing their faith, the church can help individuals find purpose, healing, and transformation in their lives. Caring for people's eternal souls, not just their temporal needs, is justice work done in Jesus's name.

GOD'S JUSTICE OVERCOMES HUMAN INJUSTICE

By most therapeutic counseling accounts, and certainly in comparison to my social and professional circles, I grew up in an unstable home and had a relatively dysfunctional childhood. I'm hesitant to describe my upbringing as traumatic because the bar for what constitutes trauma has dropped so low and has become overused and misapplied in the last several decades, so I do not want to apply the term casually. However, growing up, I knew my home life was volatile in contrast to other friends and classmates, but I had not considered it traumatic until my thirties when I became acquainted with the ACE test. ACE is an acronym for a survey that measures "adverse childhood experiences," and I first discovered the study when I was conducting human trafficking prevention research in partnership with

Baylor University and Unbound Now, a local anti-trafficking organization. As one might imagine, most human trafficking victims have had several adverse childhood experiences.

In doing human trafficking prevention research, I learned the ACE study was first conducted from 1995 to 1997 by the CDC and Kaiser Permanente (a California-based behemoth hospital network), and it was considered groundbreaking upon its publication.[2] According to the researchers, as well as the multitude of therapists and doctors who have since incorporated it into their practices, the study sheds light on the profound impact that childhood trauma can have on an individual's health and wellbeing throughout their life. Purportedly, the research uncovered startling connections between childhood adversity, chronic disease, and mental health issues. The ACE study identified several categories of childhood trauma: physical, emotional, and sexual abuse, neglect, and household dysfunction such as parental substance abuse, mental illness, divorce, incarceration, and domestic violence. Recent ACE surveys have expanded these categories to include additional variables like racism, bullying, community crime, foster care, homelessness, and even immigration.

According to the ACE study, there is a strong correlation between a person's high ACE score and low overall wellbeing in adulthood.[3] The higher an individual's score, the more likely he or she is to experience negative outcomes in physical and mental health and behavioral issues throughout life. Follow-up studies examining how the overall American population scores on ACE surveys have varied in outcomes. In 2018, Merrick and others published the largest ACE study to date with nearly 250,000 American participants over age 18. Their survey found 38.5 percent of people report no ACE, 23.5 percent reported one ACE, 13.4 percent reported two ACEs, 8.8 percent reported three ACEs, and 15.8 percent of those surveyed reported four or more ACEs.[4]

In 2020, a similar study was conducted and included the expanded categories for childhood trauma. It confirmed similar results.[5] All ACE research conducted over the last two decades arrived at the same two conclusions. First, the prevalence of ACEs is higher in samples of individuals in socially and economically disadvantaged contexts, such as poverty. And second, those with a higher score because of a traumatic childhood will have a higher likelihood of negative behaviors and symptoms—such as depression, suicide, brain injury, disease, and substance abuse—in their adult life.

The ACE survey is lengthy, complex, and it is not without criticism. One of the main critiques of the ACE test and its scores is that it can lead to an oversimplification of the complex nature of childhood adversity and its long-term effects on individuals. But whatever merit the test might hold aside, I confess, I was certainly taken aback to learn my childhood adversities scored a five. An ACE score of five places me in about 3-6 percent of Americans with a traumatic or, in the very least, an adverse childhood experience.

I reference the ACE test foremost to evidence that trauma is real, albeit difficult to define, measure, and extrapolate. And I mention the dysfunction of my own childhood not to elicit pity or garner sympathy but instead to underscore God's redemptive and restorative power in my life. And not just in my own life; I have witnessed others set free from wounds and traumas no professional could explain naturally because the indwelling of the Holy Spirit is supernatural. Discovering my ACE score in my late thirties was jarring, but it was not disorienting. The test score ostensibly explained a lot. It seemed to explain why I'm typically slow to trust and quick to skepticism. It highlighted my father wounds. It underscored my blasé detachment from casual relationships. The score helped make sense of what a therapist tried to communicate in our forced sessions after my parents' divorce when I was only nine. My ACE score resonated with the horrific statistics a different therapist rattled off about what might happen to "kids like me." I was 11 at that time. Yes, the ACE score was an explanation for some of my less desirable attributes. Yes, it provided some clarity to undesirable behaviors I had acquired or poor decisions I made in my adolescence and college years.

I am an imperfect, broken person. Learning my ACE score further confirmed this for me. But the score failed to rationalize why or how I had largely defied the adverse childhood experiences and achieved more than the statistics indicated I would. For instance, how had I managed to abstain from risky behaviors such as illicit drug use and sexual promiscuity? How had I been able to hold down professional work and meaningful relationships? How have my children not inherited any of the systemic, cyclical traumas I incurred? (Thanks be to God!) How had I managed to maintain a healthy, nourishing marriage for more than 20 years? And most quizzical, how did I earn four college degrees that culminated in a doctorate when the stats indicated I may never graduate from high school? The ACE score might reveal the level of dysfunction I endured as a kid, but it certainly could not account for how I flourished against the odds as an adult. With all sincerity, I have Jesus and His bride to thank for that. I did not overcome trauma by sheer internal grit or by listening to a TED Talk on resilience; although, by most accounts I am a rather gritty, resilient person. And I could not give an account for those who have defied the ACE statistics without faith.

THE CHURCH: GOD'S GREENHOUSE FOR FLOURISHING

As best I can discern, I overcame trauma because I found my identity in Christ and my community in His church. When I was in college and began walking with the Lord and a solid, Jesus loving church, I experienced a slow, transformative form of restorative justice that accounted for any injustices inflicted upon me in childhood. It is a picture of God making beauty from ashes through His church body. I have experienced the power of God's redemptive justice in my own life. But even more resounding, I've witnessed it in the lives of friends as I have walked with them in community and in the span of Christian history as I have studied it.

As followers of Christ, we are called to be active participants in the life and mission of the church. The church is not merely a building or an institution, but a living, breathing community of believers who gather together to worship God, grow in their faith, and share the good news of the gospel with the world. Our justification in Christ occurs the moment we accept the Lord as our Savior. But our sanctification is a process—a process that occurs by way of closely walking with the Lord and His bride, which is the church body. Recent research from Barna Group and Lifeway Research has shown that being an active member of a healthy, Jesus-following, and gospel-preaching church can have a significant impact on one's spiritual formation and overall wellbeing.[6] According to a study by Barna Group, "those who are part of a vibrant faith community are more likely to be flourishing in their spiritual, emotional, and relational lives."[7] Similarly, a Lifeway Research study found that "Protestant churchgoers who attend services at least four times a month are more likely to read the Bible daily, pray for their community and church, and share their faith with others."[8] These findings underscore the importance of being actively involved in a local church community.

When we gather with other believers to worship, pray, study God's Word, and serve others, we are shaped and transformed by the power of the Holy Spirit. We are challenged to grow in our faith, to deepen our relationship with Christ, and to live out our calling as disciples in the world. Moreover, being part of a healthy church community provides us with the support, encouragement, and accountability we need to navigate the challenges and struggles of life. We are surrounded by brothers and sisters in Christ who can pray for us, walk alongside us, and point us back to the truth of the gospel when we stumble or lose our way. In a postmodern, post-Christian Western world, one that is increasingly fragmented by hyperindividualism, the church stands as a beacon of hope for community and unity. It is a place where we can find meaning, purpose, and belonging, rooted in our identity as beloved children of God. As we actively participate in the life and mission of the church, we are formed and shaped into the image of Christ, and we have been empowered by the Holy Spirit to be agents of transformation in the world.

Since the inception of the early church, throughout church history and across the globe, Christianity has been instrumental in shaping culture and fostering human flourishing. Because of Christianity's emphasis on the inherent worth and dignity of all people made in God's image, and because of His invitation to co-labor with Him and steward what we have been given, people and whole societies thrive when they adhere to God's Word. In cultures that have not experienced a macro-move of God, where Christianity has not been the primary adopted religion, there is a lack of recognition of every human's equal value. In those cultures, slavery has been a perennial norm, and in many cases, millions are still enslaved today. There is no urgency to free people when they are considered commodities. The biblical view that all people are created in God's image is the foundation for Western human rights. Christians affirm the dignity of all human life because God Himself became flesh in Christ. They believe that every human life should be protected, and God will judge the shedding of innocent blood.

Our Western notions of religious freedom are rooted in biblical truth. Genuine worship, love, and relationship with Christ cannot be forced. It can be presented; it can be encouraged; it can even be coerced. (Lord knows I have coerced my tween boys to attend church Sunday mornings and youth group more than a time or two.) But followers of Jesus know that a true, transformative encounter with Him comes only from a heart willing to abide in Christ. Though there are examples in church history of forced conversions or threats of persecution, such as the medieval church's crusades, those are examples of patriarchal abuse. God is grieved anytime His name is evoked for the purpose of exploitation or manipulation (Exodus 22:22; Isaiah 10:2; 1 Thessalonians 4:6). Even the intentional misapplication of His Word incenses the Lord's standard of justice and righteousness (Matthew 7:21-23). As this section presents, these biblical principles of coming to Christ through willful, joyful election have facilitated the advancement of religious freedom as a universal human right, a core governing principle shared in Western countries.

TWO ROADS DIVERGE, AND WE
TOOK THE ONE...MOST BIBLICAL

Part one of this book provided context for this cultural moment. We considered how we got here and how our postmodern, post-Christian culture has made it increasingly difficult to engage in social justice work from an overt and unapologetically Christian worldview. Part two offered a framework for how a Christian worldview is distinctly different from other major worldviews and why it matters for those of us who follow Christ. Part three serves as a reminder to Christians that the global church has a track record of more than 2,000 years of cultivating good in the world—a history to which no other religion can lay claim. This section also highlights several contemporary parachurch ministries and organizations that continue to work toward human flourishing and the common good according to biblical standards. Primarily, section three is an assurance to faithful followers of Jesus that we don't need to take our cues from shifting cultural narratives to engage good for His glory. God's unchanging Word is sufficient for social justice work.

To be clear, this section does not attempt to further the culture war divide. I do not want to assert that only Christians can lay claim to what is good, true, beautiful, or just. In fact, I maintain those spiritual virtues are God's alone to define, and He often uses people who are not following Him to further His purposes. Throughout the Bible and human history, God has used imperfect, broken, sinful men and women to accomplish His purposes. There is no compelling reason to believe He does not do so in our contemporary times too. My heart posture in section three is not to establish an "us versus them" or a "Christians versus everyone else" boundary; to the contrary, I believe there is enough common ground to engage the common good through common grace. But this section does hope to encourage spiritual discernment. The aim of this section is to recapture a biblical framework for doing good work in the world and to inspire a collective, communal move of the church toward these efforts. Often this will require partnership with those who hold worldviews antithetical to Christianity. But as we share concerns on contemporary social issues like racism, poverty, and the sanctity of life, Christians must also carefully weigh secular perspectives against biblical principles of humanity, sin, salvation, and justice. As theologian Thaddeus Williams cautions, "Seeking justice is biblical, but we must take care not to confuse God's justice with ideological programs that borrow the terminology of justice but ignore the Creator who alone can define and secure it."[9]

In our pursuit of a just society, it's imperative to distinguish between the worldly philosophies of social justice and the timeless wisdom of biblical justice. While social justice ideologies may appear noble on the surface, they are ultimately rooted in human constructs and biases rather than the eternal truths of God's Word. These secular frameworks elevate certain groups and denigrate others based on ever-shifting cultural norms, rather than recognizing the inherent dignity bestowed by our Creator upon all people. As previous sections underscored, postmodern standards of social justice are often devoid of truth; they center exclusively on the temporal and negate an eternal purpose for establishing a just society. Erroneous motives or critical theories for social justice can also breed a culture of victimhood and resentment. In contrast, biblical justice flows from the very heart of God. It recognizes that true righteousness requires both personal holiness and societal reformation, anchored in the transformative power of the gospel. Only by aligning our hearts with God's redemptive purposes can we foster genuine reconciliation and human flourishing. Scripture offers the ultimate standard for pursuing true justice rooted in restoring humanity's right relationship to God and each other in Christ. As followers of Christ, we can discern against the deceptive allure of social justice ideologies by instead championing a vision of justice informed by Scripture and enacted by the multitude of saints who have come before us.

14

GOD'S JUSTICE PLAYBOOK

Seven Expressions of Biblical Justice

When I was in my doctoral program, I read a book on biblical justice recommended by my professor at the time, Dr. Perry Glanzer. After class one day, I recall bemoaning the book selection listed for a course I was scheduled to teach that fall titled "Social Issues in Education." Dr. Perry suggested I read Timothy Keller's *Generous Justice: How God's Grace Makes Us Just*. And I'm certainly thankful I did. Up to that point in my teaching experience and learning process, I had read only non-faith-based education books pertaining to enacting social change. I don't want to suggest every scholar or educational activist I had ever read was an atheist or even that they were antagonistic to Christianity. Certainly, one could make a case for how faith informs Cornel West's book *Race Matters*. Similarly, educational activist bell hooks (lowercased by her choosing) has referred to herself many times as a "Buddhist—Christian."[1] Though not explicitly biblical, themes of spirituality abound in her scholarship. But it was Keller's book, *Generous Justice*, that offered a framework and language for a

distinctly Christian vision of social justice. Not only did Keller provide explanations for why Christians are called to uphold verses like
Micah 6:8, but his book also distinguished different forms of justice
in the Bible. And of greatest significance, Keller's book underscored
for me how God uses each expression of justice to lead us closer to
His righteousness, which encompasses both a right relationship with
Him and with each other.

Keller frames his book with the biblical concept of justice by
examining key Hebrew words in the prophet Micah's answer to
"What does the LORD require of you? To act justly and to love mercy
and to walk humbly" with Him (Micah 6:8). Keller explains in his
first chapter, "What is Doing Justice?" that the Hebrew word for
justice, which is *mishpat*, is actually a different form of justice than
when the Scriptures use the Hebrew word *tzadeqah*. Keller explains
expressions of *mishpat* occur over 200 times in the Old Testament,
and that the term underscores the facet of justice attributed to "treating people fairly."[2] This equitable form of justice is used in cases of
punishment and acquittal. It calls for the rights of people based on
equal merit, fairness, and treatment, regardless of a person's status,
importance, or appearance. It creates an equal standard and is frequently invoked in a legal context. It often refers to retributive or
punitive justice, which involves the punishment of wrongdoing and
the upholding of moral standards. He cites passages such as Deuteronomy 25:1, which instructs judges to justify the righteous and condemn the wicked, as examples of *mishpat* in action.[3]

In contrast, *tzadeqah* is an expression of justice that encompasses
a broader understanding of justice. As Keller suggests, *tzadeqah* goes
beyond the retributive or punitive aspects of justice. This expression
involves actively working to create a society characterized by fairness, generosity, and social responsibility. He points to passages like
Proverbs 31:8-9, which exhorts readers to "speak up for those who
cannot speak for themselves" and to "defend the rights of the poor

and needy," as examples of *tzadeqah* in practice.[4] Commonly, this form of justice is often what both sacred and secular spaces consider "social justice." When we discuss, for instance, social inequalities pertaining to poverty or injustices stemming from abuse, we frequently paint those conversations with the broad brush of social justice. Keller rightly notes that the Bible considers multiple expressions of justice ranging from individual and collective righteousness to mercy, generosity, and sacrifice for the sake of individual and collective flourishing. Ultimately, Keller argues that Christians are called to embody both aspects of justice in their lives and in their engagement with the world, seeking to uphold moral standards while also working to create a more just and compassionate society.

SEVEN EXPRESSIONS OF BIBLICAL JUSTICE

1. Retributive Justice

This form of justice involves the punishment of wrongdoing, often based on the principle of "an eye for an eye." It emphasizes that God is just and will punish sin and evildoers. Punitive or retributive justice involves the punishment of wrongdoing, where the penalty fits the crime committed. It is based on the idea of retribution and is exemplified in verses such as Romans 13:4, which states that the government is "God's servant for your good" and "carries out God's wrath on the wrongdoer."[5] In his book *Generous Justice*, Keller highlights the concept of this type of justice, a fundamental aspect of the biblical understanding of justice. Keller explains that this form of justice is rooted in the idea that wrongdoing deserves punishment, and the severity of the penalty should correspond to the gravity of the offense. There are numerous passages in Scripture that highlight a retributive form of justice.

Contemporary Examples

Examples of retributive justice can be observed in various facets of daily life, most notably within the criminal justice system. This form of justice, which emphasizes punishment proportionate to the offense committed, remains a cornerstone of legal frameworks in many countries. One prominent example is the sentencing guidelines used in criminal courts. These guidelines often prescribe specific punishments based on the nature and severity of the crime committed. For instance, in the United States, federal sentencing guidelines provide judges with a range of recommended penalties for various offenses, considering factors such as the defendant's criminal history and the specific circumstances of the crime.

Outside the formal legal system, retributive justice can be observed in disciplinary practices within educational institutions, where I have more experience than in the legal system. I can recall a few times as a college professor where I've needed to report students to a university for blatant academic dishonesty. For example, I once had a student turn in the same paper her roommate had written for me the semester before, which was a disheartening discovery for all involved. Thankfully, it was her first offense (as far as the university was aware, anyway), and her punishment was light. When students face consequences for academic dishonesty or behavioral infractions, the punishments are often designed to be commensurate with the severity of the violation. This approach aims to deter future misconduct while also imparting a sense of fairness and accountability. Retributive justice continues to play a significant role in shaping societal norms and maintaining order in various contexts within Western society. While debates persist about the effectiveness and ethical implications of this approach, its influence remains evident in many aspects of contemporary life.

Biblical Examples

> Beloved, never avenge yourselves, but leave it to the wrath of God, for it is written, "Vengeance is mine, I will repay, says the Lord" (Romans 12:19).

Be assured, an evil person will not go unpunished, but the offspring of the righteous will be delivered (Proverbs 11:21 ESV).

God is just: He will pay back trouble to those who trouble you (2 Thessalonians 1:6).

2. Distributive Justice

This form of justice refers to the fair allocation of resources and opportunities within a society. The Bible often speaks about caring for the poor, the widow, the orphan, and the stranger, ensuring that everyone's basic needs are met. This aspect of justice involves ensuring that everyone has access to the resources and opportunities they need to thrive. It is rooted in the idea that God wants all people to flourish. For example, Leviticus 25 describes the Year of Jubilee, a time when debts were forgiven, and land was redistributed.[6] The church partaking in distributive justice is not the same as the government implementing socialism as an economic system. Biblical distributive justice and socialism both address resource allocation in society, but they differ significantly in purpose and implementation. The motivation behind biblical distributive justice is religious obedience and compassion, whereas socialism is driven by economic and political ideology aimed at addressing class inequalities. Biblical distributive justice is rooted in religious teachings, emphasizing God's desire for all people to flourish. It focuses on caring for vulnerable groups like the poor, widows, orphans, and strangers, ensuring basic needs are met. Biblical distributive justice focuses more on God's people providing for others; it requires individual and community responsibility within whatever economic framework exists and within any global context.

Contemporary Examples

As we look across the world, particularly in Western countries that have been influenced by Christianity, distributive justice can be observed in various initiatives and policies aimed at ensuring a more equitable allocation of resources and opportunities. These efforts often reflect the biblical principle of caring for the vulnerable and promoting the flourishing of all members of society. As unpopular as this might be, one prominent example is the implementation of progressive tax systems in many Western countries. These systems are designed to ensure that individuals with higher incomes contribute a larger proportion of their earnings to support public services and social programs. This approach aligns with the concept of distributive justice by attempting to redistribute wealth and resources more equitably across society. In the realm of healthcare, efforts to expand access to medical services and insurance coverage exemplify distributive justice. Programs like Medicaid in the United States or the National Health Service in the United Kingdom strive to ensure that all citizens, regardless of their economic status, have access to essential healthcare services.

Community-based initiatives also demonstrate distributive justice in action. Food banks, homeless shelters, and community development programs often work to address immediate needs while also providing resources and opportunities for long-term improvement. These efforts, often driven by churches and nonprofit organizations, echo the biblical emphasis on caring for the poor and vulnerable. I recognize these examples can be politically controversial, so it's important to note that biblical distributive justice engaged by Christians differs from socialism as an economic system enforced by the government. They are not the same. As Christians, we should feel compelled to work toward fair and just systems and to give generously to those in need regardless of our country's political or economic system.

Biblical Examples

> There will always be poor people in the land. Therefore
> I command you to be openhanded toward your

fellow Israelites who are poor and needy in your land (Deuteronomy 15:11).

Speak up for those who cannot speak for themselves, for the rights of all who are destitute. Speak up and judge fairly; defend the rights of the poor and needy (Proverbs 31:8-9).

Religion that God our Father accepts as pure and faultless is this: to look after orphans and widows in their distress and to keep oneself from being polluted by the world (James 1:27).

3. Procedural Justice

This expression of justice relates to the fair and impartial administration of justice through the establishment of courts and legal procedures. When we think about biblical justice, the court system may not be the first form of justice that comes to mind. But America's Founding Fathers actually drew significantly from biblical concepts of justice when shaping the judicial system. To offer a few examples, when we think about the notion of "equal justice under law" for all people, this principle, fundamental to the American system, echoes biblical teachings that all are equal before God and the law (Deuteronomy 1:17). Due process, the concept of fair and impartial trials in court, is found in the Constitution and also reflected in biblical principles of just judgment (Deuteronomy 19:15-20). While not explicitly biblical and most likely a reactionary response to England's monarchy, the separation of powers—including the power of the church and the state over one another—was influenced by the idea of checks and balances to prevent tyranny.

This judicial principle aligns with biblical warnings about the corrupting nature of unchecked power when it is oppressive to the people under its rule (Proverbs 29:2). The American Bill of Rights draws from the Magna Carta, a significant British human rights document written in 1215. And both documents establishing human rights are derived from biblical concepts of human dignity and individual worth as creations of God. Our Western judicial systems consider the humanity and dignity of even those deemed guilty, because of the *imago Dei* (Genesis 1:27). And if someone has been wronged, our American justice system allows not only for punishment but also for restitution, which reflects biblical notions of restoration.

Contemporary Examples

One prominent example of procedural justice is "the right to a fair trial," which is enshrined in Western constitutions and human rights documents. In the United States, for instance, the Sixth Amendment guarantees the accused the right to a speedy and public trial by an impartial jury. This reflects the biblical concept of impartial judgment, as seen in Deuteronomy 1:17: "Do not show partiality in judging; hear both small and great alike." Another contemporary manifestation of procedural justice can be observed in workplace dispute resolution mechanisms. Many companies have established formal grievance procedures through human resources that allow employees to voice complaints or concerns through a structured process. These procedures often include steps such as mediation or arbitration, ensuring that conflicts are resolved fairly and systematically. This approach echoes the biblical principle of resolving disputes justly, as outlined in Matthew 18:15-17.

In the realm of education, disciplinary procedures in schools and universities often embody elements of procedural justice. Previously, I mentioned a student who recycled and submitted her roommate's paper for my class. Other than assigning her a failing grade on the paper, I did not have the authority to punish her. She had the right to be heard by higher authorities at the university. Students facing disciplinary action are typically granted the right to a hearing, to present their side of the story, and to appeal decisions. This process reflects the biblical emphasis on hearing both sides of a dispute before rendering judgment, as expressed in Proverbs 18:17: "In a lawsuit the first to speak seems right, until someone comes forward and cross-examines." These examples demonstrate how the concept of procedural justice, with its roots in biblical principles, continues to shape and influence various aspects of contemporary society. From courtrooms to classrooms, and from workplaces and human rights, we emphasize fair processes and impartial procedures as a form of justice.

Biblical Examples

> You shall not pervert the justice due to your poor in his lawsuit. Keep far from a false charge, and do not kill the innocent and righteous, for I will not acquit the wicked. And you shall take no bribe, for a bribe blinds the clear-sighted and subverts the cause of those who are in the right (Exodus 23:6-8 ESV).

> I answered them that it was not the custom of the Romans to give up anyone before the accused met the accusers face to face and had an opportunity to make his defense concerning the charge laid against him (Acts 25:16 ESV).

> Do not admit a charge against an elder except on the evidence of two or three witnesses (1 Timothy 5:19 ESV).

4. Covenantal Justice

Sheepishly, I admit, I knew little about God's covenants with His people until I attended seminary. But if ever a seminary believed it essential to understand the purpose of God's covenants in the redemptive plan for His people, Dallas Theological Seminary would rank among the top of the list. And for this theological training, I am thankful! Seminary helped me better understand the relationship between biblical covenants, tracing God's redemptive plan throughout the Bible. And studying God's covenants offered a framework for understanding God's heart for justice on the basis of His covenantal relationship with His people. This form of justice involves both blessings for obedience and consequences for disobedience to the terms of the covenant.

Scripture begins with the Adamic covenant, establishing humanity's role and the consequences of sin (Genesis 1:28-30; 2:15-17; 3:14-19). The Noahic covenant follows, promising that God will never again destroy the earth by a flood (Genesis 8:20-22; 9:8-17). The Abrahamic covenant introduces God's unconditional promise of land, prosperity, and blessings to Abraham's descendants (Genesis 12:1-3; 15:18-21; 17:1-8). The Mosaic covenant establishes moral laws and expectations for Israel (Exodus 19:3-8; 20:1-17; 24:3-8). The Davidic covenant promises an eternal kingdom through David's lineage, pointing toward the coming Messiah (2 Samuel 7:8-16; 1 Chronicles 17:10-14). Finally, the new covenant, prophesied in the Old Testament and fulfilled through Jesus Christ, offers forgiveness, restoration, and a new relationship with God. Initially intended for Israel, it extends to all who accept Jesus, both Jews and Gentiles (Matthew 26:26-28; Luke 22:20).

God's covenants are intrinsically linked to the concept of justice throughout the Bible. In these covenants, God establishes a framework for righteous living and fair treatment among His people, as well as His own just dealings with humanity. The Adamic covenant introduces the concept of consequences for disobedience, demonstrating God's justice in holding humans accountable for their actions. The Noahic covenant shows God's commitment to maintaining order and preserving life—key aspects of justice. The Abrahamic covenant highlights God's promise to bless all nations through Abraham's descendants, pointing to a universal application of divine justice. The Mosaic covenant, with its detailed laws and commandments, provides a comprehensive system for social justice, including provisions for the poor, widows, and foreigners. The Davidic covenant promises a righteous king who will rule with justice, foreshadowing Christ's perfect reign. This idea of just leadership is central to biblical concepts of societal justice.

The new covenant, fulfilled in Christ, addresses the ultimate injustice of sin and separation from God. It offers redemption and reconciliation, satisfying both God's justice and mercy. Through Christ's sacrifice, God justly deals with sin while offering grace to sinners.

In *Generous Justice*, Keller discusses how the Old Testament laws and prophets, which are closely tied to God's covenants, emphasize care for the poor, widows, orphans, and immigrants as essential aspects of justice. He also discusses how God's covenant relationship with His people should shape our understanding of justice and our treatment of others. On this, Keller writes, "In Proverbs we see God identifying with the poor symbolically. But in the incarnation and death of Jesus we see God identifying with the poor and marginal literally."[7] Keller notes that God is not merely concerned with those who are financially impoverished. More, Jesus came to redeem those who are spiritually impoverished, which is all of us. "This was the ultimate instance of God's identification with the poor. He not only became one of the actually poor and marginalized, He stood in the place of all those of us in spiritual poverty and bankruptcy (Matthew 5:3) and paid our debt."[8]

We are invited to have an eternal relationship with the Father through His Son, Jesus. This is God's final and fulfilled covenant. It is also God's triumphant justice over the Enemy. The biblical covenants consistently emphasize God's faithfulness in keeping His promises, exemplifying the justice of His character. They also call His people to reflect this justice in their own lives and communities. In essence, God's covenants provide a progressive revelation of divine justice, culminating in the perfect justice and mercy demonstrated in Christ.

Contemporary Examples

Western culture has been significantly influenced by covenantal justice concepts, even as our Western society has become increasingly secular. Specifically, the institution of marriage in Western society reflects many aspects of covenantal justice. Traditionally viewed as a covenant between two individuals and often before God, marriage carries both personal and legal implications even outside of the church. The concept of faithfulness within marriage mirrors the faithfulness emphasized in biblical covenants. When this covenant is broken through divorce or infidelity, there are significant consequences. Legally, divorce proceedings often involve the equitable distribution of assets, alimony payments, and child custody arrangements. These legal frameworks attempt to ensure justice for both parties and any children involved, reflecting the broader societal understanding of the seriousness of the marital covenant. The personal consequences of breaking the marriage covenant can be profound. Infidelity leads to a breach of trust that can have long-lasting, damaging emotional and psychological effects on all parties involved, including children. The societal stigma associated with infidelity, though diminished in recent years, still reflects the cultural value placed on marital fidelity.

Admittedly, I have never had much interest in conversations about environmental care (sorry if that makes me a terrible person). Of all the contemporary social issues, environmental protection simply ranks low on my priority list. But I recognize this is not true for most young people. In fact, in my writing courses, environmental stewardship was among the most popular topics to research and write. My younger Millennial and Gen Z students offered cogent arguments for why creation care is a biblical mandate. And perhaps this is another area where covenantal justice influences Western culture. Environmental stewardship certainly draws parallels with the Adamic and Noahic covenants, which established humanity's role in caring for creation. Contemporary environmental laws and international agreements reflect a collective understanding of humanity's responsibility to preserve and protect the natural world. Whether consciously and overtly expressed or subconsciously and subtly implied, there is a collective understanding that we have a responsibility to steward and care for the world as a form of justice.

Biblical Examples

"This is the covenant I will make with the people of Israel after that time," declares the LORD. "I will put my law in their minds and write it on their hearts. I will be their God, and they will be my people. No longer will they teach their neighbor, or say to one another, 'Know the LORD,' because they will all know me, from the least of them to the greatest," declares the LORD. "For I will forgive their wickedness and will remember their sins no more" (Jeremiah 31:33-34).

From everlasting to everlasting the LORD's love is with those who fear him, and his righteousness with their children's children—with those who keep his covenant and remember to obey his precepts (Psalm 103:17-18).

5. Social Justice

This aspect of biblical justice involves addressing the root causes of poverty and oppression and working to create a more equitable society. In *Generous Justice*, Keller notes there are valid reasons many become concerned when they hear Christians talk about "doing justice." He writes,

Often the term [social justice] is just a slogan being used to recruit listeners to jump on some political bandwagon. Nevertheless, if you were trying to live a life in accordance with the Bible, the concept and call to justice are inescapable. We do justice when we give all human beings their due as creations of God. Doing justice includes not only righting the wrongs. But generosity and social concern, especially toward the poor and vulnerable. This kind of life reflects the character of God.[9]

Here, Keller rightly acknowledges the wariness some Christians feel when confronted with terms like *social justice*, which can indeed be co-opted for political agendas that may not fully align with biblical principles. But he also astutely points out that the concept of justice is fundamental to a life lived in accordance with Scripture. A holistic understanding of biblical social justice goes beyond merely righting wrongs or punishing evildoers. It encompasses a view that because human dignity is rooted in God's image, this truth compels Christians to honor the inherent worth of people on the individual, micro level as well as the social, macro level. This understanding of justice aligns with evangelical emphasis on personal holiness and societal transformation. It calls believers to embody Christ's love in tangible ways, recognizing that our faith must be lived out in action (James 2:14-17).

The Bible calls for justice in social structures and institutions, addressing issues such as poverty, oppression, and inequality. Aside from Keller (for whom I have an obvious partiality), a few other evangelical theologians have written books on social justice as a form of biblical justice, and their works have also informed my framework for biblical justice and orthopraxy. I'd be remiss if I didn't name Nicholas Wolterstorff's book *Justice: Rights and Wrongs*, which I read while researching for my doctoral dissertation. Wolterstorff, a brilliant theologian and professor emeritus of philosophical theology at Yale University, presents a philosophical, social, and theological examination of justice. Primarily, the book focuses on the concept of inherent human rights as a belief system stemming directly from

Judeo-Christian teachings. Wolterstorff argues against the prevailing view that social justice is a modern, secular invention.[10] When I was in college, I read Gary Haugen's book *Good News About Injustice: A Witness of Courage in a Hurting World.* I was young and impressionable, but I imagine the book would have landed the same if I had read it as an adult. Haugen is the founder of International Justice Mission (IJM) and writes about engaging social justice from both a theological and practical perspective.[11]

As these authors and many other respected theologians have noted, the Christian motivation for doing justice comes from understanding God's grace. Unlike guilt-driven approaches, grace-based justice is sustainable and deeply rooted in the gospel, in God's redemptive plan for humanity. When we truly grasp the magnitude of God's grace shown to us through Christ's sacrifice, it naturally evokes a deep sense of gratitude. This gratitude, this grasp of God's grace in our own lives, compels us to respond by extending grace and justice to others. James 2:14-26 emphasizes the inseparable nature of genuine faith and its practical outworking. Here, James argues that true, saving faith will inevitably produce good works, including acts of justice and mercy. He writes:

> What good is it, my brothers and sisters, if someone claims to have faith but has no deeds? Can such faith save them? Suppose a brother or a sister is without clothes and daily food. If one of you says to them, "Go in peace; keep warm and well fed," but does nothing about their physical needs, what good is it? In the same way, faith by itself, if it is not accompanied by action, is dead (James 2:14-17).

Engaging in social justice is not only a practical outworking of the gospel in our lives; according to James, it should also be a natural one. Biblical social justice provides an opportunity for evangelism too. While our impetus for doing social justice should not be solely for the sake of evangelism, doing good work can certainly lead people to consider the gospel message. Engaging in social justice work as an opportunity for evangelism is a concept deeply rooted in biblical teaching and exemplified in the life of Christ.

Contemporary Examples

Contemporary Western culture has been significantly influenced by biblical concepts of justice, even as society has become increasingly secular. This influence is particularly evident in the work of Christian churches and ministries that have actively engaged in social justice initiatives for the common good. Biblical social justice emphasizes care for the vulnerable, including the poor, widows, orphans, and immigrants. This principle has deeply influenced Western culture's approach to social welfare and human rights, often led by Christian organizations. The Salvation Army, for example, was founded in 1865 by Methodist preacher William Booth. And over 150 years later, it still exemplifies this Christian commitment to biblical justice. Today, it operates in more than 130 countries, providing a wide range of social services including homeless shelters, addiction recovery programs, and disaster relief. Their work embodies the biblical mandate to care for the poor and marginalized.

Catholic Charities USA, one of the largest private networks of social service organizations in the United States, serves millions of people annually regardless of religious, social, or economic backgrounds. Their services include food banks, affordable housing initiatives, and immigration and refugee services, reflecting the biblical call to welcome the stranger (Matthew 25:35). In education, organizations like Compassion International and World Vison focus on child development in impoverished areas worldwide. They provide education, healthcare, and spiritual support to millions of children. Later in our conversation, we'll consider the historical and global impact Christians have made in their efforts to engage social justice work; many of these charities have roots dating hundreds of years.

Biblical Examples

> Learn to do right; seek justice. Defend the oppressed. Take up the cause of the fatherless; plead the case of the widow (Isaiah 1:17 NKJV).

> The King will reply, "Truly I tell you, whatever you did for one of the least of these brothers and sisters of mine, you did for me" (Matthew 25:40).

> Carry each other's burdens, and in this way you will fulfill the law of Christ (Galatians 6:2).

Redemptive Justice

This form of justice is centered on God's plan of redemption through Christ. It involves God's justice being satisfied through Christ's atoning sacrifice, which provides forgiveness and righteousness to believers. As you recall from earlier readings, a biblical worldview is framed by four foundational cornerstones of the biblical narrative: creation, fall, redemption, and restoration. Redemptive justice is a profound theological concept that encapsulates God's overarching plan of salvation for humanity and all He has created. This expression recognizes that in the wake of the fall, humanity became estranged from God; we became mired in our sin and brokenness. The perfect justice of God demands that sin be addressed, and yet, His perfect love seeks reconciliation with His creation. This tension finds its resolution in the person and work of Jesus Christ. It is through Christ alone that we can be redeemed and then restored back into union with our heavenly Father.

Through Christ's atoning sacrifice on the cross, God's justice is fully satisfied. The cross is where justice and peace kiss each other (Psalm 85:10). Christ, the sinless one, bears the full weight of God's righteous judgment against sin, thereby making a way for forgiveness and righteousness to be extended to believers. This ultimate act of love and atonement demonstrates that God is both "just and the justifier of the one who has faith in Jesus" (Romans 3:26 ESV). God's grace, manifested through this redemptive act, reaches into the depths of human sin and brokenness. It offers not just forgiveness, but a complete transformation: a new identity in Christ. God's grace doesn't just save us; it also sanctifies us. Our redemption leads to sanctification, to a transformation of the heart. God's grace redeems us from the power of sin, setting us free to live in righteousness and to participate in God's redemptive work in the world.

Redemptive justice, however, doesn't end at our individual salvation. It extends to God's plan for the restoration of all creation. This connects deeply with the concept of stewardship. As recipients of God's grace, we recognize that all we have—our resources, talents, and privileges—are all gifts from God. This recognition compels us to use these gifts for the benefit of others and the advancement of God's kingdom. We become conduits of God's redemptive work, seeking justice and showing mercy in tangible ways.

Redemptive justice offers eschatological hope. The promise of ultimate justice in God's coming kingdom isn't just a future reality we passively await. Rather, it is a powerful motivator for believers to work toward justice in the present, to co-labor with the Lord while we are here on earth. Redemptive justice provides a theological framework for understanding God's plan for the world. That plan encompasses both personal salvation and societal transformation. This view of justice, grounded in God's grace and propelled by future hope, has the power to transform individuals, communities, and ultimately, the entire creation.

Contemporary Examples

In examining contemporary expressions of redemptive justice within the Christian context, we observe a multifaceted approach that seeks to address complex societal issues through the lens of biblical theology. This approach is characterized by a commitment to both individual transformation and systemic change, rooted in the understanding that God's redemptive work encompasses all aspects of creation. What first comes to my mind is the church's engagement with anti-human-trafficking efforts. I've had the honor of working with numerous Christian anti-trafficking organizations, many of which also partner at the state and national levels. This faith-based involvement represents a profound application of the *imago Dei* doctrine, recognizing the inherent dignity of every human being. Organizations such as International Justice Mission, A21, and Unbound Now exemplify a holistic, global, and biblical approach that combines direct intervention, legal advocacy, and long-term care. These efforts not only address the immediate needs of trafficking survivors but also work toward systemic change, reflecting the biblical narrative of God's justice and restoration.

To offer another example, the Christian response to substance abuse and various forms of trauma demonstrates a nuanced understanding of human brokenness and the need for comprehensive healing. Programs like Celebrate Recovery integrate clinical insights with biblical principles, acknowledging that true transformation involves both spiritual renewal and practical life skills. This approach aligns with the biblical concept of sanctification, emphasizing ongoing growth and healing rather than mere behavioral modification. With redemptive justice, I think also of the work my sister-in-law does for Prison Fellowship Ministries. Often, inmates were first victims of abuse long before they were perpetuating abuse. Christian prison ministry programs go beyond traditional evangelism to encompass discipleship, reintegration support, and advocacy for criminal justice reform. This multifaceted approach echoes the biblical themes of redemption and reconciliation, asserting that no individual is beyond the scope of God's transformative grace.

These contemporary examples demonstrate how the church is enacting a theology of redemptive justice in contemporary contexts. By addressing both individual and systemic aspects of brokenness, these initiatives reflect a robust understanding of the gospel's implications for social engagement. They exemplify a distinctively Christian approach to justice that is grounded in the biblical narrative of creation, fall, redemption, and restoration. They offer a compelling witness to the comprehensive nature of God's redemptive work and provide a model for how Christian theology can inform and transform public engagement in meaningful ways.

Biblical Examples

> It was to show his righteousness at the present time, so that he might be just and the justifier of the one who has faith in Jesus (Romans 3:26 ESV).

> Steadfast love and faithfulness meet; righteousness and peace kiss each other (Psalm 85:10 ESV).

> If anyone is in Christ, he is a new creation. The old has passed away; behold, the new has come (2 Corinthians 5:17 ESV).

7. Restorative Justice

Last, restorative justice seeks to move beyond redeeming broken people and places and moves toward their restoration. Rather than merely identifying what is broken or punishing wrongs committed, restorative justice restores relationships. It brings healing to both the victim and the perpetrator. Even more, it offers reconciliation back to the Lord. It is exemplified in passages that discuss forgiveness, reconciliation, and the restoration of community. The Bible offers several examples of God restoring His people unto Himself throughout both the Old and New Testament. Restorative justice is a biblical concept rooted in God's desire for reconciliation and healing back to Himself and back to His original plan for humanity. This expression of God's justice seeks to address the harm caused by wrongdoing, heal broken relationships, and restore both offenders and victims to the community. Scripture provides ample examples of how consequences for actions are important; God allows consequences to lead us to repentance and ultimately our spiritual sanctification. But the aim of restorative justice is transformation rather than simply punishment. This expression of biblical justice seeks restoration, specifically the restoration of our hearts to the Lord. But it also includes the restoration of all creation, of all that has been broken by the fall. This comprehensive view motivates Christians to address broken systems that impose injustice.

Contemporary Examples

In contemporary examples of restorative justice within the church, we observe a multifaceted approach that seeks to embody the biblical principles of reconciliation, healing, and transformation. Ultimately, these expressions of biblical justice seek to provide holistic healing. These efforts reflect a profound understanding of God's restorative work in creation and humanity, addressing both individual and systemic aspects of brokenness. Previously, I referenced the church's engagement with incarcerated individuals, but often, these ministries also work with those emerging from incarceration too. For instance, Prison Fellowship's reentry programs exemplify a holistic approach to restoration. These initiatives go beyond mere rehabilitation by offering long-term spiritual mentorship, vocational training, and community support. By facilitating reconciliation between offenders and their communities, these programs mirror the biblical narrative of restoration, recognizing that true justice involves not only accountability but also the opportunity for genuine transformation and reintegration into society.

The church's response to domestic abuse survivors demonstrates a nuanced application of restorative justice principles. Faith-based organizations like Restoring Relationships provide comprehensive support systems that address the physical, emotional, and spiritual needs of abuse survivors. Outside of abuse, there are ministries that also facilitate marriage reconciliation where there has been infidelity, pornography, or general breakdown of trust. As an example, my mother remarried after she and my father divorced. My mother and stepfather had a rocky, tumultuous beginning, but for the last two decades, they have led a marriage recovery class through their church. God used both the brokenness and healing they experienced in their relationship to offer hope and restoration to others. These programs often incorporate trauma-informed care with biblical counseling, fostering an environment where healing and restoration can occur. By offering safe spaces for recovery and empowerment, these initiatives reflect God's heart for the vulnerable and His desire for the restoration of human dignity.

Beyond marriage restoration, the church's role in restoring families affected by tragedy—whether through economic loss, bereavement, or natural disasters—showcases the community-oriented aspect of restorative justice. Ministries like Samaritan's Purse disaster relief efforts or local church benevolence funds exemplify this approach. These initiatives not only provide immediate material assistance but also offer long-term support through financial resources, counseling, community rebuilding efforts, and spiritual care. Such comprehensive responses reflect the biblical understanding that restoration encompasses all aspects of human needs—financial, physical, emotional, social, and spiritual.

These restorative justice examples demonstrate how the church operationalizes restorative justice in contemporary contexts. By addressing both immediate needs and underlying issues, these initiatives reflect a robust theology of restoration that is grounded in the biblical narrative. They offer a compelling witness to the transformative power of God's grace and provide a model for how Christian engagement can foster genuine healing and reconciliation in a broken world.

Biblical Examples

All this is from God, who reconciled us to himself through Christ and gave us the ministry of reconciliation: that God was reconciling the world to himself in Christ, not counting people's sins against them. And he has committed to us the message of reconciliation (2 Corinthians 5:18-19).

Peter came to Jesus and asked, "Lord, how many times shall I forgive my brother or sister who sins against me? Up to seven times?" Jesus answered, "I tell you, not seven times, but seventy-seven times" (Matthew 18:21-22).

Bear with each other and forgive one another if any of you has a grievance against someone. Forgive as the Lord forgave you (Colossians 3:13).

In the tapestry of biblical justice, we find a rich and multifaceted design, woven with threads of divine love, human responsibility, and the redemptive narrative that spans creation to restoration. This comprehensive framework, as elucidated by theologians like Timothy Keller, offers a nuanced understanding of justice that transcends simplistic notions of punitive measures or social equality. The seven expressions of biblical justice—retributive, distributive, procedural, covenantal, social, redemptive, and restorative—form a holistic paradigm that reflects the very character of God. Each facet illuminates a different aspect of His nature and His intentions for human flourishing.

These expressions of justice are not isolated concepts but intertwining strings of yarn woven carefully, purposefully from the Lord. They find their ultimate fulfillment in the person and work of Jesus Christ, who embodies perfect justice and mercy.

In our contemporary context, these biblical expressions of justice continue to shape and inform Western societal norms and institutions, even as their religious roots are often unacknowledged. From legal systems that strive for impartiality to social programs that seek to address inequity, the influence of biblical justice persists. The challenge for the modern believer, then, is to embrace this comprehensive vision of justice, recognizing that it is not merely about righting wrongs or punishing evildoers, but about participating in God's grand design for the restoration of all creation. It calls us to a life of active engagement, where our pursuit of justice is grounded in grace, motivated by gratitude, and oriented toward the ultimate hope of God's kingdom fully realized.

15

EXPRESSIONS OF SOCIAL JUSTICE THROUGHOUT CHURCH HISTORY

Good Work and God's People

O ver the year it has taken me to write this book, I have written from various locations: coffee shops around Waco, Texas, airplane rides to and from speaking engagements, poolside at home while watching my kids, and even in the car on long road trips to family camps. But at present, I write this from my hotel room in Oaxaca, Mexico, on a mission trip. Today is our free day, and my team has taken an excursion to see ancient indigenous ruins, but I hung back to write since I am already nine months over my writing contract deadline. To be transparent, this book has been a big project for me, my family, and currently for my mission trip team too. To be even more transparent, though, writing alone in my hotel room has provided me a break from an even more stretching mission trip. I can think of numerous reasons to complain right now:

- The hotel Wi-Fi doesn't work well

- The air-conditioning window unit doesn't work well either

- There is a faint sewage smell permeating the walls and floors of this hotel

- The food in Oaxaca hasn't set well with my stomach or my boys' stomachs

- We're all a little dirty, smelly, and tired

But for every uncomfortable complaint, I can think of even more beautiful aspects of this mission trip:

- Watching my kids share the gospel through drama presentations

- Praying over others in need of encouragement and healing

- Handing out food, water, and clothes to migrants and refugees

- Playing with kids of these families

- Worshipping in Oaxaca, Mexico, with our Waco, Texas, team and the global body of Christ

As I write this in the tension of the uncomfortable and the beautiful, I'm reminded this is exactly what doing mission work has looked like for more than 2,000 years, since the inception of the church. The discomfort we experience—whether it's faulty air conditioning, unpleasant odors, or stomach ailments—are all so minor compared to the harsh realities missionaries have faced throughout church and world history. On this mission trip, I have worried some about our safety, but I have not feared for my life or my kids' lives. But even in our relative safety, I am reminded in these moments of weakness that we often find ourselves most receptive to the Holy Spirit's work, both in us and through us. Amid these challenges, we witness glimpses of God's kingdom breaking through in profound ways. The joy on a child's face as they are offered a balloon, toy, and face painting. The hope in the eyes of their parents when they hear the gospel, perhaps for the first time or the hundredth time. Each time, the gospel's message provides eternal hope that is unrivaled by anything else the world can offer. Recalling the tears of gratitude from a refugee receiving a meal and clean clothes brings tears to my own eyes. The unity experienced in worship that transcends language and cultural barriers. These moments are not mere coincidences but divine appointments orchestrated by a loving Father who desires all to come to repentance and knowledge of the truth.

This is the heart of missions. This is the heart of biblical justice: We keep sharing the gospel, we keep seeking and saving the lost, we keep redeeming and restoring what has been broken by the fall because we know Christ did so for us. We're called to a deeper understanding of what it means to be the body of Christ in a world that is both beautiful and broken. Our discomfort and sacrifices, however small they may seem or even be, connect us in a small way to the sufferings of Christ and to the daily realities faced by many of our brothers and sisters around the world who lack the basic comforts we often take for granted. In embracing this tension, we find ourselves living out the paradox of the Christian life—that in our weakness, God's strength is made perfect. I am not perfect. My husband and kids are not perfect. My team is not perfect either. As we minister from our weakness, we've made a multitude of mistakes. Namely, I have had to fight having a bad attitude about the aforementioned list of gripes. But I am reminded all the more that the mission of God has never been about our comfort or convenience; it has always been about co-laboring with the Lord for the redemption and restoration of all the Enemy has stolen and sin has broken. This is the crux of biblical justice work. This is what has transformed people and societies since the death and resurrection of Christ.

THE EARLY CHURCH (AD 1-500)

In the whole of human history, no one has left more of an impact on doing justice in the world than Jesus. His life, His teachings, and His actions are not only the bedrock of Christian orthodoxy (right thinking, according to Scripture and doctrine), but they are also the touchstone for Christian orthopraxy (right doing, according to Scripture and doctrine). Not unlike our own time and culture, Jesus was born into a world sharply divided by social, economic, and religious injustice. And yet, He consistently confronted these inequalities without compromising His faith. In fact, as revolutionary as Jesus was, His life, teachings, and actions in the gospel were a fulfillment of the Old Testament. In reading Rebecca McLaughlin's book *The Secular Creed*, I was reminded anew that Jesus's first sermon to His hometown was on His fulfillment of Scripture and the call on His life to bring justice to an unjust, fallen world. I bet I've read this passage in Luke 4 over a dozen times in my life, but watching this provocative moment depicted in *The Chosen* television series helped me better understand the gravity of the context in which Jesus preached. It is a scene worth watching, especially with children over about age eight. We watched it with our boys, and they, too, could discern the significance of Jesus claiming to be the long-awaited Messiah amid a crowd of people who thought His assertion heretical. As Luke depicts, on the Sabbath, Jesus entered the synagogue and proceeded to read from the prophet Isaiah:

> The Spirit of the Lord is on me,
>   because he has anointed me
>   to proclaim good news to the poor.

> He has sent me to proclaim freedom for the prisoners
> and recovery of sight for the blind,
> to set the oppressed free (Luke 4:18).

Scripture tells us the religious leaders were amazed by Jesus's sermon. Initially, they were impressed. In fact, "All spoke well of him and were amazed at the gracious words that came from his lips. 'Isn't this Joseph's son?' they asked" (verse 22). They were astonished that a carpenter's son from Nazareth could speak with such wisdom and authority. But when they demanded a miracle, Jesus pointed out the religious leaders' hypocrisy. They wanted the miracle, but they denied the divine authority of the miracle worker. They wanted the good work, but they wanted the results without having to partner in any of the good work themselves in their community (verses 24-30). Jesus refused. And the audience's positive reception subsided. Quickly, the conversation escalated to hostility. Jesus's hometown, a crowd comprised of lifelong mentors and role models, then threatened His life. Scripture tells us Jesus evaded the angry mob that wanted to throw Him off a cliff (verse 30). McLaughlin notes that social justice was the theme of Jesus's first official sermon to his home church in Nazareth, a point I had not before observed. When Jesus held up a mirror to the religious leaders' hypocrisy—that they wanted the fruit of Jesus's ministry without having to submit to Jesus's authority—He was rejected and despised. On Jesus's sermon theme, McLaughlin writes, "Instead of performing a miracle or celebrating Jewish history, however, Jesus started showcasing how God has always cared for Gentiles (Luke 4:25-27). Jesus's fellow countrymen were so furious they tried to kill him. His multiethnic message was the last thing they wanted to hear. But this didn't put Jesus off; quite the reverse."[1] McLaughlin rightly concludes that the shame heaped upon Jesus—by the very community of people who raised Him—did not deter Him. In fact, justice according to God's definition was the foundation of Jesus's ministry.

In our church circles, many of us have become so accustomed to stories about how Jesus ministered to others that we might be inclined to forget how countercultural His approach to ministry was then and even now. Not only did He engage others with love, but He did so without compromising truth. The Pharisees and Sadducees called people to a standard of truth and holiness, one that even they could not meet. Often, they were full of hubris and lacked humility. Their approach was not compassionate or loving. Jesus flipped the script on what it looks like to honor God. He assured us that in God's economy, the first will be last and the last will be first. Jesus elevated people who have historically been marginalized. Consider His interaction with the woman caught in adultery (John 8:1-11). Amid the bustle of Jesus's preaching, a commotion erupted in the crowd. The Pharisees and teachers of the law, eager for opportunities to ensnare Jesus and decry Him a false teacher, dragged an adulterous woman before Him. They demanded Jesus respond to the crime, since adultery was punishable by death under Mosaic law. The Pharisees' plot was not a holy quest for upholding justice according to God's standard. Rather, this was a carefully laid trap. That the Jewish leaders brought the adulterous woman but not the adulterous man evidences their desire to trap Jesus more than uphold the law. If Jesus expressed leniency, He'd be accused of disregarding Jewish law. On the other hand, if He called for her execution, Jesus would supersede Roman authority.

But Jesus's response confounded them all. He stooped down, tracing patterns in the dust, seemingly indifferent to their demands. When He finally spoke, His words cut to the heart of the matter: "Let any one of you who is without sin be the first to throw a stone at her" (verse 7). One by one, the accusers melted away, leaving Jesus alone with the woman. Where others saw only guilt and shame, Jesus offered grace and a new beginning. "Neither do I condemn you," He said, balancing mercy with a call to transformation: "Go now and leave your life of sin" (verse 11). This encounter vividly illustrates how

Jesus upheld justice and mercy, truth and love. It also challenges us to examine our own hearts, reminding us that we all stand in need of God's forgiveness. In the context of the woman caught in adultery, we see the essence of the gospel: Condemnation is overcome by compassion, sentencing is an opportunity for redemption, and truth ("go and sin no more") comes from a place of love ("your identity is not your sin").

Jesus's ministry was predicated on fulfilling God's Word, and in that fulfillment, He spoke identity and truth over people. Most of us are familiar with the Samaritan woman at the well too (John 4:1-42). In this encounter, Jesus again shattered multiple societal norms: engaging with a Samaritan (who were a despised ethnic group to Jews), conversing publicly with a woman (which broke gender customs), and offering spiritual truth and comfort to someone deemed unworthy (by Jewish religious leaders). The encounter between Jesus and the Samaritan woman at Jacob's Well is a profound illustration of God's grace transcending cultural and moral boundaries. This unnamed woman who had been married five times emerges from the story as both a model of spiritual curiosity and then evangelistic fervor. Here, like in the previous example with the woman caught in adultery, Jesus did not ignore the Samaritan woman's sin. He knew she had to realize her sin to recognize her need for a Savior. So Jesus engaged her in a theological conversation. He noted that she was drawing water from the well in the heat of the day because she was not welcome to do so with more respectable women because of her multiple marriages and affairs. Their dialogue showcases the transformative power of truth spoken in love, without condemnation. Jesus's loving kindness led her to truth, and the woman recognizes Him as the Messiah. She then became an evangelist to her town. In many parables we read, we learn that encounters with Christ not only change people, but these encounters also compel them to share that transformative experience with others.

This pattern of boundary-crossing justice underscored Jesus's ministry. He touched lepers, dined with tax collectors, and defended adulterers—actions that simultaneously scandalized the powerful and offered hope to the marginalized. In doing so, Jesus wasn't merely being kind; He was demonstrating a kingdom ethic that valued every individual as a bearer of God's image, regardless of their social status or moral record. Jesus's model of social justice extends beyond individual interactions. His teachings, particularly His most celebrated teachings in the Sermon on the Mount (Matthew 5–7), offer us a comprehensive vision for a justice on kingdom principles, not a model based on societal constructs. Jesus's approach to justice was not merely reactive but proactively restorative. The parable of the Good Samaritan (Luke 10:25-37) illustrates this beautifully. In this story, Jesus expands the concept of neighbor beyond cultural and religious boundaries, calling His followers to active compassion that seeks to restore dignity and wholeness to even those we consider our enemies.

For the early church, Jesus's model of justice was transformative for not only His followers but the whole of society too. We see its impact in the communal life described in Acts, where believers shared possessions and ensured that no one among them was in need (Acts 2:42-47, 4:32-35). This wasn't just charity; it was a radical reimagining of society based on Jesus's teachings. As we look to the future, Jesus's model of social justice continues to challenge the church. In essence, Jesus modeled a holistic approach to social justice, one that addressed individual needs and challenged unjust systemic practices. But even more than overthrowing injustices, Jesus led people to Himself. Jesus is our ultimate source of justice, goodness, truth, and beauty. The book of Acts paints a vivid picture of a community where resources were shared, needs were met, and divisions based on ethnicity or social status were actively challenged. This wasn't a utopian political or economic ideal. It was a lived reality that drew both admiration and persecution from the surrounding culture. As the church grew, so did its influence and cultural transformation. Jesus's approach remains as relevant and revolutionary today as it was two millennia ago, and it calls the church to be a beacon of hope and an agent of transformation in a fallen, broken world still plagued by inequality and injustice.

EARLY CHURCH LEADERS

When I was in seminary, I took a course on early church history as an elective. I elected to take the class because I knew there were significant gaps in my knowledge of early church history up until the Reformation. (I know that's such a Protestant confession to make, but in the spirit of transparency, I had not studied church history prior to Martin Luther until seminary.) As one can imagine, a great deal of church history occurred in the first 1,500 years after Jesus's resurrection. Thankfully, in the course, we were permitted to take our final in groups with four or five classmates, which allowed us to break up the material. To be even more transparent, I doubt I would have passed the course otherwise! While studying at Dallas Theological Seminary, I had the idea for this book in mind. So, in my courses, I paid particular attention to the ways the radical, countercultural ethics of Jesus took root in the early church. I was especially surprised to see how these practices flourished in contrast to the prevailing and hostile Roman society. Some church historians suggest the early church flourished not in spite of Roman persecution but because of it. For example, the late Rodney Stark, a renowned Christian sociologist and former colleague of mine at Baylor University, detailed the rise of Christianity under the oppression of the Romans in his famed book *The Rise of Christianity: How the Obscure, Marginal Jesus Movement Became the Dominant Religious Force in the Western World in a Few Centuries*. In his work, Stark argues that Christianity's growth was not primarily attributed to conversions or political power. Instead, social and cultural factors made Christianity more attractive to Romans than the dying pagan faith in the Greco-Roman gods and goddess. (And after watching the 2024 Paris Olympics' tribute to these Greco-Roman gods, it's easy to see how Christianity stood in contrast to the immorality and decadence of these false idols.) In Stark's book, he contends Christianity offered a more appealing worldview and lifestyle, particularly with how Christians responded to disease, poverty, infanticide, and general social inequality.[2]

I don't recall when I first heard about the impact first-century Christians had on ending the Roman practice of infanticide. I imagine it was in a sermon. But I do remember reading about it in Stark's book. Accordingly, one of the most profound impacts of early Christianity's emphasis on social justice was the practice of rescuing abandoned infants. In a Roman society where killing unwanted babies was commonplace, particularly for female or disabled children, Christians would often take in these vulnerable little ones when they had been left to die in fields. This practice not only saved countless lives but also served as a powerful witness to the sanctity of all human life, which is a cornerstone of Christian social ethics. Similarly, the early church's care for widows and orphans, which is explicitly commanded in James 1:27, became a hallmark of Christian communities. Because of the gospel, which adopts all who accept Christ into God's family, the church offered a radical, revolutionary alternative to how society should care for orphans, widows, and others in need of support and love.

Early church leaders were also known for their care for the sick and disabled, which was not a standard practice in the Roman Empire. In the third century, for instance, Saint Basil the Great established one of the first hospitals in history. This hospital, known as the Basiliad, provided care for the sick, shelter for the homeless, and support for travelers. It employed trained caregivers. The Basiliad was a concrete manifestation of Christ's teachings on compassion and service even to those who could never repay the kindness. Within the Catholic church, Saint Basil is now remembered as the patron saint of hospitals.[3] Similarly, Saint John Chrysostom was known for his powerful sermons on alleviating poverty and elevating people. He emphasized charitable giving and was concerned with both the spiritual and temporal needs of the poor. He spoke against abuse of wealth and personal property. Saint Chrysostom didn't merely call for charity; he advocated for a fundamental restructuring of society based on Christian principles of justice and equality. He frequently preached against excessive displays of wealth, particularly in the church. The early church implemented Jesus's teachings of care and service to both our neighbors and our enemies. These foundational teachings of social justice established medical centers, ended the once socially accepted practice of infanticide, and encouraged generous giving of time and treasure.

THE MIDDLE AGES (500-1500)

When I think on the church in the Middle Ages, my initial reflection is not a positive one. Perhaps you, too, think more about the atrocities committed by the Catholic church—like the crusades, the suppression of biblical literacy, and the excommunication of those who disagreed with church leadership—than the positive aspects of this period of church history. But in retrospect, there is more to celebrate than lament. In the shadows of medieval cathedrals, stained glass windows bathed cold stone in hues of divine light. In the Dark Ages of history, the church carved out an unparalleled influence on the course of Western civilization. This period of church history established institutions of human flourishing from which we are still benefiting today. Far beyond the stiff rituals of worship or the strict governance of ecclesiastical affairs, the medieval church championed a vision of human flourishing that was intricately woven into our theological orthodoxy and orthopraxy. The medieval church perceived its role not merely as a conduit for sharing the gospel but also as a catalyst for human development and societal justice. This perspective was rooted in the conviction that human dignity and worth are derived from the divine. Consequently, the church's endeavors to foster the common good were profoundly interconnected with its theological commitments.

When I studied higher education in graduate school, I was surprised to learn about the medieval church's influence in establishing universities. Prior to formally studying this, I had no idea how influential Christianity has been in the history of higher education. Essentially, for more than a thousand years, the church has helped found most of our renowned colleges. For example, in Italy, the church played a pivotal role in the development of the first and oldest established college, the University of Bologna, in 1088.[4] The University of Bologna emerged during a time when the church was the primary custodian and gatekeeper for learning and intellectual life in Europe. Many of the early Christian scholars and teachers at Bologna were also clergymen. These scholars brought with them a theological perspective that shaped the university's curriculum and academic discourse. In England, the University of Oxford (established around 1096) and the University of Cambridge (founded in 1209) emerged as bastions of faith and learning. This early collegiate system, with its emphasis on communal living and learning, mirrored the monastic traditions established in the early church period. The University of Paris, which was founded in 1150, boasted faculty members such as Thomas Aquinas. The university was a beacon of intellectual rigor, drawing students from across Europe to engage in the deep questions of faith and existence. In America, institutions like Harvard University (1636) and Princeton University (1746) were testaments to the Puritan and colonialist regard for integrating theology in every facet of study. Though their religious affiliations would evolve and some completely dissolve over time, their initial purpose was clear: to train students to articulate and defend the Christian faith in various professional contexts.

The church's early involvement in higher education was not merely about the accumulation of knowledge but about the formation of character. These institutions sought to cultivate wisdom, virtue, and a deep sense of purpose in their students. And the medieval church's vision for education influenced from a Christian perspective is a legacy from which we still reap social benefits.

In addition to giving us a model for higher education, the medieval church played a pivotal role in advancing social justice through its numerous charitable and educational institutions. Monastic orders, particularly the Benedictines and Franciscans, were particularly instrumental in establishing hospitals, orphanages, and safe houses. By providing care for the sick, the poor, and the destitute, the church manifested a tangible expression of justice, demonstrating that the love of God could be lived out in practical ways. The Catholic church placed an emphasis on community life and service. They created a blueprint for societal care, nurturing a culture of empathy and support. Although I am not Catholic, in learning about the foundations of the early church, I have a deep appreciation for all the Catholic church has done in the areas of orthodoxy and orthopraxy. Many of the creeds and doctrines we continue to uphold today were established through councils that met during these instrumental ecclesiastical years. That's true not just in the way we frame our Christian thinking but also in the ways we put our faith into action.

In seminary, I recall reading about Bernard of Clairvaux, a particular monk who was a beacon of justice and reform. Among the many Benedictine monks who dedicated themselves to justice work during the medieval period, Saint Bernard of Clairvaux stands out as one of the most renowned and influential figures. He was born in 1090 and became a transformative force in 12th-century Europe.[5] Bernard was distinguished not only by his prolific spiritual writings and his vigorous reform efforts within the church but also by his impactful work for social justice. University of Cambridge professor and church historian G.R. Evans writes extensively about his life in a scholarly book titled by his name. Evans writes about how Bernard's advocacy for the poor was particularly notable. He persistently denounced the exploitation of the impoverished by the wealthy elite, urging nobles and clergy alike to direct their resources toward aiding those in need. His commitment to social justice extended to his role as a mediator, where he was frequently called upon to resolve conflicts between the church and nobility, thereby preventing wars and fostering peace. Evans also notes that Bernard's efforts in church reform were tireless; he challenged ecclesiastical corruption and championed a return to the simplicity and piety of early Christian practice. His defense of Jewish communities during the Second Crusade further underscores his commitment to justice; Bernard's vocal opposition to the persecution of Jews highlighted his dedication to protecting marginalized groups.

As I reflect on the medieval church's contributions to human flourishing, it's apparent to me how flawed this period of church history was. But it is also evident that their approach was integrative. In this timeframe, the church sought to align biblical truths with temporal realities. Its institutions and practices were not isolated from the broader societal context. Rather, the church intended to nurture a vision of human life that was both profoundly spiritual and deeply practical. Through its educational, charitable, and legal endeavors, the medieval church endeavored to manifest a comprehensive understanding of justice that resonated with its theological convictions, ultimately seeking to advance common good in the world and share the gospel.

THE REFORMATION AND POST-REFORMATION ERA (1500- EARLY 1800)

Recently, our home church, Antioch Community Church, celebrated its 25-year anniversary. It was a joy to attend the Sunday morning service and hear our senior leadership share the beautiful and miraculous work the Lord has done. We recalled the story heard around the world when two of our missionaries, Heather Mercer and Dana Curry, were imprisoned in an Afghan jail for more than 100 days on charges of sharing Christianity in a country that was closed to the gospel then and now. Their imprisonment occurred just weeks before September 11, 2001, which made diplomatic efforts to free them after the terrorist attacks especially difficult. But through the work of President George W. Bush's cabinet, global prayer, and the goodness of the Lord, Mercer and Curry were safe and finally freed. We remembered servant-minded stories such as going to Haiti after the earthquake in 2010, rebuilding a village in India after the 2012 tsunami, and rushing to provide medical assistance after Turkey's horrific earthquake in 2023. Our church also recalled the domestic and global launch of more than 100 churches and the numerous sacrificial missionaries willing to live out the Great Commission to see those come to fruition. We also highlighted several local ministries that have made an impact on addressing the needs of our local community.

Antioch has faithfully given time and resources to combating human trafficking, establishing reading groups in underperforming elementary schools, providing addiction rehabilitation homes, alleviating hunger, and decreasing crime surrounding the church's community. And that work just scratches the surface. For 23 of those 25 years, my husband and I have had the honor of attending our church family by way of our Boston, San Diego, and Waco church plants, so the celebration day was a powerful walk down memory lane. What was especially meaningful, though, was having our boys by our side during that Sunday morning service. I wept sweet, thankful tears as I worshipped the Lord, praising Him for my little family, my local church family, and the global body of Christ. In that moment, and as I type this now, I deeply longed for everyone on earth to taste the goodness of God and the beauty of being grafted into an eternal family. Can you imagine how different, how much better the world would be if everyone felt that sort of deep identity and connection to the Lord and His bride?

If my church is even a tiny, micro sample of the larger, macro narrative, I imagine thousands of years of church history is similarly beautiful and messy. It's beautiful because the church body is blessed and loved by a covenant with the Lord. But it's also messy because the church consists of broken, sinful people. And perhaps that's an applicable description of the social change enacted by the Protestant Reformation. It was a seismic shift in the landscape of Western Christianity. The Protestant Reformation brought forth not only theological upheaval but also profound social transformations that reverberated through the centuries. Many of the reformers' ideas, particularly those of Martin Luther and John Calvin, sowed the seeds for a renewed understanding of social justice and individual responsibility in the Christian faith. Martin Luther's proclamation of the doctrine of the priesthood of all believers was nothing short of revolutionary. By asserting that every Christian has direct access to God, without the need for priestly intermediation, Luther effectively popularized the theological notion of a "personal relationship with Christ." This idea, radical for its time, had far-reaching implications for social justice. No longer was spiritual authority solely in the hands of the ecclesiastical elite; instead, each believer bore the responsibility to understand Scripture and live out their faith in the world. This theological shift empowered individuals to see their daily work and interactions as opportunities for divine service, laying the groundwork for what we now understand as the integration of faith and work.[6]

Similarly, John Calvin further developed the Protestant tradition's emphasis on social responsibility. Calvin's theology, with its focus on God's sovereignty over all aspects of life, led to a more holistic view of Christian engagement with society. He argued that believers were called to be active participants in the transformation of their communities, seeing every sphere of life—be it politics, economics, or culture—as an arena for God's redemptive work.[7] This worldview fostered a sense of divine calling in all vocations, elevating the dignity of labor and encouraging believers to seek the welfare of their cities. This reframing of vocation as a form of social justice and engagement with society had profound implications. The Protestant Reformation reminded Christians that we're not called to withdraw from the world but to actively participate in its renewal and redemption. As these Reformation ideas permeated the church, they began to bear fruit in society.

Perhaps one of the most significant social justice outcomes of this period in church history was the Christian-led abolition of slavery in England. William Wilberforce stands as a towering figure in the abolitionist movement. He was a devout evangelical Christian, well educated, and a politician. Wilberforce dedicated decades of his work to ending the slave trade in the British Empire in the late 18th century. His efforts were deeply rooted in his Christian faith—a faith that shaped an emphasis on personal responsibility and social engagement. Wilberforce's work exemplifies how the Reformation inspired Christians to take on systemic injustices, even when such efforts were politically and economically costly. The abolition of slavery set a precedent for modern human rights movements. The success of the British abolitionist movement, especially the passage of the Abolition of the Slave Trade Act in 1807 and the Slavery Abolition Act in 1833, drew international attention to the issue. Wilberforce's efforts in England to end the transatlantic slave trade had a significant influence on the broader abolitionist movement, particularly in America. American abolitionist figures, like Frederick Douglass, who traveled to Britain and spoke with abolitionists there, were influenced by Wilberforce's work, and they used these connections to further their cause in the US. Wilberforce's work evidenced that ending slavery was not only a moral imperative because it was a human rights violation, but his work also showed that ending slavery was achievable through legislative action. Of most significance for Christians, Wilberforce's integration of faith and public policy demonstrated how our Christian faith, when fully lived out, could not only challenge but also transform entrenched societal evils.[8]

THE MODERN ERA (LATE 1800-1950)

Have you ever noticed how many hospitals and charities have been influenced by Christianity? Admittedly, I had not until my early twenties when I moved to Boston, Massachusetts, shortly after finishing my undergraduate work. For the first time, I noticed the influence of Christianity, specifically Catholicism, etched on buildings all over the city. For instance, my new doctor was located at Saint Elizabeth's Women's Hospital. And to get to her, I drove by a YMCA, the Saint Francis House homeless center, and Saint Anne's Home, a counseling center for children. As I drove and observed, it occurred to me just how influential early American Christians had been in many of our country's social needs, especially in terms of medical care.

In early 19th century America, the medical landscape was starkly different from what it is today. Hospitals were few and far between, often seen as places of last resort rather than centers of healing. Often, only the wealthy could afford medical attention. But the Christian imperative to care for the sick and suffering is deeply embedded in the teachings of Jesus, as we considered earlier, and in the 1800s, Christians catalyzed a transformation in this field. One seminal figure was the Catholic Sister of Charity Elizabeth Seton, who founded the first Catholic hospital in New York. Her work was a direct outgrowth of her faith's call to serve the marginalized and sick. The Catholic church named her the patron saint of widows and orphans.[9]

Much like Seton's contribution, I recently learned the beautiful story of Frances Cabrini, who gave her life to similar work. My

son and I watched a movie based on Cabrini's life as we were fly-
ing home from our mission trip in Mexico. The film portrays her
efforts to improve the plight of neglected immigrant children during the height of America's industrial revolution.[10] In 1889, Mother
Frances Xavier Cabrini, a nun with tuberculosis, persistently sought
to establish her own missionary order despite rejection from the
Vatican. After a personal appeal to Pope Leo XIII, she was directed
to New York, where she began her mission to serve impoverished
Italian immigrants. Her initial challenges included hostility from
local officials and dangerous conditions, and yet, she persevered
with a spirit of unwavering faith. Cabrini's work, often conducted
at great personal risk to her health, included setting up hospitals
and orphanages and confronting systemic injustices in New York
City. Despite health struggles and adversity, including a violent
confrontation involving her associates and confrontations with
city officials, she triumphed with the help of other key Christian
leaders. Her efforts led to significant improvements in the lives
of immigrants, particularly the then-despised Italian immigrants.
Her work was honored worldwide and throughout history by her
eventual canonization as the first American saint. She is remembered as the patron saint of immigrants. Her legacy endures and
speaks to her profound commitment to faith-driven social justice
and humanitarianism.

Medicine was not the only social issue influenced by Christianity in our early American history. In terms of caring for impoverished people, the establishment of the Salvation Army by William
Booth marked a significant leap in social justice. The Salvation Army
was founded in England in 1865, but by 1880, the charity had more
than 1,000 volunteers and a center in ten countries, including in the
United States.[11] Booth's vision extended beyond charity; he sought
to address systemic issues through holistic care. And by the late 19th
century, the Salvation Army had provided millions of meals and

extensive social services. This model of compassionate service rooted in Christian values set a precedent for hospital care that emphasized both medical treatment and holistic wellbeing. The influence of Christianity in this domain underscored a broader commitment to improving human conditions through institutionalized care, laying the groundwork for a more organized and widespread healthcare system in America.

Adoption Care

The first computer game I ever played was *The Oregon Trail*, and I played it on a 1990s Dell desktop in junior high. I always looked forward to the end of typing class when our teacher would allow us to play the game or catch up on homework. The premise of the game was for the user to traverse the harsh Western landscape from the East Coast to the West Coast (Oregon, specifically) and arrive with as many family members as possible alive. I don't recall a round of the game when all my people made it alive. Someone, and sometimes everyone in my horse drawn buggy, always died from dysentery or was killed by a Native American or died of starvation. *The Oregon Trail* was a fairly morbid game, now that I think about it. Playing was an enjoyable way to fill time at the end of my typing class, but I can also see how the game provided some context for this portion of American history.

America rapidly expanded West in the early 1800s, and our urbanized cities experienced unpreceded growth in the late 1800s. In these 100 years, America underwent tremendous social and economic transformations. And as a result, people experienced unparalleled shifts in the demographic and familial structures, which included a rise of orphaned children. The great migration across America and to America from other countries was driven by the American dream—the promise of greater economic opportunity. But the pursuit frequently resulted in fractured family units, where parents succumbed to the harsh conditions of urban life or were separated from their children amid the chaos of labor exploitation and health epidemics.

Reverend Charles Loring Brace felt the plight of the orphaned and homeless children who were affected by America's changing landscape. These vulnerable young ones were often warehoused in the dehumanizing institutions like orphanages and poorhouses, places that offered no hope, no future, and no family unit. Brace was driven by his Christian convictions to intervene, to protect and nurture vulnerable lives. And in 1853, he founded the Children's Aid Society, which became a pioneering institution in child welfare. The young minister, just 26 years old, launched the revolutionary "Orphan Train" program. The program sent an estimated 100,000 orphaned children Westbound to be adopted by families.[12] I imagine the program was not without flaw; I'm certain there is reason to question the motives of some adoptive parents. But Brace's program was revolutionary. It not only provided orphans with families and homes but also offered these children educational opportunity and vocational training. Brace aligned Christian principles of charity and stewardship to address a great social injustice, and his efforts laid a foundation for a more compassionate and effective adoption system in America that moved away from housing children in orphanages.

Christianity Influenced K-12 Education

Since the birth of the early church, Christians have always placed significant emphasis on studying truth and developing an apologetic for it. As we considered earlier, the Catholic church established several universities during the medieval and Renaissance periods. The first Puritans to land in America in 1620 founded Harvard University as a place of seminary training in 1636, just 16 years later. After the American Revolution, towns began partnering with churches to provide free public school. By the mid-19th century, Horace Mann, who is considered the father of the Common School movement, worked for legislation to provide free, nonsectarian public schools in cities and rural communities. Mann's work was arguably the beginning of secular public education.

What is particularly notable about this portion of American history is the collective shift in thought on the role of education for women and African Americans, a shift largely influenced by professing Christians. Until the early 19th century, providing women with an education was not common or valued beyond the primary grades.[13] The woman's education movement was made possible by suffragettes such as Emma Willard, Mary Lyon, and Catherine Beecher, all of whom cited their Christian faith in their efforts. These women were instrumental in establishing schools called female seminaries. These schools provided social and intellectual opportunities not previously accessible to women. The primary purpose for women's seminaries was to prepare students for domestic roles, and vocational opportunities for women were limited to teaching young children in primary grades. The curriculum in female seminaries centered principally on the intellectual, religious, and social standards for women.[14] Schools for African Americans were also established in the mid-1800s and became law in 1896 with *Plessy v. Ferguson*.[15]

Booker T. Washington fought tirelessly for the educational advancement of African Americans and frequently cited his faith in God as the catalyst for his work. In his autobiography, *Up from Slavery*, he stated the following about the influence of church unity in the work of improving Black lives: "If no other consideration had convinced me of the value of the Christian life, the Christlike work which the Church of all denominations in America has done during the last thirty-five years for the elevation of the black man would have made me a Christian."[16] Washington founded the Tuskegee Normal and Industrial Institute and focused on equipping students with vocational trades such as farming, irrigating, and carpentry. Washington believed African Americans would be better served educationally by providing them with vocational skills.

Christians Helped End Segregation During the Civil Rights Movement

The culpability of the American church in upholding slavery and segregation, particularly in Southern states, cannot be denied. And that is a deeply embarrassing and heartbreaking reality. We do not have to affirm the teachings of critical race theory to apologize for the church's partnership in such historical and theological atrocities. But there is another, more redemptive side to the story that often does not get told. The struggle for civil rights in the United States was significantly shaped by Christian activism. During the 1950s and 1960s, leaders like Martin Luther King, Jr. emerged as pivotal figures in the fight against racial segregation and injustice. King's theological convictions and his interpretation of Christian teachings on justice and equality provided a powerful moral foundation for the civil rights movement. Both White and Black Christian organizations and churches played a crucial role in this struggle. For instance, Reverend William Sloane Coffin and Robert Graetz were two prominent White Christian ministers and activists who championed the civil rights movement and worked alongside King on various policy reforms. The Southern Christian Leadership Conference (SCLC), founded by King and other leaders in 1957, harnessed Christian teachings to advocate for civil rights and social justice. The Christian doctrine of the inherent dignity of every individual resonated deeply within the movement, providing both a spiritual and ethical framework for challenging segregation and discrimination. The moral authority of Christianity lent credibility and urgency to the demands for racial equality, influencing both public opinion and legislative change.[17]

From the early church's hospitals and orphan care, to medieval universities' desire to provide students with a Christian education, to our more modern efforts to eradicate slavery, human trafficking, and poverty, the church has had a significant influence in social justice for 2,000 years. By acknowledging that reality, we do not dismiss the church's failures. Indeed, we lament them; we acknowledge where church leaders have missed the mark. Yet church history vindicates the Christian worldview. Throughout history, the Christian worldview has proven itself as a trustworthy, sturdy foundation on which to build social justice endeavors.

CONTEMPORARY CHRISTIAN SOCIAL JUSTICE EFFORTS

May We Not Grow Weary

Like most of the world, my family and I huddled around the television watching the 2024 Paris Olympics. We really enjoyed watching gymnastics. It's inspiring to watch world-renowned gymnasts display incredible skills and creative floor routines. We also found the track heats enthralling. Watching the fastest men and women in the world contend in parallel rivalry is captivating. Even if for just a moment in time, the Olympics can be such a unifying event for the world and for families. I won't speak for my boys, and perhaps this is the English professor in me, but my favorite aspect of watching the Olympics is learning the athletes' backstories. I love learning where these men and women come from and how they reached such extraordinary achievements. In listening to the commentators, I learned some funny information about the athletes. For instance, Yaroslava Mahuchikh, a women's high jumper from Ukraine, takes her sleeping bag to track meets. In it, she has been known to take naps between her events. And during the Olympic Games, she could be seen warming herself in her sleeping bag after each jump. According to Mahuchikh, she uses the sleeping bag and power naps to rest and refocus in between competitions.[1]

In listening to the athletes' stories, I learned about more than their quirky habits. I learned, for example, decorated gymnast Simone Biles and track runner Kenney Benarek are both adopted from foster care. Biles was adopted by her grandparents when they learned her mother could not care for her, and Benarek was adopted by a woman who brought in him, his brother, and two others from foster care. Given the high percentage of Christians who choose to adopt (compared to those who do not identify as Christian), I couldn't help but wonder the faith background of their parents. A few web searches confirmed my suspicion: Biles and Benarek both hail from Christian homes.[2]

ADOPTION

Christian families in the United States have historically been at the forefront of adoption, both domestically and internationally. But it turns out, adoption is not just a part of church history; Christians are still the largest demographic to adopt. In fact, according to Barna Research, practicing Christians are more than twice as likely to adopt than the general population, with 5 percent of practicing Christians having adopted compared to 2 percent of the general population. Catholics are three times as likely to adopt, and evangelicals are five times more likely. The same Barna study found that 77 percent of practicing Christians believe that Christians have a personal responsibility to adopt.[3] This practice stems from a combination of theological, cultural, and practical factors. Theologically, many Christians view adoption as a reflection of God's love and their own spiritual adoption into God's family. Biblical passages emphasizing care for orphans resonate deeply within Christian homes.

Culturally, the pro-life stance aligns with adoption as an alternative to abortion. This has led to increased support for adoption within Christian circles, including financial and emotional support from church communities. Practically, Christian networks and organizations have developed robust systems to facilitate adoption processes. Many churches partner with adoption agencies or have their own adoption ministries, providing resources and guidance to prospective adoptive parents.

As the early church modeled, adoption is a form of biblical social justice, one that emerges from a deep-rooted theological understanding of God's love and care for children. By welcoming children into their families, Christian adoptive parents actively participate in addressing societal inequalities and providing opportunities for those who might otherwise be disregarded. The biblical mandates to care for orphans reflects the Christian belief in being adopted into God's family through Christ (John 1:12). Adoption is a tangible expression of faith, demonstrating God's love in action and the value He places on us being woven into families. Christian adoption often extends beyond mere provision of a home. It frequently involves cross-cultural and interracial adoptions, which breaks down social and racial barriers, thereby promoting diversity and inclusion. By opening homes to children from various backgrounds, Christian families model a form of biblical hospitality that challenges societal norms and prejudices. In the context of Scripture, adoption becomes not just a personal act of love, but a powerful statement of social justice, embodying the Christian call to "defend the cause of the fatherless" (Isaiah 1:23).

For years, my husband and I prayed about whether the Lord was calling us to adopt. We even attended two weekend adoption training classes within an eight-year timeframe. Ultimately, as best we could discern, the Lord was not necessarily calling us to adopt, but He was asking us to help fund others' adoption processes. After our second training, we both felt compelled to donate to another family what it would have cost us to adopt domestically.

POVERTY ALLEVIATION AND COMMUNITY DEVELOPMENT

Adoption certainly isn't the only biblical justice cause in which contemporary Christians partake. The modern church and contemporary Christians have increasingly engaged in other social issues as an integral part of their faith commitment. For instance, poverty alleviation and community development have been at the forefront of Christian social justice efforts. Organizations like Compassion International, World Relief, and World Vision have pioneered child sponsorship programs, connecting individual donors with children in need to provide education, healthcare, and spiritual support. This model has not only addressed immediate needs but has also fostered long-term development in impoverished communities. Similarly, Habitat for Humanity, founded on Christian principles, has made significant strides in providing affordable housing. By engaging volunteers in home-building projects, they've not only addressed housing needs but have also built community and raised awareness about housing insecurity. I've been able to witness firsthand many of these Christian organizations partner with Baylor University and then connect college students and alumni with these programs.

ANTI-TRAFFICKING

When I taught at Baylor University, I had the honor of connecting the university to local, domestic, and global efforts to combat human trafficking. The fight against human trafficking has robust Christian involvement. For example, the Christian organization International Justice Mission (IJM) has been a leader in this space, working to rescue victims, prosecute perpetrators, and strengthen justice systems in vulnerable regions. Their multifaceted approach combines direct intervention with systemic change. The A21 Campaign, founded by Christine Caine, is another Christian-based organization. It has focused on prevention and awareness efforts, educating communities about the risks of trafficking and providing support to survivors. The A21 Campaign and Christine Caine were my first introduction to the horrific and nefarious practice of modern-day slavery.

ENVIRONMENTAL CARE

If I were to make a top-five list of position paper topics my college students have wanted to write about in their argumentative and research papers, environmental care would be situated somewhere near abortion and same-sex marriage. To be honest, I don't fully understand why younger Millennials and Gen Z care so deeply about this social issue. And I certainly do not understand why 60 percent of this demographic reports having "ongoing environmental anxiety."[4] Twenty years ago, when I was their age, none of my classmates expressed interest in these conversations. Contemporary discussions about global warming and environmental care are contentious—if not outright controversial—in some evangelical circles. So I am not here to weigh in on the validity of either side's claims. Trust me, I have no authority or knowledge in this area, so you do not want my opinion. But what I can say with confidence is, there is a clear biblical mandate for God's people to steward and cultivate His creation (Genesis 1:28, 2:15). But given Scripture's clarity on our responsibility to care for the earth, I'm thankful conversations about environmental stewardship have gained traction within Christian circles. Organizations like the Evangelical Environmental Network have been instrumental in promoting the "creation care" movement, framing environmental protection as a Christian responsibility. They've advocated for policies addressing climate change and environmental degradation, grounding their work in biblical teachings.[5]

CARING FOR REFUGEES AND IMMIGRANTS

Refugee and immigration care is another area of social concern where I have witnessed Christians rise to address a need. This area of care can also be controversial for Christians, whether they lean toward Republican or Democratic policies. Sadly, much of what has historically been considered theological has become political (ending slavery, protecting life in the womb, and allocating resources to citizens here legally or illegally). I had the honor of joining Women of Welcome, a Christian ministry housed under World Relief, on a four-day border immersion trip in the summer of 2022. It was a firsthand glimpse into America's complex and nuanced border crisis. Before this opportunity, I'd been to Mexico numerous times, sometimes for vacation but also for mission trips. Because I've lived in Texas and California, both of which share borders with Mexico, and because I've engaged in anti-human-trafficking efforts for years, I had given the border challenge more than just a passing thought. Even still, I had much to consider after meeting with actual women fleeing violence—with infants in tow—from countries like Honduras and Columbia. I left the trip with more questions than solutions. But I also left with a softer heart. Women of Welcome embodies a profound commitment to the wellbeing of refugees and immigrants from a faith-based perspective. They encourage women in the church to channel their compassion into tangible action. One of the ways they do so is through creating resources to equip local churches and community groups to assist refugees and immigrants. Illegal border crossing and claiming refugee status remains politically problematic, and I won't pretend to have the definitive geopolitical solution. But I appreciate organizations like Women of Welcome that exemplify the integration of faith and social action, underscoring the transformative power of compassionate advocacy by pressing into a humanitarian crisis.

NAVIGATING CHRISTIAN SOCIAL
ENGAGEMENT IN A POST-CHRISTIAN WORLD

The landscape of contemporary Christianity is marked by an abundance of ministries and organizations committed to addressing various social issues—by sheer numbers alone, arguably more than in any other time in church history. The aforementioned groups are merely a sample of the hundreds upon hundreds of faithful Christian organizations seeking to love people and meet their needs in Jesus's name. This surge in justice-minded movements in the last several decades further underscores our biblical understanding and desire to "seek the welfare of the city" (Jeremiah 29:7 ESV). These ministries also stand as a testament to the church's role as "salt and light" (Matthew 5:13-16) in a world darkened by the schemes of the Enemy.

Our increased engagement with social justice issues presents the body of Christ with a profound theological and political tension. On one hand, we are called to proclaim the gospel of Jesus Christ, recognizing that true and lasting transformation comes only through the regenerating work of the Holy Spirit. On the other hand, we're attempting to do biblical justice work in a culture increasingly antagonistic to Christianity. But this tension is not new to the church. It echoes the early church's struggle to balance gospel-driven ministry and cultural hostility. As we navigate this challenge with wisdom and discernment, we can take confidence in knowing that gospel proclamation and social engagement are not competing mandates but complementary aspects of our kingdom mission. As we continue to engage in social justice initiatives, we must do so from an unapologetically biblical worldview. This approach honors the *imago Dei* in every human being, the reality of sin and its systemic effects, and the ultimate hope found in Christ's redemptive work. It calls us to collaborative efforts with those outside the faith, while maintaining our distinct identity and message. As we navigate this cultural tension, may we do so with theological clarity, cultural discernment, and unwavering commitment to the gospel of Jesus Christ.

HOW CAN CHRISTIANS BE INVOLVED IN JUSTICE WORK? PRACTICAL AND BIBLICAL WAYS

The Great Commandment, which Jesus presents not merely as a moral imperative but as the very essence of biblical justice, is central to understanding how to engage the world for God. When approached by a Pharisee, an expert in Mosaic law, Jesus was asked to identify the greatest commandment (Matthew 22:34-36). His response was both profound and transformative: "Love the Lord your God with all your heart, with all your soul, and with all your mind. This is the greatest and most important commandment. The second is like it: Love your neighbor as yourself. All the Law and the Prophets depend on these two commandments" (Matthew 22:37-40 csb). This declaration by Christ is not a platitude, but a radical reorientation of our understanding of God's law and justice. It compels us to consider: What does it truly mean to love our neighbor? And how do we reconcile this command with the often-challenging directive to love our enemies?

The concept of loving one's neighbor finds its roots in Leviticus 19:18, which states, "Do not seek revenge or bear a grudge against anyone among your people, but love your neighbor as yourself." The temptation for people then, and indeed still today, is to narrowly define "neighbor" as those within our immediate community or those who share our beliefs and values. But Jesus expands this definition dramatically through the parable of the good Samaritan (Luke 10:25-37). This narrative subverts cultural expectations by portraying a Samaritan as the exemplar of neighborly love. The parable teaches us that our neighbor is not defined by proximity, ethnicity, or shared beliefs, but by the opportunity to show mercy and compassion. This expansive view of neighborly love challenges us to reconsider our approach to those we might even consider enemies. Jesus pushes this concept even further in the Sermon on the Mount, instructing His followers to "love your enemies and pray for those who persecute you" (Matthew 5:44). This command is not just counterintuitive; it's countercultural, calling us to a standard of love that reflects the character of God Himself.

However, to be clear, we should be careful not to misconstrue God's command to love with culture's demand to affirm or acquiesce to false narratives. Biblical love is inextricably linked to truth. As followers of Christ, we are called to "[speak] the truth in love" (Ephesians 4:15). This means that loving our neighbors sometimes involves challenging these false narratives, lies about identity, or harmful behaviors. Our aim as followers of Jesus should always be to point people toward the ultimate truth found in Him. It's crucial to recognize that our capacity to love others in this way stems from our love for God and our understanding of His love for us. John reminds us, "We love because he first loved us" (1 John 4:19). Our love for neighbors and enemies is not something we can muster in our own strength—at least, I certainly cannot. Our love for others is a supernatural overflow of the transformative, sanctifying grace we have received through Christ's sacrifice on the cross.

Perhaps of even greater importance than discerning who is our neighbor or our enemy, we need to understand what "love" is according to God's standard, not ours. Authentic love for our neighbors is rooted in biblical teaching, and it transcends mere agreement or approval seeking. Instead, it manifests in a genuine pursuit of others' holistic wellbeing. It a love that addresses physical, emotional, and spiritual needs. At its core, loving others well is intrinsically linked to loving God supremely. It requires a humble acknowledgment that God's wisdom surpasses our limited understanding. Fundamentally, we cannot love others well unless we love God more.

If loving our neighbor is a form of doing good work for others and unto God's glory, we can accomplish biblical justice through everyday, simple acts of love. Not all of us will be called to grandiose justice efforts like becoming an overseas missionary, or starting a hospital, or ending human trafficking. But we can engage biblical justice through simple, modest acts of love. This is by no means an exhaustive list, but the following are a few ways the Lord has taught me to engage biblical justice by obeying God's greatest commandment.

Showing Grace Rather Than Upholding Punishment

With 20 years of teaching under my belt, I have endless stories of students who have turned in late assignments or even outright cheated. And although I distributed varied forms of consequences, I never implemented the "law" to the full extent. And I always tried to approach my students from a posture of grace. Because ultimately, I was more interested in setting them up to flourish than holding them back. Yes, consequences help us grow; yes, punishments can be a form of justice. Parenting and living my own life have underscored these truths for me. But where there is room for grace, in Jesus's name, I want to offer it.

Acting with Compassion and Humility

The Latin definition of *passion* is to become so overcome with emotion one suffers for it, which helps explain why Mel Gibson named his film about Jesus's crucifixion *The Passion of the Christ. Compassion* in Latin means to suffer with someone or on someone's behalf. When my friend Jennifer lost her sweet baby just a few hours after the baby was born, my heart broke every time I prayed. Deep guttural cries poured out of me. It had been more than ten years since I had miscarried, but I remembered that pain through her pain. I fasted and prayed for three days as a humble, meager offering to the Lord. Compassion compelled me to carry her pain to the cross. Practically, Christians can demonstrate compassion by providing meals during illness, offering childcare to exhausted parents, accompanying someone to difficult appointments, or simply sitting in solidarity with those experiencing grief. The acts themselves may not appear distinctly Christian at face value, but as Christians, our motivations flow from a distinct theological foundation that transcends the acts themselves. Christians engage in these compassionate acts as a reflection of Christ's sacrificial love and in obedience to His command to "bear one another's burdens" (Galatians 6:2 ESV), rather than from general humanitarianism or social obligation. Additionally, we offer prayer, hope, wisdom, and eternal comfort that is found in Christ alone.

Looking Out for Another's Wellbeing

My husband exhibits this well in our marriage. If not for him, I would likely never take my vitamins, have gas in my car, or make it to my dentist appointments. As I have taken on the lion's share of caring for our kids in similar areas, my husband has stepped up to care for me. Even outside the context of marriage and kids, we can all relate to the loyal, devoted friends and coworkers who look out for our wellbeing. Think of the folks in your neighborhood, your actual and literal neighbors. Is there a single mom who could use help with carpooling kids? Is there an elderly man who needs help bringing his trash cans to and from the curb? What about the lonely kid who rarely gets invited to a playdate? These are all small acts of love, and they are also extensions of biblical justice because we are redeeming and restoring broken parts of our world. As we extend ourselves in these seemingly mundane yet profoundly impactful ways, we fulfill Jesus's teaching that "whatever you did for one of the least of these brothers and sisters of mine, you did for me" (Matthew 25:40).

Speaking Kindly and Engaging Charitably

Not a week goes by that I don't consider quitting social media. I never cease to be shocked or disheartened by how professing Christians treat each other online. People I would likely enjoy in person over a cup of coffee can be vicious and cruel in the comments. And the duplicity is demoralizing. I am not the perfect arbitrator of dissenting discourse; I still have much to learn about how to disagree well and in an honoring way. As a personal rule of engagement, I try to be conscientious about whether I am addressing an idea or attacking a person. I never want to do the latter. I want to engage with others in a way that seeks truth without disparaging the person holding an oppositional perspective. Even with the written word, I think about the tongue having the power of life and death. Proverbs 18:21 states: "The tongue has the power of life and death, and those who love it will eat its fruit." This verse emphasizes the profound impact our words can have. They can either build others up and bring encouragement (life) or tear others down and cause harm (death). It's a powerful reminder of the responsibility we have when we speak and how our words can significantly influence others and ourselves.

Forgiving Others Who Have Committed an Offense

Since my Title IX stance went viral a few years ago, not one person who slandered me online, or signed a petition to get me fired, or threatened to harm my kids at their school, has ever apologized. Many have apologized on their behalf, but I've given up on hoping the actual offenders will realize the error of their attacks and ask for forgiveness. I've reconciled that hurt people really do in fact hurt people. Offended people project their wounds onto others. That's an unfortunate aspect of living in a fallen, broken world. Thankfully, though, our healing is not contingent on anyone's apology. That's not just good news; it's great news! Our emotional health is not dependent on others. Rather, it is dependent on our willingness to forgive others and draw close to the Lord. Forgiveness, as modeled by Christ, is not contingent on the offender's repentance but on the forgiver's obedience to God. Jesus exemplified this on the cross, saying, "Father, forgive them, for they do not know what they are doing" (Luke 23:34). This act of forgiveness can also serve as a powerful witness, potentially leading the offender to recognize their error. As Romans 2:4 suggests, it is God's kindness that leads to repentance. Our extension of forgiveness, therefore, may be the very catalyst that opens the eyes of those who have wronged us to their own need for repentance and reconciliation.

Stewarding Our Resources for Kingdom Impact

As followers of Christ, we're called to be good stewards of all God has entrusted to us. This includes our time, talents, and treasures. Supporting Christian ministries and organizations that address social needs is a powerful way to live out this calling. Whether by volunteering at a local food bank, mentoring at-risk youth, or financially supporting missionaries, these acts of service extend Christ's love in tangible ways. By investing in ministries that align with biblical values, we participate in God's redemptive work in society. My husband and I give 20 percent of our finances to our church and to various faith-based ministries. We intentionally give our time and donations to organizations working from a biblical worldview. This doesn't mean neglecting secular entities. We're still paying taxes, for example. But we prioritize giving to orthodox charities because we recognize the unique role they play in holistic social and spiritual transformation. When we give, we're not just meeting immediate needs; we're sowing seeds of hope and pointing people to the ultimate source of healing and restoration in Jesus Christ. The church's generosity, often in partnership with non-faith-based organizations, can be a catalyst for lasting change in individuals and communities. We need the church and the state to work in partnership to address social injustices.

Throughout church history and across the global contemporary church, Christians have meaningfully engaged in social justice work like adoption, poverty alleviation, anti-trafficking initiatives, environmental stewardship, refugee care, and many more human flourishing endeavors. Through organizations like Compassion International, International Justice Mission, and Women of Welcome, the modern church continues the biblical tradition of seeking justice, demonstrating Christians' commitment to addressing societal needs. While it is important to acknowledge that theological and political tensions arise when doing justice work in an increasingly post-Christian culture, ultimately we take heart in knowing the gospel proclamation and social engagement are complementary aspects of our kingdom mission. As Christians, we're called to participate in biblical justice through everyday acts of love—showing grace, acting with compassion, caring for others' wellbeing, speaking kindly, forgiving offenses, and stewarding resources. These acts, rooted in the Great Commandment, allow believers to be salt and light in a broken world, reflecting Christ's redemptive work and offering hope that transcends mere earthly, social solutions.

DIVINE JUSTICE

When Heaven's Arc Meets Earthly Action

Perhaps more than any other religion, followers of Jesus often receive this criticism: *You claim to be a Christian, but you don't act in accordance with it.* Sometimes the criticism is warranted. For instance, when I think about the horrors of the medieval crusades or the modern-day scandals of pastors who show grave moral failure, such as sexual abuse, I can see why Christians receive this sort of disparagement. The church and those who comprise it are far from perfect. Christians are still human and sinful. What fundamentally sets us apart from other religions is our confession in Christ. We know we are sinners in need of a Savior. We acknowledge Jesus is our Savior and our only way to eternity. And yes, followers of Christ who abide in Him should be transformed (sanctified) into more of His likeness as they walk with Him.

But what's interesting to me is how we're seeing this strange reverse phenomenon emerging where non-Christian thought leaders publicly admit they like the fruits of Christianity, but they don't believe in the existence of the tree. Or they don't adhere to the tree's teaching, anyway. There is an emerging group of thinkers who are unwilling to say that they believe in the actual truth of Christianity and yet they want to be Christian-adjacent. They lament that culture is no longer Christian. Jordan Peterson, to some degree, embodies this. As I watch his videos on Christianity, it is not lost on me that he knows Christian theology arguably better than I do and even many respected pastors. And yet he does not claim to be a Christian. (Although, I believe his daughter does, and I have hopes Peterson will someday submit his life to Christ.) Podcaster Joe Rogan, professor Jonathan Hadit, and public historian Tom Holland are other examples who come to mind. In various forms, all have recently expressed belief in the cultural benefits of Christianity, but they do not confess to following Christ.

To expound, in 2024, Richard Dawkins, the famous atheist and author of the anti-Christian book *The God Delusion*, admitted to being a "cultural Christian." This unexpected revelation came during an interview where Dawkins expressed concern about the fading Christian influence in Western society. Dawkins, known for his fierce criticism of Christianity, found himself in an awkward and contradictory position. He confessed to enjoying Christian hymns, Christmas carols, and feeling at home in the Christian ethos, despite not believing in God.[1]

Specifically, Dawkins told the interviewer he was horrified to see Islamic holidays and mosques taking the place of Christian feasts and cathedrals in Europe. It's an understandable position; I get it. But then Dawkins said the quiet part out loud. He continued, "If I had to choose between Christianity and Islam, I'd choose Christianity every single time. It seems to me to be a fundamentally decent religion in a way that I think Islam is not."[2] His stance sparked a flurry of reactions online. Some pointed out the irony of Dawkins enjoying the fruits of Christianity while rejecting its roots. On Twitter/X, thought leader Henry George wrote that "Rebuilding [civilization] means accepting the source, not [just] the effect, of Christianity." George then quoted historian Remi Brague who said, "We owe European civilization to people who believed in Christ, not to people who believed in Christianity."[3]

Quizzically, Dawkins claimed to love the taste of pears, but he doesn't believe in the existence of the pear tree. But as Christians, we know this fundamental reality: We cannot have a Christian culture without Christ. We cannot produce the fruit after cutting a tree off from its roots. The values, art, and traditions Dawkins appreciates weren't birthed out of good-will humanism; they flourished from centuries of Christian belief and practice, from Christian orthodoxy and orthopraxy. We cannot divorce the values from the beliefs. For Christians, hearing people claim to enjoy the fruit of Christ but not believe in the existence of Him can feel frustrating. How does one not see the connection? A good-tasting pear comes directly from a good pear tree. But if we're willing to exchange our hubris for a bit of humility, we can also see this as an opportunity for sharing the transformative power of the gospel. Instead of gloating, it's an opportunity for conversation about why Christianity matters beyond just tradition and culture. Our Christian values come from Christ. He is the source of the fruit. The tree is our belief in Christ, that He rose from the dead, and that we need Him as our Savior because we are broken, lost, and bound for eternal separation from the Lord without Him.

The tree and its fruit produce far more good in the world than mere cathedrals, hymns, and Christmas carols. Jesus is the embodiment of a radical philosophy of forgiveness, compassion, and justice through relationship with Him. In fact, the human longing for justice is evidence that we understand that the world is not as it should be. The reason we all recoil at racism, oppression, and abuse is because we know, deep down, that this is not how the world is supposed to be. Truth is written on our hearts. But often our eyes are blinded.

We may be blinded by contemporary narratives that stand in opposition to God's Word. We may be blinded by leaders who steer us astray. Mostly, we are blinded by the Enemy, the father of lies, who comes to steal, kill, and destroy all that God has said is good, true, and beautiful. Doing justice isn't merely a matter of engaging good work for the sake of the common good; rather, doing justice is a battle against the Enemy. Each time we bring light to darkness, living water to the thirsty, the bread of life to the hungry, Satan loses territory and the gospel of Jesus is advanced.

As Christians, we should absolutely leverage our influence for good in all facets of society, including the government. Faith integration and civic engagement from a biblical worldview is not Christian nationalism. That accusation is frequently used against Christians who publicly cite their faith as the basis of their actions. But no one I know and certainly no one worth listening to is arguing for a Christian theocracy, which is the crux of the Christian nationalism indictment. Even if we were to establish a Christian theocracy, it would fail us; just ask the medieval church. When we put our ultimate hope in human governments and leaders to save us, we are bound to be disappointed. In fact, the more power we give to the state to enforce an ideological vision of justice, the more we run the risk of creating new forms of oppression. World history is full of examples of governmental movements that promised a just society but ended in tyranny. So if history is our teacher, we can safely learn that the church should be leading justice-based causes, not the state. There is room to partner with public sectors; there is room for common good work from a pluralistic perspective, even. But that posture is far different from hoping or expecting the government to lead like Jesus.

The Bible calls us to be salt and light in the world, to care for the poor and oppressed, to uphold the cause of the marginalized. On issues like racial discrimination, economic opportunity, ending human trafficking, and criminal justice reform, Christians should be leading the charge. And we lead with the truth of the gospel. Only the gospel can transform hearts and systems. The Christian view of justice is rooted in the cross. In Christ's death, we see the ultimate fusing of God's perfect justice and perfect love. On one hand, evil is punished and sin is condemned in full; this is justice upheld. On the other hand, mercy triumphs as Christ bears that punishment on our behalf. Justice is both accountability and mercy.

As followers of Christ, may we be a people characterized by a zeal for justice in all its forms because of our hope in Christ. May we steward our earthly citizenship for kingdom-minded, eternal good. May we extend the reconciling love of God to everyone we meet. Not just to our neighbors but also to those we're tempted to cast as our enemies. We speak up for the marginalized, the oppressed, the forgotten. We labor to build systems and structures that reflect God's heart for human flourishing. We pray and work and advocate and serve, not because the world tells us to but because we know every act of compassion is a foretaste of God's coming eternal and perfect kingdom. As Christians, we know there is no true form of social justice apart from the redemptive and restorative power of Christ. Doing biblical justice in a world often antagonistic to God's truth is not an easy road to walk. The needs of the world are great, and the opposition often seems even greater. But we draw strength from Jesus, who has overcome the world, confident that His purposes will prevail. In the face of injustice, we choose to hope, to love, and to persevere because we believe God's justice will have the final word. Our responsibility as Christians is not to please the world; instead, we are called to faithfully steward what He has given us unto His glory.

As you reflect on the rich heritage of Christian justice work throughout history and into our present day, consider how God might be inviting you to participate in His redemptive plan. Biblical justice isn't reserved just for churches, ministries, or faith-based nonprofits. Biblical justice work begins in everyday moments where Christ's love meets our human need. Perhaps it starts with bringing meals to a new mother, offering rides to an elderly neighbor, or mentoring a child from a single-parent home. Maybe it means examining your spending habits and redirecting resources toward ministries addressing injustices in your community. Or it could involve using your professional skills to volunteer at a crisis pregnancy center, refugee resettlement agency, or anti-trafficking organization. Whatever shape it takes, your participation matters because each act of justice, however small, bears witness to the coming kingdom where all things will be made right. When Christians faithfully engage in justice work from a biblical worldview, we offer more than temporary relief—we point to the ultimate Redeemer who alone can heal our broken world. As image-bearers called to reflect God's character and share His truth, embracing biblical justice isn't optional; rather, it is essential to discipleship. It demonstrates to others that our faith extends beyond our salvation and to God's plan of restoration. Unlike secular social justice, which often focuses solely on restructuring power systems and achieving equal outcomes, biblical justice is rooted in God's unchanging character and redemptive purposes. Discerning the difference matters because true social justice cannot be achieved apart from the gospel's power to transform hearts and minds.

PART THREE: REFLECTION QUESTIONS

1. Biblical justice is rooted in the totality of Scripture and encompasses multiple expressions: retributive, distributive, procedural, covenantal, social, redemptive, and restorative justice. This holistic view has motivated Christians throughout history to engage in transformative social action. In what ways has your understanding of biblical justice been challenged or expanded by considering its multiple expressions (retributive, distributive, procedural, etc.)? How might this more comprehensive view impact your engagement with social issues?

2. Throughout church history, Christians have worked for human flourishing and God's glory. From the early church's radical embodiment of Christ's teachings to modern-day efforts in poverty alleviation, anti-human-trafficking efforts, and environmental stewardship, Christianity has consistently been a catalyst for social reform and human rights. Reflecting on the rich history of Christian social engagement, where do you see yourself fitting into this ongoing narrative? Are there particular areas of injustice that God may be calling you to address in your community or beyond?

3. The Christian approach to justice is distinct in its motivation and scope, stemming from gratitude for God's grace rather than guilt or political ideology. It seeks both individual transformation and systemic change, recognizing that true justice requires addressing heart issues as well as social structures. How does the motivation of gratitude for God's grace, rather than guilt or political ideology, change your

approach to social justice work? In what ways can you cultivate this grace-driven perspective in your own life and church community?

4. As Western culture becomes increasingly post-Christian, there's a growing recognition of Christianity's positive societal influence, even among skeptics. This presents an opportunity for Christians to articulate why the "fruit" of Christianity cannot be separated from its "root" in Christ. In an increasingly post-Christian culture that may appreciate the fruits of Christianity without acknowledging its roots, how can you effectively articulate the inseparable connection between Christian faith and its social benefits?

5. The Great Commandment (Matthew 22:37-40) is central to understanding biblical justice, calling us to love God supremely and our neighbors as ourselves. This love extends beyond our immediate circles and even encompasses our enemies, while remaining inseparable from God's truth. Consider the practical ways of engaging in biblical justice mentioned (showing grace, acting with compassion, looking out for others' wellbeing, giving of our time and finances). Which of these resonates most with you, and how might you more intentionally incorporate it into your daily life as an expression of loving God and your neighbor?

NOTES

FOREWORD

1. Rodney Stark, *The Rise of Christianity: A Sociologist Reconsiders History* (Princeton University Press, 1996).

PREFACE: LIGHT IN THE DARKNESS

1. Benedetta Berti, "The Syrian Refugee Crisis: Regional and Human Security Implications," https://www.inss.org.il/wp-content/uploads/sites/2/systemfiles/SystemFiles/adkan17_4ENG_7 _Berti.pdf.

2. Nell Gabiam, "Humanitarianism, Development, and Security in the 21st Century: Lessons from the Syrian Refugee Crisis," *International Journal of Middle East Studies* 48, no. 2, (2016): 382-386, doi:10.1017/S0020743816000131.

INTRODUCTION

1. International Justice Mission (IJM), https://www.endslaverynow.org/international-justice -mission-ijm.

2. Jesse Smith and George Yancey, "Measurement and Conceptualization of Christian Nationalism: A Critical Examination and Alternative Approach," *Review of Religious Research*, May 21, 2025, doi: 10.1177/0034673X251336460.

3. Evangelicals were far and away the group most likely to donate money, items, or time as a volunteer. More than three-quarters of evangelicals (79 percent) have donated money in the last year, and 65 percent and 60 percent of them have donated items or volunteer time, respectively. Additionally, only 1 percent of evangelicals say they made no charitable donation in the last 12 months. David P. King, "What Role Can Religious Leaders Play in the Generosity Conversation?," Lake Institute on Faith and Giving, https://lakeinstitute.org/resource-library/insights/ oct-8-2024/.

CHAPTER 1: FAITH UNDER FIRE

1. Parker Palmer, *The Courage to Teach: Exploring the Inner Landscape of a Teacher's Life* (Jossey-Bass, 2017), 10.

2. Katherine Knott, "What's Next for Colleges After Judge Vacates Biden's Title IX Rule," *Inside Higher Ed*, January 9, 2025, https://www.insidehighered.com/news/government/student-aid-policy/2025/01/09/federal-judge-throws-out-bidens-title-ix-overhaul.

3. RAINN, "Children and Teens: Statistics," https://www.rainn.org/statistics/children-and-teens.

4. Crime Victims' Institute, https://www.crimevictimsinstitute.org/.

5. U.S. Department of Justice, "Sexual Victimization Reported by Adult Correctional Authorities, 2012–15," Bureau of Justice Statistics, July 2018, https://www.bjs.ojp.gov/content/pub/pdf/svraca1215.pdf.

6. Abigail Shrier, "Male Inmates in Women's Prisons," *Wall Street Journal*, May 31, 2021, https://www.wsj.com/articles/male-inmates-in-womens-prisons-11622474215.

7. National Network to End Domestic Violence Fact Sheet, "Domestic Violence, Housing, and Homelessness," https://azmag.gov/Portals/0/Domestic-Violence/NNEDV-Fact-Sheet.pdf.

8. E.L. Bassuk, S. Melnick, and A. Browne, "Responding to the Needs of Low-Income and Homeless Women Who Are Survivors of Family Violence," *Journal of the American Medical Women's Association*, 53, no. 2 (1998): 57-64.

9. Ipsos Survey, "Topline & Methodology," https://static01.nyt.com/newsgraphics/document tools/f548560f100205ef/e656ddda-full.pdf.

10. Michael Lipka and Patricia Tevington, "Attitudes About Transgender Issues Vary Widely Among Christians, Religious 'Nones' in U.S.," Pew Research Center, July 7, 2022, https://www.pewresearch.org/short-reads/2022/07/07/attitudes-about-transgender-issues-vary-widely-among-christians-religious-nones-in-u-s/.

11. American Psychiatric Association, *Diagnostic and Statistical Manual of Mental Disorders*, 5th ed. (American Psychiatric Publishing, 2013).

CHAPTER 2: WHAT EVEN IS "SOCIAL JUSTICE"?

1. Thomas Patrick Burke, "The Origins of Social Justice: Taparelli d'Azeglio," *Modern Age* 52, no. 2 (2010): 97-106. This article provides a detailed exploration of Taparelli's life, work, and his development of the concept of social justice.

2. Charles E. Curran, *Catholic Social Teaching, 1891-Present: A Historical, Theological, and Ethical Analysis* (Georgetown University Press, 2002), 7.

3. C.H. Kang and Ethel R. Nelson, *The Discovery of Genesis: How the Truths of Genesis Were Found Hidden in the Chinese Language* (Concordia, 1979), 98.

4. Michael W. Goheen and Erin G. Glanville, eds. *The Gospel and Globalization: Exploring the Religious Roots of a Globalized World* (Regent College Press, 2009), 125-140.

5. Jennifer Pitts, "Legislator of the World? A Rereading of Bentham on Colonies," *Political Theory* 31, no. 2 (2003): 200–234, http://www.jstor.org/stable/3595700.

6. James E. Crimmins, "Bentham on Religion: Atheism and the Secular Society," *Journal of the History of Ideas* 47, no. 1 (1986): 95–110, https://doi.org/10.2307/2709597.

CHAPTER 3: CHRISTIANITY AND CONTEMPORARY SOCIAL ISSUES

1. To offer more about the learning loss of children due to school closures and lockdowns from the COVID-19 pandemic, I recommend these three academic articles.
   Emma Dorn, Bryan Hancock, Jimmy Sarakatsannis, and Ellen Viruleg, "COVID-19 and

student learning in the United States: The hurt could last a lifetime," McKinsey & Company, June 1, 2020, https://www.mckinsey.com/industries/education/our-insights/covid-19-and -student-learning-in-the-united-states-the-hurt-could-last-a-lifetime. This article uses empirical data to estimate that due to school closures, students in the US may have lost 3 months of learning in math and 1.5 months in reading on average. Learning losses have likely been greater for minority and low-income students.

Per Engzell, Arun Frey, and Mark D. Verhagen, "Learning loss due to school closures during the COVID-19 pandemic," Proceedings of the National Academy of Sciences, 118, no. 17 (April 2021), https://www.pnas.org/doi/10.1073/pnas.2022376118. This study analyzed learning loss between 2019 and 2021 across several countries. They found substantial learning losses, especially in mathematics and for students from low-income families. Students lost over 20 percent of average school year gains in the Netherlands and Switzerland.

Karyn Lewis, Megan Kuhfeld, Erin Ruzek, and Andrew McEachin, "Learning during COVID-19: Reading and math achievement in the 2020-21 school year," NWEA, July 2021, https://www.nwea.org/uploads/2021/07/Learning-during-COVID-19-Reading-and-math -achievement-in-the-2020-2021-school-year.research-brief-1.pdf. This report examines reading and math achievement on standardized tests in the US during the 2020-21 school year. Students scored 5-10 percentile points lower compared to pre-pandemic achievement growth trends, indicating substantial learning loss.

2. McKinsey Global Institute, "COVID-19 and gender equality: Countering retrogressive effects," McKinsey & Company, July 15, 2020, https://www.mckinsey.com/featured-insights/ future-of-work/covid-19-and-gender-equality-countering-the-regressive-effects.

3. UN Women, "Whose time to care? Unpaid care and domestic work during COVID-19," UN Women: Women Count, November 25, 2020, https://data.unwomen.org/publications/ whose-time-care-unpaid-care-and-domestic-work-during-covid-19.

4. UN Women, "Whose time to care?"

5. UN Women, "Whose time to care?"

6. Damian F. Santomauro, et al. "Global Prevalence and Burden of Depressive and Anxiety Disorders in 204 Countries and Territories in 2020 Due to the COVID-19 Pandemic," The Lancet 398, no. 10312 (2021): 1700-1712, doi: 10.1016/S0140-6736(21)02143-7.

7. National Institute on Drug Abuse, "COVID-19 and Substance Use," https://www.drugabuse .gov/drug-topics/comorbidity/covid-19-substance-use.

8. CDC, "U.S. Overdose Deaths in 2021 Increased Half as Much as in 2020—But Are Still Up 15%," May 11, 2022, https://www.cdc.gov/nchs/pressroom/nchs_press_releases/2022/202205 .htm.

9. National Center for Missing and Exploited Children, "2018 Year in Review" NCMEC Annual Review, 2019, 1–10, https://www.missingkids.org/ourwork/ncmecdata.

10. Megan Idle, "Child Pornography Crimes as Reported to Law Enforcement Agencies," December 2019, https://jscholarship.library.jhu.edu/server/api/core/bitstreams/46990b05-3826-4f1a -8490-b3a29a1caeab/content.

11. Idle, "Child Pornography Crimes."

12. Christina Maxouris, Holly Yan, and Ralph Ellis, "Cities Extend Curfews for Another Night in an Attempt to Avoid Violent Protests over George Floyd's Death," CNN, May 31, 2020, https://www.cnn.com/2020/05/31/us/george-floyd-protests-sunday/index.html.

13. Abby Budiman, "Americans are More Positive About the Long-Term Rise in U.S. Racial and Ethnic Diversity than in 2016," Pew Research Center, October 1, 2020, https://www.pewresearch

.org/short-reads/2020/10/01/americans-are-more-positive-about-the-long-term-rise-in-u-s-racial
-and-ethnic-diversity-than-in-2016/.

14. George Yancey and Y. J. Kim, "Interethnic Congregations and the Reconciliation of Outgroup Attitudes," *Sociological Perspectives* 62, no. 5, (2019): 758–778.

CHAPTER 4: THE CASE FOR BIBLICAL JUSTICE

1. William G. McLoughlin, "Revivals, Awakenings, and Reforms: An Essay on Religion and Social Change in America, 1607–1977," *Chicago History: The Magazine of the Chicago Historical Society*, 5, no. 5, (1976): 130–141.

2. John D. Wilsey, "Was America Founded as a Christian Nation? A Historical Introduction," *Themelios* 37, no. 2, https://www.thegospelcoalition.org/themelios/review/was-america-founded-as-a-christian-nation-a-historical-introduction/.

3. Kimberle Crenshaw, "Demarginalizing the Intersection of Race and Sex: A Black Feminist Critique of Antidiscrimination Doctrine, Feminist Theory and Antiracist Policies," University of Chicago Legal Forum, 1989, no. 1, https://chicagounbound.uchicago.edu/cgi/viewcontent.cgi?article=1052&context=uclf.

4. David Aikman, *The Delusion of Disbelief: Why New Atheism is a Threat to Your Life, Liberty, and Pursuit of Happiness* (Tyndale House, 2008).

CHAPTER 5: EQUIPPING THE NEXT GENERATION
FOR BIBLICAL JUSTICE

1. Barna Group, "The Connected Generation: How Christian Leaders Around the World Can Strengthen Faith and Well-Being Among 18–35-Year-Olds," Barna Group ebooks, 2019, https://access.barna.com/studies/the-connected-generation/.

2. Barna Group, "Gen Z Finding Beauty in Brokenness Could Be Key to Leading Populist Movements," Barna Group, March 16, 2022. https://www.barna.com/research/gen-z-populists/.

3. Barna Group, "How the Church Can Fuel Black Gen Z's Desire for Justice," February 22, 2023, https://www.barna.com/research/black-gen-z-justice/. Barna, "Gen Z and Morality: What Teens Believe (So Far)," October 9, 2018, https://www.barna.com/research/gen-z-morality/.

4. Barna Group, *Gen Z: The Culture, Beliefs, and Motivations Shaping the Next Generation* (Barna Group, 2018).

5. J.I. Packer, *Concise Theology: A Guide to Historic Christian Beliefs* (Tyndale House, 1993), 187, https://files.tyndale.com/thpdata/firstchapters/978-0-8423-3960-5.pdf.

6. Dietrich Bonhoeffer, *Life Together: The Classic Exploration of Christian Community* (HarperOne, 2009), 19.

7. Timothy Keller, *Generous Justice: How God's Grace Makes Us Just* (Penguin Books, 2012), 1-18.

CHAPTER 6: HOW IN THE WORLDVIEW DID WE GET HERE?

1. Richard M. Weaver, *Ideas Have Consequences* (University of Chicago Press, 1948).

2. John Stonestreet, "Breakpoint: Why Freedom Is so Fragile," Breakpoint Colson Center, October 2, 2018, https://breakpoint.org/breakpoint-why-freedom-is-so-fragile/.

3. Tracy Munsil, "Biblical Worldview Among U.S. Adults Drops 33% Since Start of COVID-19 Pandemic," Arizona Christian University, February 28, 2023, https://www.arizonachristian

.edu/2023/02/28/biblical-worldview-among-u-s-adults-drops-33-since-start-of-covid-19
-pandemic/.

4. George Barna, "American Worldview Inventory 2023: How the Pandemic Reshaped Christian Beliefs and Behaviors," Cultural Research Center at Arizona Christian University, November 22, 2023, https://georgebarna.com/2023/06/american-worldview-inventory-2023-release
-5-how-the-pandemic-reshaped-christian-beliefs-and-behaviors/.

CHAPTER 7: A SECULAR WORLDVIEW AND A CHRISTIAN WORLDVIEW

1. J.P. Moreland and William Lane Craig, *Philosophical Foundations for a Christian Worldview* (InterVarsity, 2003).

2. Moreland and Craig, *Philosophical Foundations for a Christian Worldview*.

3. David S. Dockery and Gregory Alan Thornbury, eds., *Shaping a Christian Worldview: The Foundations of Christian Higher Education* (Broadman & Holman, 2002).

4. James W. Sire, *The Universe Next Door: A Basic Worldview Catalog*, 6th ed. (IVP Academic, 2020).

CHAPTER 8: ONE OF THESE THINGS IS NOT LIKE THE OTHER

1. Nancy Pearcey, *Total Truth: Liberating Christianity from Its Cultural Captivity* (Crossway, 2004).

2. David S. Dockery, *Faith and Learning: A Handbook for Christian Higher Education* (B&H, 2012), 17.

3. 2 Corinthians 5:20 NASB: "Therefore, we are ambassadors for Christ, as though God were making an appeal through us; we beg you on behalf of Christ, be reconciled to God." Ephesians 6:20 NASB: "For which I am an ambassador in chains; that in proclaiming it I may speak boldly, as I ought to speak."

4. Meredith G. Kline, *Images of the Spirit* (Baker, 1980). See also Jack Deere for how God administers supernatural spiritual gifts. Jack Deere, *Surprised by the Power of the Spirit* (Zondervan Publishing, 1996).

5. Walter A. Elwell, *Evangelical Dictionary of Theology* (Baker, 1987), 60. "They are God's messengers or ambassadors. They belong to his heavenly court and service. Their mission in heaven is to praise him."

CHAPTER 9: DIVINE DESIGN OR COSMIC CHANCE?

1. J.P. Moreland, *Kingdom Triangle: Recover the Christian Mind, Renovate the Soul, Restore the Spirit's Power* (Zondervan, 2007).

2. Brennan Manning, *Abba's Child: The Cry of the Heart for Intimate Belonging* (The Navigators: 2015), 95.

3. Hendricks Center, "Should Christians Use IVF?," The Table Podcast, https://hendrickscenter
.dts.edu/podcast/should-christians-use-ivf/.

CHAPTER 10: MODERNISM AND POSTMODERNISM

1. Friedrich Nietzsche, *The Gay Science*, Section 125, 1882, Walter Kaufmann, trans. (Vintage Books, 1974).

2. *Time Magazine*, "Is God Dead?," https://content.time.com/time/covers/0,16641,19660408,00 .html.

3. William Grimes, "John T. Elson, Editor Who Asked 'Is God Dead?' at *Time*, Dies at 78," *The New York Times*, September 17, 2009, https://www.nytimes.com/2009/09/18/business/ media/18elson.html.

4. Richard John Neuhaus, *The Best of the Public Square*, vol. 3 (Wm B. Eerdmans, 2007).

5. Os Guinness, *The Global Public Square: Religious Freedom and the Making of a World Safe for Diversity* (IVP Books, 2013), 145.

6. Alasdair MacIntyre, "Relativism, Power and Philosophy," *Proceedings and Addresses of the American Philosophical Association*, 59, no. 1 (1985): 5–22. For other scholars who have written on relativism philosophies, see John MacFarlane, 2003, "Future Contingents and Relative Truth," *Philosophical Quarterly*, 53, no. 212 (2003): 321–336. And Alvin I. Goldman, "Epistemic Relativism and Reasonable Disagreement," in *Disagreement*, Richard Feldman and Ted A. Warfield, eds. (Oxford University Press, 2010), 187–215.

7. Gerald L. Gutek, *Philosophical and Ideological Voices in Education* (Pearson, 2004), 86.

8. Erroll Hulse, *Post-Modernism: Attack on the Heart of Biblical Christianity* (Mount Zion, 2008), 28.

9. Richard Rorty and Stanley Fish, *There's No Such Thing as Free Speech: And It's a Good Thing, Too* (Oxford University Press, 1994). Rorty and Fish critique notions of universal rights and neutral truth underpinning classical conceptions of free speech. They argue speech protections emerge from particular communities rather than absolute foundations. They also advocate an anti-foundationalist, relativist view denying that neutral universals shape notions of rights. Rather, rights derive meaning from specific traditions and historical contexts.

10. Stanley Fish, "Is There a Text in This Class?" in *Is There a Text in This Class?: The Authority of Interpretive Communities* (Harvard University Press, 1980), 319.

11. Richard Rorty, *The Consequences of Pragmatism* (University of Minnesota Press, 1982), 166.

12. Nicholas Wolterstorff, "True Words," in *But Is It All True: The Bible and the Question of Truth*, ed. Alan G. Padgett and Patrick R. Keifert (Eerdmans Publishing Company, 2006), 34–43.

13. Wolterstorff, "True Words," 34–43.

14. D.A. Carson, *The Gagging of God: Christianity Confronts Pluralism* (Zondervan, 2002).

15. Pew Research Center, "How U.S. Religious Composition has Changed in Recent Decades, September 13, 2022, https://www.pewresearch.org/religion/2022/09/13/ how-u-s-religious-composition-has-changed-in-recent-decades/.

16. Barna, "*Only Half of Protestants Have A Biblical Worldview*," 2018.

17. Barna, 2018.

18. Barna, 2018.

19. Barna, 2018.

20. Barna, 2018.

CHAPTER 11: FOUNDATIONS OF FAITH

1. Saint Augustine, *Confessions*, trans. Maria Boulding, ed. John E. Rotelle, 2nd ed. *The Works of Saint Augustine: A Translation for the 21st Century* (New City Press, 2012), 1.

2. Cultural Research Center, "American Worldview Inventory 2023," February 28, 2023, https:// www.arizonachristian.edu/wp-content/uploads/2023/02/CRC_AWVI2023_Release1.pdf.

3. Tracy Munsil, "Barna, CRC Research Identify 'Seven Cornerstones' for Restoring Biblical Worldview," Arizona Christian University, March 14, 2023, https://www.arizonachristian .edu/2023/03/14/barna-crc-research-identify-seven-cornerstones-for-restoring-biblical-worldview/.

4. Cultural Research Center, "American Worldview Inventory 2023."

5. Cultural Research Center, "American Worldview Inventory 2023."

6. Munsil, "Barna, CRC Research Identify 'Seven Cornerstones.'"

7. C.S. Lewis, "The Weight of Glory," in *The Weight of Glory and Other Addresses* (HarperOne, 2001), 45-46.

CHAPTER 13: THE BRIDE OF CHRIST AS
THE CATALYST FOR SOCIAL JUSTICE

1. C.S. Lewis, *Mere Christianity* (Simon & Schuster Touchstone, 1996), 171.

2. CDC, Violence Prevention, "About the CDC-Kaiser ACE Study," https://www.cdc.gov/vio-lenceprevention/aces/about.html.

3. Karen Hughes, et al., "The effect of multiple adverse childhood experiences on health: a systematic review and meta-analysis," *Lancet Public Health* 2, no. 8 (2017): 356-66.

4. Melissa T. Merrick, et al., "Prevalence of Adverse Childhood Experiences From the 2011-2014 Behavioral Risk Factor Surveillance System in 23 states," *JAMA Pediatrics* 172, no. 11 (2018): 1038-44.

5. Zachary Giano, Denna L. Wheeler, and Randolph D. Hubach, "The frequencies and disparities of adverse childhood experiences in the U.S.," *BMC Public Health* 20, no. 1327 (2020), https://doi.org/10.1186/s12889-020-09411-z.

6. Barna Group, "5 Things You Need to Know About Gen Z in 2024," Barna, September 12, 2024, https://www.barna.com/research/gen-z-2024/.

7. Barna Group, "Introducing the State of the Church 2020," Barna, February 3, 2020, https://www.barna.com/research/state-of-the-church-2020/.

8. Lifeway Research, "Few Protestant Churchgoers Read the Bible Daily," Lifeway Research, 2019, https://research.lifeway.com/2019/07/02/few-protestant-churchgoers-read-the-bible-daily/.

9. Thaddeus J. Williams, *Confronting Injustice Without Compromising Truth: 12 Questions Christians Should Ask About Social Justice* (Zondervan Academic, 2020), 27-28.

CHAPTER 14: GOD'S JUSTICE PLAYBOOK:
SEVEN EXPRESSIONS OF BIBLICAL JUSTICE

1. Nadra Nittle, "New Book Explores the Influences Behind the Life and Work of bell hooks," 19th News, November 8, 2023, https://19thnews.org/2023/11/bell-hooks-spiritual-vision-nadra-nittle/.

2. Tim Keller, *Generous Justice: How God's Grace Makes Us Just* (Dutton, 2010), 3.

3. Keller, *Generous Justice*, 3.

4. Keller, *Generous Justice*, 4.

5. Keller, *Generous Justice*, 10.

6. Keller, *Generous Justice*, 27-28.

7. Keller, *Generous Justice,* 185.

8. Keller, *Generous Justice,* 188.

9. Keller, *Generous Justice*, 18.

10. Nicholas Wolterstorff, *Justice: Rights and Wrongs* (Princeton University Press, 2008). Wolterstorff contends that human rights are grounded in the inherent worth of individuals, which stems from God's love for each person. Wolterstorff challenges both secular theories of justice and Christian alternatives that reject rights-based thinking. The book explores the historical development of rights theory, critiques competing views of justice, and offers a theistic foundation for human rights. Wolterstorff argues that this approach provides a more robust basis for human rights than secular alternatives. *Justice: Rights and Wrongs* offers a nuanced, philosophically rigorous defense of rights-based justice from a Christian perspective, contributing significantly to contemporary discussions on justice and human rights.

11. Gary A. Haugen, *Good News About Injustice: A Witness of Courage in a Hurting World* (InterVarsity, 1999). Haugen's book is a compelling call to action for Christians to engage in the fight against global injustice. Haugen draws from his experience as a human rights attorney and founder of International Justice Mission. He presents a biblical framework for understanding justice and God's heart for the oppressed. He shares powerful stories of individuals confronting various forms of injustice worldwide, from slavery to police brutality. Haugen argues that God's people are called to be agents of justice and offers practical guidance on how ordinary Christians can make a difference. The book emphasizes that there is hope in the face of overwhelming injustice through faith, courage, and action.

CHAPTER 15: EXPRESSIONS OF SOCIAL
JUSTICE THROUGHOUT CHURCH HISTORY

1. Rebecca McLaughlin, *The Secular Creed: Engaging Five Contemporary Claims* (Gospel Coalition, 2021), 10.

2. Rodney Stark, *The Rise of Christianity: How the Obscure, Marginal Jesus Movement Became the Dominant Religious Force in the Western World in a Few Centuries* (Princeton University Press, 1996).

3. Catholic Medical Association, "St. Basil the Great," https://catholicmedicalassociation.org.uk/resources/saints-in-healthcare/st-basil-the-great/.

4. Charles Homer Haskins, *The Rise of Universities*, 2nd ed. (Harvard University Press, 1957).

5. G.R. Evans, *Bernard of Clairvaux* (Oxford University Press, 2000).

6. Gene Edward Veith Jr., *God at Work: Your Christian Vocation in All of Life* (Crossway, 2002).

7. Gene Edward Veith Jr., *God at Work*.

8. Eric Metaxas, *Amazing Grace: William Wilberforce and the Heroic Campaign to End Slavery* (HarperCollins, 2007). This biographical work examines Wilberforce's Christian faith as central to his antislavery activism and political career.

9. Ashlee Anderson, "Elizabeth Ann Seton," National Women's History Museum, https://www.womenshistory.org/education-resources/biographies/elizabeth-ann-seton.

10. Richard Roeper, "'Cabrini': Sweeping Biopic Depicts the Altruistic Nun Who Would Later Be a Saint," *Chicago Sun-Times*, March 6, 2024, https://chicago.suntimes.com/movies-and-tv/2024/03/06/cabrini-review-mother-chicago-cristiana-dellanna.

11. Salvation Army, "History of the Salvation Army," https://www.salvationarmyusa.org/usn/history-of-the-salvation-army/.

12. J.E. Hansan, "Charles Loring Brace (June 19, 1826 – August 11, 1890): Congregational Minister,

Child Welfare Advocate, Founder of the New York Children's Aid Society and Organizer of the Orphan's Train," Virginia Commonwealth University, https://socialwelfare.library.vcu .edu/people/brace-charles-loring/.

13. Andrew J. Milson, Chara Haeussler Bohan, Perry L. Glanzer, and J. Weseley Null, eds., *American Educational Thought: Essays from 1640-1940* (Information Age Publishing, 2010).

14. Milson et al., *American Educational Thought*.

15. Milson et al., *American Educational Thought*.

16. Booker T. Washington, *Up from Slavery* (Doubleday, Page & Co., 1901), 218.

17. Charles Marsh, *The Beloved Community: How Faith Shapes Social Justice from the Civil Rights Movement to Today* (Basic Books, 2005). *The Beloved Community* by Charles Marsh examines how Christian faith and theology provided the foundational motivation and framework for the Civil Rights Movement, particularly through the leadership of figures like Martin Luther King Jr. and other faith-based activists. Marsh argues that the movement's vision of racial reconciliation and social justice was deeply rooted in Christian concepts of love, redemption, and community, and traces how these religious principles continue to influence contemporary social justice movements. The book demonstrates how the "beloved community" ideal— a society based on justice, equal opportunity, and love—emerged from Christian theological traditions and shaped both the strategies and goals of civil rights activism.

CHAPTER 16: CONTEMPORARY CHRISTIAN SOCIAL JUSTICE EFFORTS

1. Sean Gregory, "This Ukrainian High Jumper Rested in a Sleeping Bag. Then She Won Gold," *Time*, August 4, 2024, https://time.com/7007642/yaroslava-mahuchikh-sleeping -bag-ukraine-high-jump-paris-olympics/.

2. Escher Walcott, "Simone Biles Opens Up About Growing Up in Foster Care and Understanding 'Hardships' Kids 'Go Through,'" *People*, December 16, 2023, https://people.com/ simone-biles-opens-up-about-childhood-in-foster-care-8417141. The Foundation, "Going for the Gold for Children Waiting in Foster Care: Kenny Bednarek's Story," Dave Thomas Foundation for Adoption, July 25, 2024, https://www.davethomasfoundation.org/resource/ going-for-the-gold-for-children-waiting-in-foster-care-kenny-bednareks-story/.

3. Jedd Medefind, "New Barna Research Highlights Christian Adoption & Foster Care Among 3 Most Notable Vocational Trends," Christian Alliance for Orphans, February 12, 2024, https:// cafo.org/new-barna-research-highlights-christian-adoption-foster-care-among-3-most-notable -vocational-trends/#:~:text=Practicing%20Christians%20(5%25)%20are,adopt%20as%20 the%20average%20adult.

4. Deloitte, "Gen Z's and Millennials Doing, Demanding More Around Climate Change, June 12, 2023, https://action.deloitte.com/insight/3378/gen-zs-and-millennials-doing -demanding-more-around-climate-change.

5. Again, I recognize there is controversy within the creation care movement, as Megan Basham addresses in her book *Shepherds for Sale*. I am not equipped to assess each of her claims, as I have not read the book. But I have gathered the gist of her arguments from listening to podcasts on which she has discussed it.

CONCLUSION: DIVINE JUSTICE

1. LBC (@LBC), "'If I had to choose between Christianity and Islam, I'd choose Christianity every single time.' Self-proclaimed 'cultural Christian' @RichardDawkins, tells @RachelSJohnson

he's 'slightly horrified' to hear Ramadan lights were hung on Oxford Street rather than Easter lights," X, March 31, 2024, https://x.com/LBC/status/1774510715975368778.

2. LBC (@LBC), "'If I had to choose between Christianity and Islam."

3. Henry Georgy (@intothefuture45), "Rebuilding means accepting the source, not the effect, of Christianity: 'Faith produces its effects only so long as it remains faith and not calculation. We owe European civilisation to people who believed in Christ, not to people who believed in Christianity.' - Remi Brague," X, April 1, 2024, https://x.com/intothefuture45/status/1774803832091906292.

ACKNOWLEDGMENTS

Every author arrives at this place by way of countless hours of study, writing, and relationships—each contributing to the culmination of what becomes a book. In a deeply profound sense, no work is ever truly individual; it is communal. So I am forever thankful for and indebted to those who edify, sanctify, and fortify me. I pray this book reflects and honors those who have influenced it.

First and foremost, I am incredibly thankful for my husband and sons. Craig, Christopher, and Corban, you have been faithful witnesses to this journey, bearing with patience the cost that writing extracts from our family life. Your belief in me persisted even when my own faltered. You've cheered me on when I've wanted to quit. Thank you for the gift of your encouragement and all the sacrifices you made for this vision to materialize. It is not lost on me how many times I failed to do the laundry, make a decent dinner, or took hours away on a Saturday (and even on vacations) during the writing process. Thank you for your grace and support. You three are more than I deserve and all I've ever wanted. I'd also like to acknowledge my mother, whose life has been a testament to courage and conviction. Mom, you have exemplified what it means to pursue life with bravery—serving in the Army, moving across the world, and earning a master's degree while raising two young daughters as a single mom. Even through life's storms, you anchored our family to the church, instilling in me both the irreplaceable value of Christian community and the necessity of Christ as my Savior.

To the many friends who have contributed their wisdom and perspective, I extend my gratitude. Jonathan Pokluda (Pastor JP), God has anointed you as a prophetic voice to Millennials and Gen Z. You stand as a welcoming voice at the threshold of the church, inviting younger generations to experience the transformative goodness of

God. I asked you to write the foreword precisely because you draw others toward Christ and point them to His definition of what is good, true, and just. To my own pastor, Jimmy Seibert, I've had the privilege of sitting under your spiritual formation and exceptional leadership for more than 20 years. I've watched you navigate trials that would have defeated most men. But you've always emerged graciously, not embittered by the world but humbled by God's grace. And with each year, you've become all the more emboldened for the gospel. Your consistent devotion to Jesus and His church is a compelling witness. Your servant leadership over the Antioch Church global movement embodies biblical justice.

To my Waco mom friends, the community of mothers who have surrounded me, you deserve special recognition. Often operating in the background, perhaps even unaware of your full contribution, you've provided the practical support necessary for this work. You've collected my sons from school, driven them to out-of-town games, and held my life together in so many small but meaningful ways. Even during shared family vacations, when writing pulled me away from communal activities, you seamlessly extended your maternal care to my kids. My husband and I often gush and brag that "Waco, Texas, is the cradle of fellowship." Indeed, this fellowship has made my professional and parenting responsibilities not only manageable but also enjoyable. And to friends outside my local community, thank you for your support and encouragement from afar.

To the many colleagues who have advocated for me in various capacities, I am forever grateful. Thank you to former Baylor professors who became trusted friends, to Dallas Seminary leaders who provided opportunities for theological growth and broader influence, to my fellow Christian academics who have collaborated with me over the years. To those who gathered around me in 2021, you helped me discover my voice at a time when many wanted to silence me.

I extend sincere thanks to my editor, Audrey Greeson, whose

discernment and unwavering confidence in this project guided me through multiple revisions. Your ability to envision the book's potential and to champion it humbles me. Thank you for your patient guidance and constructive feedback throughout our collaboration. Similarly, I am grateful to everyone at Harvest House Publishers. From marketing to editing, design to promotion, your behind-the-scenes efforts have been indispensable. Thank you for treating this work with exceptional care.

Finally, to you who have opened these pages: Thank you for trusting me, for allowing these reflections into your intellectual and spiritual life. I pray this book serves as both a reminder and an encouragement that God's eternal purpose for humanity is redemption and restoration through Christ. He alone is the foundation and methodology for biblical justice, a form of social justice that leads to spiritual transformation and eternal salvation.

To learn more about Harvest House books and
to read sample chapters, visit our website:

www.HarvestHousePublishers.com

HARVEST HOUSE PUBLISHERS
EUGENE, OREGON